Elucidating Law

OXFORD LEGAL PHILOSOPHY

Series Editors
Timothy Endicott, John Gardner, and Leslie Green

Oxford Legal Philosophy publishes the best new work in philosophically oriented legal theory. It commissions and solicits monographs in all branches of the subject, including works on philosophical issues in all areas of public and private law, and in the national, transnational, and international realms; studies of the nature of law, legal institutions, and legal reasoning; treatments of problems in political morality as they bear on law; and explorations in the nature and development of legal philosophy itself. The series represents diverse traditions of thought but always with an emphasis on rigour and originality. It sets the standard in contemporary jurisprudence.

In memory of John Gardner
1965–2019

ALSO AVAILABLE IN THE SERIES

Coercion and the Nature of Law
Kenneth Einar Himma

Property Rights: A Re-Examination
JE Penner

The Right of Redress
Andrew Gold

Faces of Inequality: A Theory of Wrongful Discrimination
Sophia Moreau

A Theory of Legal Personhood
Visa AJ Kurki

Imposing Risk: A Normative Framework
John Oberdiek

Law and Morality at War
Adil Ahmad Haque

Ignorance of Law: A Philosophical Inquiry
Douglas Husak

Reason and Restitution: A Theory of Unjust Enrichment
Charlie Webb

Allowing for Exceptions: A Theory of Defences and Defeasibility in Law
Luís Duarte d'Almeida

The Ends of Harm: The Moral Foundations of Criminal Law
Victor Tadros

Corrective Justice
Ernest J. Weinrib

Conscience and Conviction: The Case for Civil Disobedience
Kimberley Brownlee

The Nature of Legislative Intent
Richard Ekins

Why Law Matters
Alon Harel

Imposing Risk: A Normative Framework
John Oberdiek

Elucidating Law

JULIE DICKSON

Great Clarendon Street, Oxford, OX2 6DP,
United Kingdom

Oxford University Press is a department of the University of Oxford.
It furthers the University's objective of excellence in research, scholarship,
and education by publishing worldwide. Oxford is a registered trade mark of
Oxford University Press in the UK and in certain other countries

© Julie Dickson 2022

The moral rights of the author have been asserted

First Edition published in 2022

Impression: 2

All rights reserved. No part of this publication may be reproduced, stored in
a retrieval system, or transmitted, in any form or by any means, without the
prior permission in writing of Oxford University Press, or as expressly permitted
by law, by licence or under terms agreed with the appropriate reprographics
rights organization. Enquiries concerning reproduction outside the scope of the
above should be sent to the Rights Department, Oxford University Press, at the
address above

You must not circulate this work in any other form
and you must impose this same condition on any acquirer

Public sector information reproduced under Open Government Licence v3.0
(http://www.nationalarchives.gov.uk/doc/open-government-licence/open-government-licence.htm)

Published in the United States of America by Oxford University Press
198 Madison Avenue, New York, NY 10016, United States of America

British Library Cataloguing in Publication Data

Data available

Library of Congress Control Number: 2021953280

ISBN 978–0–19–872776–7

DOI: 10.1093/oso/9780198727767.001.0001

Printed and bound by
CPI Group (UK) Ltd, Croydon, CR0 4YY

Links to third party websites are provided by Oxford in good faith and
for information only. Oxford disclaims any responsibility for the materials
contained in any third party website referenced in this work.

*This book is dedicated to the memory of
William Barker, Janet Dickson, and John Gardner*

Series Editors' Preface

Julie Dickson's exciting book takes as its object analytical legal philosophy: its domain and aims, the constraints within which it works, its criteria of success, and its prospects for progress. Professor Dickson defends and elaborates her landmark idea that legal philosophy is 'indirectly evaluative', now setting it within a wider view that sees philosophical explanation as an *elucidation* of its subject matter.

Elucidating law is neither a social science nor an applied ethics. It approaches law as an artefact with an objective existence, but which has an essential nature in a modest, domain appropriate, sense of the term. In explaining that nature, legal philosophy needs to be sensitive to values—in the first instance, to the values that determine what is significant among the myriad facts about law. It must also attend to the views about significance expressed or presupposed in the self-understandings of those who engage with the law. Because law is complex and because judgements of significance are dynamic, there is no fixed list of eternal questions for jurisprudence to answer. The subject adapts to changes in its object and in our knowledge of that object and its role in society. Nonetheless, a philosophical elucidation of law should be a 'staged inquiry': we begin by trying to identify and understand the object before we assess it as good or bad, just or unjust, efficient or inefficient. *En route*, Dickson scrutinizes what leading analytic philosophers actually argue and how they actually proceed, showing that familiar complaints about their insularity or indifference to empirical inquiry are unfounded. The approach to legal philosophy she defends often consistent with, or even latent in, the work of her critics.

Dickson's theory of law is not moralistic, but like Bentham and Weber she proposes a demanding ethics of inquiry about law. Legal philosophers should approach their subject alert to the complexity and value-relevance of law, but also with an attitude of 'due wariness'. Law is not only a thing that can be dangerous, it is a thing that cloaks its dangers in claims to authority or justice. Legal philosophers are called on to elucidate law's claims, and to test them, always wary that law is often in the business of obfuscating its nature. *Elucidating Law* sheds light on modern jurisprudence as it is, but also as it should be. It is significant new work from one of the subject's leading exponents.

Timothy Endicott
Leslie Green

Acknowledgements

So many people have helped and encouraged me during the years when I was writing this book and I can mention only some of them here. First and foremost, I would like to thank my partner, Richard Broadhead, for his constant support and encouragement. I am indebted to various friends and colleagues who carefully read the original proposal for this book and encouraged me in various ways to persist with it when my own enthusiasm faltered, and I would particularly like to thank Wil Waluchow, Juan Vega Gómez, Joseph Raz, Sophia Moreau, Mike Giudice, Clare Fitzpatrick, and Georgia Testa in this regard.

I presented material from this book at various seminars and workshops, including the Legal and Political Philosophy Colloquium at Queen's University, Kingston, Ontario; the Law and Philosophy Group Seminar at Universitat Pompeu Fabra, Barcelona; and the Law and Philosophy Workshop at the University of Chicago Law School. I would like to thank all those who participated for their thoughtful feedback and enthusiastic engagement, and Grégoire Webber, Jean Thomas, José Juan Moreso, Chiara Valentini, Brian Leiter, and Max Etchemendy for inviting me and looking after me so well.

For their unfailing good humour and collegiality, which was particularly needed during the Covid-19 pandemic, I would like to thank my Somerville law colleagues Chris Hare and Achas Burin.

The series editors of the *Oxford Legal Philosophy* book series, Timothy Endicott, John Gardner, and Leslie Green, each read and commented extensively on parts of the book, and their help throughout the project has been invaluable. I would especially like to thank Leslie Green for his incredibly thorough and frequently entertaining comments on the entire manuscript.

This book is dedicated to the memory of my grandad William Barker, my mum Janet Dickson, and my colleague and friend John Gardner, who helped me more than they knew.

Julie Dickson, September 2021

Contents

1. Elucidating Law: Motifs and Motivations ... 1
   1. Introduction: The Philosophy of Legal Philosophy ... 1
   2. Why Elucidating Law? ... 3
   3. Why 'Elucidating Law'? ... 11
   4. The End of a Beginning ... 13
2. Legal Philosophy and the Nature of Law: Some Initial Considerations ... 15
   1. Introduction ... 15
   2. Legal Philosophy and the Nature of Law: Some Initial Considerations ... 16
3. Legal Philosophy and the Nature of Law: Some Challenges Considered ... 25
   1. Legal Philosophy about the Nature of Law: Theoretically Imperialist? ... 26
   2. Legal Philosophy about the Nature of Law: 'Guild Exclusivity'? ... 31
   3. Legal Philosophy about the Nature of Law: Impossible? ... 37
   4. Legal Philosophy about the Nature of Law: Too Abstract/Neglectful of Law's Social Character? ... 50
   5. Legal Philosophy about the Nature of Law: Static, Staple Questions? ... 52
   6. Conclusion: A Metaphysically Modest and Domain-apt Understanding of Legal Philosophy about the Nature of Law ... 52
4. The Questions of Legal Philosophy: Diversity, Development, and Distribution of Emphasis ... 54
   1. Introduction: The Questions of Legal Philosophy ... 54
   2. Two Roles for Choice in Theory Construction in Legal Philosophy ... 55
   3. Subject-matter Selectivity in Legal Philosophy ... 57
   4. Distribution of Emphasis Selectivity in Legal Philosophy ... 65
   5. Conclusion ... 81
5. Approaching Law: A Constraining Duality and an Attitude of Due Wariness ... 82
   1. Introduction: Towards Indirectly Evaluative Legal Philosophy ... 82
   2. An Important Duality: Law's Social and Normative Nature ... 85
   3. Law's Duality in Indirectly Evaluative Legal Philosophy ... 87
   4. Failing to Do Justice to the Duality: An Example Considered ... 90
   5. Approaching Law: An Attitude of Due Wariness ... 94
   6. Conclusion: Further Towards Indirectly Evaluative Legal Philosophy ... 101

xii CONTENTS

6. Self-understandings and the Limits of Revisionism   104
   1. Self-understandings Introduced   104
   2. Self-understandings as Constraints on Successful Theories of Law I:
      What to Do with Them and Why   107
   3. Self-understandings as Constraints on Successful Theories of Law II:
      What *Not* to Do with Them and Why   122
   4. Conclusion: Self-understandings and the Limits of Revisionism   133

7. Indirectly Evaluative Legal Philosophy: The Value of Staged
   Inquiry   135
   1. Evaluation in Legal Philosophy   135
   2. Indirectly Evaluative Judgements in Staged Inquiry   142
   3. The Advantages of the Indirectly Evaluative Approach to Legal
      Philosophy   153

8. Continuity and Complementarity in Legal Philosophy   161
   1. Introduction   161
   2. Some Challenges Considered   162
   3. IELP and Law as It Ought to Be   167
   4. The Province of Jurisprudence Enlarged?   175

Index   177

1
Elucidating Law

Motifs and Motivations

1. Introduction: The Philosophy of Legal Philosophy

What do we do when we do legal philosophy? This book explores this question and develops and defends my own answer to it. I hope that the discussions which follow will interest and engage students, academics, and indeed anyone who has ever wondered what it is that philosophers of law think they are doing, and what it is that they are doing, when they take up their keyboards in the service of jurisprudential inquiry.

As soon as we consider it, this opening question disperses into an intriguing array of puzzles and challenges about what legal philosophy is, and why and how we ought to engage in it. What are the aims of legal philosophy? What can it hope to achieve? How should legal philosophers approach and engage with their subject matter, and what constraints are incumbent on them as they do so? Which questions should philosophy of law seek to address? What are its relations with neighbouring disciplines, such as political, moral, and social philosophy, and are there important sub-divisions of inquiry *within* the domain of legal philosophy itself? What are the criteria of success of legal philosophy, and how do we know if they have been met? To what extent are different jurisprudential explanations of the same phenomena compatible? Can there be progress in legal philosophy? Does the discipline have a finite or a never-ending task?[1]

These are deep-rooted and philosophically rich questions. Much writing in the philosophy of law—including some of my own—has referred to these sorts of questions as *methodological* in character, and as concerning a part of

---

[1] It should be noted from the outset that I use 'legal philosophy', 'philosophy of law', and 'jurisprudence' interchangeably throughout this book. As is discussed in ch 3, ss 1 and 2, in my view these terms do not demarcate significant and/or context-independent differences between types of inquiry. I have previously discussed aspects of my views on their interchangeability in J Dickson, 'Ours is a Broad Church: Indirectly Evaluative Legal Philosophy as a Facet of Jurisprudential Inquiry' (2015) 6 *Jurisprudence* 207–.

our discipline designated 'the methodology of legal philosophy' or 'the methodology of jurisprudence'.[2] This terminology, however, may connote an overly restrictive view of the ambit, and kind, of questions I am interested in here. Specifically, referring to the 'methodology' of legal philosophy may give the misleading impression that the relevant inquiries concern only *how* or the *way in which* legal philosophy ought to be done, rather than encompassing, in a broad sense, inquiry into *what legal philosophy is*: its aims, criteria of success, constraints incumbent upon it, prospects for progress, and indeed how we should determine and understand its very domain and subject matter. As it is this broader understanding of the relevant questions and puzzles which I endorse and engage with here, I try, for the most part, to refer to this aspect of the discipline as 'the philosophy of legal philosophy'.[3]

This book explores certain aspects of the philosophy of legal philosophy. As will emerge from the account I develop and defend, such selectivity is a valuable feature of jurisprudential inquiry.[4] My approach explores what it is to understand law by *elucidating* it. In my view, elucidating law encompasses four main motifs:

(i) the legal philosopher's task is to identify, illuminate, and explain aspects of something—law—which (in a sense which receives further specification in Chapters 2, 3, 5, and 6 of this work) exists in our social reality and has a character that legal philosophy attempts to capture;

(ii) law is a multi-faceted and complex phenomenon, different aspects of which can be illuminated from different theoretical directions, at different times, and for different reasons. Accordingly, the questions of legal philosophy are various, diverse, arise in and change over time, and its quest is never-ending;

(iii) legal philosophers have much work to do, and many judgements—including evaluative judgements—to make, in developing their theories of law. Elucidation is an active process and involves bringing out

---

[2] Examples include SR Perry, 'Hart's Methodological Positivism' (1998) 4 *Legal Theory* 427; B Leiter, 'Beyond the Hart/Dworkin Debate: The Methodology Problem in Jurisprudence' (2003) 48 *American Journal of Jurisprudence* 17; J Dickson, 'Methodology in Jurisprudence: A Critical Survey' (2004) 10 *Legal Theory* 117; A Halpin, 'The Methodology of Jurisprudence: Thirty Years Off the Point' (2006) 19 *Canadian Journal of Law and Jurisprudence* 67.

[3] Owing to the prevalence of the term 'methodology' in the relevant literature and debates, I will not seek to avoid it entirely. No harm should come of this, so long as 'methodology' is read and understood in the broad sense just indicated. Note that, although the phrase 'the philosophy of legal philosophy' may evoke echoes of Timothy Williamson's, The Philosophy of Philosophy (Blackwell 2007), and although I admire that work, I do not intend the phrase to indicate commonalities of approach or of substance, with it.

[4] This point is discussed in ch 4.

from law its most important and significant features and offering illuminating accounts of those features which speak to that which concerns us, given the distinctive character of law, and its impact upon our social world;

(iv) developing an explanatorily apt understanding of law can, in turn, help to identify, bring into focus, and shed light on other important issues including other important moral issues. In particular, understanding law's character bears importantly on puzzles and questions we face such as how law bears upon our practical reasoning processes, whether and when we ought to take it as having authority over us, and what we ought to do, morally speaking, given the presence of law and its requirements.

2. Why Elucidating Law?

My choice of the term 'elucidating' is important in characterizing the approach to understanding law that I champion. In selecting this term, and in using it throughout this book, I draw partly on aspects of its existing usage in philosophical and legal philosophical discourse, but also aim to move beyond these, and to develop the ideas which 'elucidating' connotes in exploring my own philosophy of legal philosophy.

As regards existing usage and connotations: while some of these seem irrelevant for present purposes,[5] others—such as the use of this term in works by Peter Strawson, HLA Hart, and various legal philosophers engaging with Hart's views—exhibit interesting affinities with aspects of my approach in this book. In *Analysis and Metaphysics*,[6] Strawson uses 'elucidation' to denote, and to indicate his support for, an approach to philosophical explanation which eschews what he refers to as the 'reductive mode.'[7] of analysis—which involves

---

[5] For example, the debate concerning what Wittgenstein may or may not have meant by 'elucidations' at various points in the *Tractatus* (L Wittgenstein, Tractatus Logico-Philosophicus (CK Ogden tr, Routledge & Kegan Paul 1922)), and whether or not any of his views in this regard carried over to his later philosophy, seems, to me at least, to be too specific to Wittgenstein's conception of philosophy, and to questions concerning the relationship between his earlier and later work, to be of significant use in considering what it is for legal philosophers to elucidate law. For discussion concerning Wittgenstein's various uses of 'elucidations', see eg PMS Hacker, 'Frege and Wittgenstein on Elucidations' (1975) 84 *Mind* 601; J Conant, 'Elucidation and Nonsense in Frege and Early Wittgenstein' in A Crary and R Read (eds), The New Wittgenstein (Routledge 2000); PMS Hacker, 'Wittgenstein, Carnap and the New American Wittgensteinians' (2003) 53 *Philosophical Quarterly* 1

[6] P Strawson, Analysis and Metaphysics, An Introduction to Philosophy (OUP 1992) especially chs 1 and 2.

[7] ibid 18.

dismantling complex structures into simpler elements[8]—and which embraces instead a 'connective model'[9] wherein philosophical explanations of concepts proceed by exploring and understanding their place in a complex network of interlinking concepts.[10] My own philosophy of legal philosophy, wherein multiple questions and puzzles stand to be illuminated by different shafts of philosophical light, each producing explanations capable of being mutually supporting and leading to greater understanding of how various aspects of the phenomena under investigation fit together, has certain affinities with these ideas.[11] Moreover, Strawson is also wary of philosophical explanations that are excessively revisionist in character and result in accounts of familiar phenomena which stray problematically far from our ordinary thinking.[12] As is explored in Chapter 6, this theme, too, has echoes in my own approach to elucidating law.

Turning from general philosophy to legal philosophy: HLA Hart is also associated with, and at times explicitly refers to, the idea that our theories of law should seek to elucidate various aspects of the phenomena they address.[13] Hart's use of the term in *The Concept of Law* often occurs at points where he seeks to reject overly simplistic and/or reductive views of what law is, and of what legal philosophy must do to understand law successfully. This is evident, for example, in his embracing the notion of elucidation in explaining why a definitional methodology would be inapposite and fruitless in understanding law,[14] and in contending that the overly simplistic elements of orders, threats, sanctions, and general habits of obedience that are so central to John Austin's nineteenth-century command theory of law cannot sufficiently capture what it is to follow a rule, to be guided by law, and to be under an obligation to follow it. Elucidating law, insists Hart, demands that we understand it in a manner appropriate to its character as a normative conduct-guiding phenomenon: legal philosophers must do adequate explanatory justice to how those living under

---

[8] ibid ch 2, especially at 18–19.
[9] ibid 21.
[10] ibid ch 2, especially at 19–21. In this discussion, Strawson indicates that it might be better to be somewhat revisionist as regards the terminology used in this area, and to replace 'analysis' with 'elucidation', in referring to the approach to philosophical explanation he advocates. He notes, however, that in intellectual work we are to an extent constrained by existing usage of terms, and the philosophical orientation they provide. This being so, Strawson settles for a different form of revisionism: he attempts to reclaim 'analysis' from the narrowness of the 'dismantling model', and to bring out its broader sense (ibid 19).
[11] This point is discussed further in the remainder of this chapter, and in ch 4.
[12] Strawson (n 6) 15–16, 21–24.
[13] See eg HLA Hart, The Concept of Law (3rd edn, OUP 2012) with a Postscript edited by PA Bulloch and J Raz, and with an Introduction and Notes by L Green 12, 17, 20, 80, 82, 110, 123, 155, 168, 169, 213, 292, 274.
[14] ibid 12–17, 213.

and administering law view it.[15] The need to achieve an adequately internal understanding of law, and not to ride roughshod over how it is already understood by those subject to it, is also strongly embraced in the present work.[16] Hart also turns to the idea of elucidation where, by contrast with overly simplistic and reductive approaches, he seeks to emphasize his embrace of a diversiform approach to understanding and exploring the multiple elements which together constitute law. He emphasizes repeatedly the need to understand and explore the character of a cluster of law's features—including social rules, legal obligations, the internal point of view, primary and secondary rules, power and authority, the open texture of law, and the interstitial character of judicial lawmaking—and indicates that only by properly understanding a sufficient range of such elements, and, crucially, the relations between them, can our theories of law have a chance of success.[17]

Various other legal philosophers also employ the notion of elucidating law, both in considering the general character of Hart's approach to understanding law, and in critically engaging with and developing further certain of his arguments. Such commentators frequently associate elucidation with various of the characteristics mentioned above, such as a desire to avoid a reductive and/or definitional approach to understanding law, and a commitment to exploring in a pluralistic way a range of law's features, and the relations between them, in order better to illuminate its character.[18]

As I note above, there are affinities between several of the above themes and aspects of my own views regarding the philosophy of legal philosophy. I regard these affinities as a strength, and, where appropriate in the discussions to come, I emphasize the sense in which we are all 'standing on the shoulders of giants' in our jurisprudential endeavours. That said, we partly repay our intellectual debts to those upon whose shoulders we stand by attempting to focus and develop our own distinctive view from that vantage point. In this spirit, let us return to and explore further the four motifs running through my own view of elucidating law:

---

[15] ibid 54–61, 80, 82–90, 110–17, 155, 202.
[16] See chs 5 to 8, and especially ch 6.
[17] Hart (n 13) 12, 17, 80, 82, 110, 169, 202, 274.
[18] See eg S Brown, 'Review of *The Concept of Law* by HLA Hart' (1963) 72 *The Philosophical Review* 250; RS Summers, 'Professor HLA Hart's Concept of Law' [1963] *Duke Law Journal* 629; N MacCormick, HLA Hart (1st edn, Stanford University Press 1981) eg 1, 5, 18, 23, 25, 28, 32, 34, 38, 43, 82, 90, 103, 106, 144, and 166; TAO Endicott, 'The Generality of Law' and J Gardner, 'Why Law Might Emerge: Hart's Problematic Fable', both in L Duarte d'Almeida, J Edwards, and A Dolcetti (eds), Reading HLA Hart's 'The Concept of Law' (Hart Publishing 2013).

(i) the legal philosopher's task is to identify, illuminate, and explain aspects of something—law—which exists in our social reality (in a sense which receives further specification in Chapters 2, 3, 5, and 6 of this work) and has a character that legal philosophy attempts to capture.

To elucidate something, as the word's origins indicate, is to cast light upon it, to illuminate it, to explain it in a way that makes its character clearer.[19] Elucidation, then, appears to envisage an explanandum to be elucidated, ie a *something* which exists, upon which light can be shed, and which has a character capable of being illuminated. This point accords well with my own understanding of the sense in which legal philosophy attempts to elucidate law. As I discuss in Chapters 2 and 3, one crucially important part of the philosophy of law is the attempt to identify and understand the nature of law, ie those properties which make law into what it is, and in virtue of which it is what it is. This enterprise, both in abstract terms, and as it is instantiated in the work of many legal philosophers from across the jurisprudential spectrum, presupposes that law has a nature, and that it is a possible and important task of a theory of law to try to identify and explain what that nature is.[20]

That said, and as Chapter 3 particularly explores, the part of legal philosophy which is concerned with the nature of law is just that, ie a *part* of—to borrow Austin's phrase—the province of jurisprudence as a whole.[21] It is, however, a very important part of that province, and a vital precursor to some other types and lines of inquiry which are also vital in our quest to understand, evaluate, and decide how to think and to act in light of, law.[22] This being so, a significant part of the philosophy of legal philosophy expounded in this book is concerned with what legal philosophers are doing, and how they ought to be doing it, when they develop and defend theories of the nature of law.

Of course, not all legal philosophers seek to ascertain and explain the nature of law. Moreover, some of those who do not—for example Brian Tamanaha, Frederick Schauer, and Kevin Walton—*also* claim that it is impossible to do so,

---

[19] '[e]lucidate, v Etymology: late Latin *ēlūcidāt-* participial stem of *ēlūcidāre*, *ē* out + *lūcidus* bright... *trans*. To render lucid;... to throw light upon, clear up, explain' OED Online (OUP 2020) www.oed.com/view/Entry/60622 (accessed 4 February 2021).

[20] For example, and to name but a few, I would count Jeremy Bentham, John Austin, HLA Hart, Hans Kelsen, John Finnis, Mark Murphy, Joseph Raz, Michael Moore, Nicos Stavropoulos, Leslie Green, Veronica Rodriguez-Blanco, Wil Waluchow, Mark Greenberg, and Scott Shapiro as all attempting to capture and explain the nature of law, in spite of their very different views on what it is for law to have a nature, and what its nature is. Some of these theorists' views are discussed in later chapters.

[21] John Austin, The Province of Jurisprudence Determined (first published 1832, W Rumble (ed), CUP 1995).

[22] These points receive further attention in chs 7 and 8.

that there is no point in doing so, that attempting to do so yields problematic consequences, or some variation on these claims.[23] These contentions, and the challenges they present to the philosophy of legal philosophy championed in this book, must be taken seriously, faced, and either overcome or legitimately by-passed. In facing and exploring such challenges, this book seeks to uncover and engage with further puzzles concerning what 'the nature of X' might mean, when the X in question is a human-made social institution.[24]

> (ii) law is a multi-faceted and complex phenomenon, different aspects of which can be illuminated from different theoretical directions, at different times, and for different reasons. Accordingly, the questions of legal philosophy are various, diverse, arise in and change over time, and its quest is never-ending.

Although elucidating law involves casting light on phenomena which exist in our social reality, this should *not* lead us to think that, as a result, there can be only one correct theory of the nature of law, or that all theories of law address the same unchanging questions or exhibit the same theoretical interests. Rather, the way to think of the situation, to speak metaphorically for a moment, is in terms of different theories of law, or indeed different aspects of the same theory of law, shining distinctive beams of light of different wavelengths on different areas and aspects of the complex and manifold phenomena comprising law.

As is explored in Chapter 4, because law is a multi-faceted phenomenon, there is reason to think that its significant and important features will be many, various, and possibly open-ended in number. Different sets, and subsets, of law's features will appear puzzling, and of interest, to different theorists at different times, partly in response to changing concerns about the character and operation of law in society. The questions which legal philosophy addresses, as well as the answers it attempts to give, hence arise in and alter over time. Moreover, certain aspects of law's character and operation, and the puzzles and concerns that they animate, may only reveal themselves to individuals, theoretical movements, and societies with particular experiences and/or sensitivities which afford them access to previously unnoticed, or at least under-emphasized and under-attended to, facets of law. Elucidatory shafts of light of varying 'theoretical wavelengths' thus illuminate legal phenomena

---

[23] These theorists' views are explored in ch 3.
[24] See the discussion in chs 2, 3, 5, and 6.

from multiple directions and seek to reveal more about facets of law hitherto in shadow. There is not, even in principle, one single, comprehensive, and entirely correct theory of law waiting to be discovered, and our discipline is the richer and more fertile for it. All this being so, the idea of elucidating law should be understood as consonant with a vision of legal philosophy, and of its questions and answers, which is pluralistic, dynamic, and open-ended.

> (iii) legal philosophers have much work to do, and many judgements—including evaluative judgements—to make, in developing their theories of law. Elucidation is an active process and involves bringing out from law its most important and significant features and offering illuminating accounts of those features which speak to that which concerns us, given the distinctive character of law, and its impact upon our social world.

In one respect, the 'casting light of different wavelengths from a variety of directions on legal phenomena which exists in our social reality' metaphor featuring in (i) and (ii) above, has the potential to mislead. It may do so if it is understood in a way which gives the impression that the role of the legal philosopher is a passive one: for example, if it is taken to connote that all the legal philosopher need do is direct a 'beam of intellectual light' over those aspects of law which interest her, and then just observe and record what she sees.

I believe that this misleading view of legal philosophy as a somewhat passive endeavour plays a role in some theorists' characterization of it as *descriptive* in character.[25] As I have argued elsewhere, this use of 'descriptive' is a misnomer, and one which is liable to generate significant misunderstandings.[26]

Two misconceptions are particularly relevant here:

> (a) that those ill-advisedly characterized as 'descriptive legal theorists' hold that legal philosophy is value-free, and maintain that theorists are not required to make or defend evaluative judgements in explaining aspects of law's character.

---

[25] This point is explored in ch 6, s 2.
[26] See eg J Dickson, Evaluation and Legal Theory (Hart Publishing 2001); Dickson, 'Methodology in Jurisprudence' (n 2); J Dickson, 'Descriptive Legal Theory' in M Sellers and S Kirste (eds), Encyclopedia of the Philosophy of Law and Social Philosophy (Springer 2017) https://doi.org/10.1007/978-94-007-6730-0_52-1.

(b) that those ill-advisedly characterized as 'descriptive legal theorists' are fundamentally uninterested in exploring certain aspects of the relations between law and morality, such as whether law has any moral properties, including any necessary moral properties, whether law has a moral task or aim, and what, morally, we—both citizens and legal officials—ought to do given the presence of law.

I return to (b) in discussing the fourth motif of elucidating law. As regards (a), it is pivotal to my philosophy of legal philosophy, as espoused in the present work and elsewhere, that *no part of* legal philosophy is value-free, and that successful theories of law, including successful theories of the nature of law, crucially and significantly involve their authors making a range of evaluative judgements.[27] Such evaluative judgements are necessary to pick out those features of law which are important and significant to explain, and feature throughout the course of offering and defending illuminating explanations of aspects of law's character. This renders the process of *elucidating law* a proactive and engaged activity, and one which must be appropriately guided by the distinctive sort of phenomenon that law is. For instance, legal philosophers must accord sufficient emphasis to the way in which law is viewed, understood, and acted in light of, by those who create, administer, and are subject to it. As a result, I contend, there are limits on the kind and degree of revisionism which can feature in successful theories of law.[28]

These schematic remarks are developed in the chapters to come. In the course of so doing, I also explore the ways in which my views on these issues differ from those of other legal philosophers, including Brian Leiter, Liam Murphy, Mark Greenberg, and Nicos Stavropoulos.[29] The crucial point to note from the outset is that to elucidate law is *not* merely to shine a flat and invariant intellectual light upon it, and then passively record those attitudes towards, and beliefs about it, which appear. Elucidating law, in the sense explored in this book, should be understood as an active and dynamic process requiring the legal philosopher to make and defend a range of evaluative judgements about her subject matter.

---

[27] See those works cited in n 26 above and also J Dickson, 'On Naturalizing Jurisprudence: Some Comments on Brian Leiter's View of What Jurisprudence Should Become' (2011) *30* Law and Philosophy 477. I explore these points in chs 7 and 8.
[28] These points are explored in ch 6.
[29] See ch 3 and, especially, ch 6.

(iv) developing an explanatorily apt understanding of law can, in turn, help to identify, bring into focus, and shed light on other important issues including other important moral issues. In particular, understanding law's character bears importantly on puzzles and questions we face such as how law operates upon our practical reasoning processes, whether and when we ought to take it as having authority over us, and what we ought to do, morally speaking, given the presence of law and its requirements.

Two ways in which the above can occur are particularly relevant for present purposes. The first arises when certain features of law are compared and contrasted with features of other phenomena with which they appear to share similarities, but regarding which we also perceive there to be important differences. As a result, both law, and that which it is being contrasted with, can be brought better into focus and understood in greater depth. For instance, garnering an understanding of the normativity of law—including an understanding of the character and meaning of legal 'oughts', what they demand of us, how they come into existence, and how we ascertain their content—can shed light on, and, in turn, can themselves be better understood, by examining what is similar, but also what is significantly different, as regards the character and operation of moral oughts, and of moral normativity.

A second way in which an understanding of the character of law can assist in illuminating other matters is evident when the nature of law is pivotal to focusing, and to ascertaining what is relevant to answering, certain question(s) about those matters. For example, take the question of what we ought to do in a given situation. If law exists which is relevant to the situation at hand, then, like the presence of many other things in our social and moral lives (family and business relationships, promises we have made, etc.), this will affect in certain ways our deliberations and decisions about what we ought to do. This being so, we cannot begin properly to answer the question: 'what ought I to do in this situation, given the presence of law which is relevant to it?', until we have an accurate and explanatorily apt understanding of certain aspects of law's character, such as the character and content of the claims that law makes including its claim to authority, and the manner in which it purports legitimately to intervene in our practical reasoning processes. We cannot properly consider what role law should properly play in our practical reasoning processes, and what, morally speaking, should be our response to law's claims, until we know precisely the character of those claims, and exactly what they do and do not demand of us.

All this being so, one of the most important roles of an account of aspects of the nature of law is to throw light upon, and to focus, and facilitate, further inquiries such as what, morally speaking, we ought to do, given the presence of law. Such further inquiries are significantly advanced when we conduct them in light of an accurate and explanatorily apt account of law's character, because the light cast by such an account brings those further questions we seek to ask and answer more precisely into focus and aids our understanding of what bears upon them.[30]

3. Why 'Elucidating Law'?

The discussion above introduces four motifs which are central to my philosophy of legal philosophy, and which begin to explain why I chose *Elucidating Law* as the title of this book. Before offering—in section 4 below—an outline of the book's structure, I want to say a few words about why I chose to write it at all. Beginning with my book, *Evaluation and Legal Theory*,[31] I have harboured a long-standing interest in issues such as the criteria of success of theories of law, the questions such theories should address, and the compatibility or otherwise of different jurisprudential approaches.[32] However, in much of my work, I have addressed these topics in a rather piecemeal fashion, tackling aspects of them across various articles, and in chapters in edited collections. This being so, and given that I hope I have developed over the years both a broader and deeper understanding of such issues, the time seemed ripe not only to draw together my views on these matters but also to further advance them. The character of and impetus generated by a book-length project seemed an appropriate genre in which to do so.

In addition, recent years have seen many thought-provoking challenges emerge which cast doubt on the very possibility of, and/or call into question the current manner of engaging in, that part of the philosophy of law which

---

[30] I have discussed certain aspects of these issues in previous work; see eg Dickson, *Evaluation and Legal Theory* (n 26) ch 7. Chapters 7 and 8 of the present work are dedicated to exploring them further.
[31] Dickson (n 26). This work has also been published in a Spanish language edition as *Evaluación en la teoría del derecho*, Spanish language edition of J Dickson, Evaluation and Legal Theory (Juan Vega Gomez tr, UNAM Press 2006).
[32] See eg J Dickson, 'The Central Questions of Legal Philosophy' (2003) 56 Current Legal Problems 63; Dickson, 'Methodology in Jurisprudence' (n 26 above); J Dickson, 'Is Bad Law Still Law? Is Bad Law Really Law? in M Del Mar and Z Bankowski (eds), Law as Institutional Normative Order (Ashgate 2009); Dickson, 'On Naturalizing Jurisprudence' (n 27); J Dickson, 'Law and Its Theory: a Question of Priorities in RP George and J Keown (eds), Reason, Morality and Law: the Jurisprudence of John Finnis (OUP 2013); Dickson, 'Ours is a Broad Church', (n 1); J Dickson, 'Who's Afraid of Transnational Legal Theory? Dangers and Desiderata' (2015) 5 Transnational Legal Theory 565.

attempts to identify and understand law's nature. Theorists with such varied jurisprudential leanings as Michael Giudice, Nicola Lacey, Brian Leiter, Dennis Patterson, Liam Murphy, Roger Cotterrell, Fred Schauer, and Brian Tamanaha have mounted challenges relevant to this issue. Some of these theorists are wary of the idea that a human-made social construction such as law can have a nature which legal philosophers can attempt to identify and explain. Others mount challenges in respect of what they regard as the key method employed by legal philosophers attempting to ascertain law's nature, namely conceptual analysis, and regard that method, either in principle, and/or as currently practised in jurisprudence, with sceptical eyes, doubting that it can yield an accurate and explanatorily adequate understanding of the nature of law, and, according to some, even well-founded knowledge of the concept of law.[33]

A different set of challenges hails from another direction. Once again, a diverse range of legal philosophers—including Nicos Stavropoulos, John Finnis, Veronica Rodriguez-Blanco, Mark Greenberg, Ronald Dworkin, Dan Priel, Maris Köpcke Tinturé, and Jeremy Waldron—have criticized certain approaches to legal philosophy—including my own—on the grounds that they are *insufficiently morally evaluative* in character. According to this line of criticism, an appropriate philosophy of legal philosophy must take a stance, at an early point in the inquiry, and throughout the course of it, on issues concerning the moral value, justification, and obligatoriness of law. Moreover, for some of these theorists a theory of law must also explain law in a way which recognizes, and grants a central place to, the thesis that law does possess inherent moral value, and does generate moral reasons for action, and moral duties to obey it.[34]

Developing and defending my own philosophy of legal philosophy, which maintains that it is an important part of jurisprudential inquiry to identify and explain aspects of the nature of law, and also insists on the importance of resisting prematurely engaging in moral evaluation, let alone moral justification of law, depends on successfully addressing thoughtful challenges such as these. The discussion in this book gives me the opportunity to meet such challenges in a variety of ways: sometimes by engaging directly with various of the interlocuters mentioned above, and sometimes in a more indirect manner, by exploring and arguing in support of my own stance on the philosophy of legal philosophy.

---

[33] Aspects of these challenges are considered in chs 2, 3, and 6.
[34] Aspects of these challenges are addressed in chs 5 to 8.

4. The End of a Beginning

This book comprises eight chapters. As the chapters proceed, there is a sense in which the discussion moves from a consideration of some more general issues in elucidating law, to arguments developing and defending a specific philosophy of legal philosophy of my own. In later chapters of the book, I refer to my philosophy of legal philosophy as 'indirectly evaluative legal philosophy'. This movement in the book from the more general to the more specific is not entirely linear or progressive in character, however. Where relevant in the course of the discussion, I indicate aspects of elucidating law which might be shared by a variety of methodological approaches, and also highlight where I am advocating my own more specific approach. Indirectly evaluative legal philosophy (IELP) can perhaps be thought of—albeit loosely and metaphorically speaking—as the species of legal philosophy which I particularly champion within the more general genus of elucidating law. In particular, IELP focuses in on and seeks to explain the character of, and reasons behind, the kinds of evaluative judgements that legal philosophers should undertake at various stages in their jurisprudential inquiries.

In this opening chapter, I have introduced some of the main motifs of the present work, and have done so by considering what is involved in elucidating law. In Chapter 2 entitled 'Legal Philosophy and the Nature of Law: Some Initial Considerations', I consider what legal philosophers might have in mind when they claim to be seeking to identify and explain the nature of law. I also outline my own view of what would need to be the case for such a quest to make sense. Chapter 3, 'Legal Philosophy and the Nature of Law: Some Challenges Considered', explores further the possibility and plausibility of legal philosophy attempting to identify and explain law's nature and does so by engaging with some thought-provoking contemporary challenges to aspects of this idea.

When the discussion reaches Chapter 4, 'The Questions of Legal Philosophy: Diversity, Development, and Distribution of Emphasis', it begins to focus more specifically on ideas that I regard as distinctive of my philosophy of legal philosophy. I argue that the questions of legal philosophy arise in and change over time and admit of great variety and differential focus. I explore various factors contributing to this state of affairs and maintain that it is compatible with the idea of legal philosophy about the nature of law, and emblematic of a flourishing discipline.

Chapters 5 to 8 each open up further and distinctive areas of the territory of exploring, developing, and defending my own philosophy of legal philosophy: IELP. Chapter 5, entitled 'Approaching Law: A Constraining Duality, and an Attitude of Due Wariness', explores the manner in which legal philosophers should approach and begin to explain law. I argue that one important test of a successful theory of law is its ability to illuminate, and do adequate justice to, both aspects of an important duality running through law. I then put forward my view that legal philosophers should not approach understanding law from what we might call a neutral, or 'uninvolved' starting point. Instead, I argue, they should proceed by adopting from the outset an 'attitude of due wariness' as regards taking at face value the claims that law makes for itself. I justify this stance by exploring those features of law which make adoption of such an attitude appropriate. Chapter 6, 'Self-Understandings and the Limits of Revisionism', explores the idea that a significant part of what we study in philosophy of law are people's *self-understandings* and that hence we have a responsibility in our theories of law to accord adequate emphasis to those self-understandings in terms of law held by those living under and administering it. I examine aspects of this idea, and the consequences which flow from it as regards how 'revisionist' a theory of law can and should be. Chapter 7, 'Indirectly Evaluative Legal Philosophy: The Value of "Staged Inquiry"', investigates some important questions concerning the appropriate order of explanation in legal philosophical inquiry, and whether addressing certain questions before others helps or hinders the inquiry at hand. I advocate what I term 'staged inquiry'— an approach which counsels understanding different aspects of law's character at different stages in legal philosophical inquiry, and which requires legal philosophers to make different sorts of evaluative judgement at each stage. Crucially, I advocate postponing moral evaluation, and/or moral justification, of aspects of law until certain other questions about law's character have been addressed. Chapter 8, 'Continuity and Complementarity in Legal Philosophy', addresses claims made by some legal philosophers that IELP and cognate methodological approaches are isolationist in character and seek hermetically to seal legal philosophy from the rest of political, social, and moral philosophy. Such views significantly misunderstand the position I espouse, and attribute to it some version of the view that it is up for grabs whether legal philosophy is situated in the context of, continuous with, and fruitfully related to, inquiries in political, social, and moral philosophy. The reality is that none of this is in doubt, certainly not as regards my own views, and possibly not as regards anyone's views. The issue is not *whether* legal philosophy is part of, situated in the context of, and, in a certain sense, continuous with inquiries in political, social, and/or moral philosophy. The issue is: what is the character of the relations between these enterprises, and in what sense is legal philosophy part of, continuous with, and tied to them?

2
Legal Philosophy and the Nature of Law
Some Initial Considerations

1. Introduction

In Chapter 1 I put forward the view that elucidating law involves the idea of law being something that exists in our social reality, and that has a character that legal philosophy attempts to identify and explain. But what does it mean to say that a human-made social institution such as law 'exists in our social reality'? Clearly it cannot mean that law would exist irrespective of the presence of human beings and their intentions, attitudes, actions, beliefs, and attempts at societal governance. Notwithstanding this point, a significant number of legal philosophers—hailing from across the jurisprudential spectrum—argue over the truth and explanatory adequacy of their accounts of law, and in so doing many of them claim to be identifying and explaining law's *nature*: those properties which make it into what it is, and which it must possess to be law.

This chapter and the next try to make sense of such claims, in a manner which neither explains them away as over-reaching or self-delusion, nor commits us to an implausible account of the ontology of law. A discussion exploring what it is for law to have a nature, and what role the concept of law plays in legal philosophers' attempts to understand that nature, is in danger of biting off much more, philosophically speaking, than it can possibly chew. Examining issues such as these can draw us into intractable puzzles in metaphysics and epistemology, puzzles which occupy tomes of the work of excellent philosophers who specialize in the issues concerned. Such puzzles cannot be fully addressed, let alone solved here, in a work exploring and developing my own view on a range of issues in jurisprudential methodology, of which the issue of whether legal philosophy about the nature of law is possible is but one. This being so, I proceed as follows. In the remainder of this chapter, I proceed by raising some initial considerations relevant to whether legal philosophy about the nature of law is a possible and plausible enterprise. With these considerations outlined, a domain-apt and appropriately metaphysically modest understanding of what it would be for law to have a nature begins to emerge. Chapter 3 then aims to render this understanding more persuasive by examining and countering a series of challenges to the idea that one important part of legal philosophy is properly concerned with elucidating law's nature. My strategy in this chapter and the next is thus to propose and explore the idea that law has a nature which legal philosophers can attempt to explain, and then to argue that certain attempts to challenge this idea do not persuasively hit home against their intended target, and/or are not successful in their aims. This strategy is further bolstered by the discussions of the character of law which feature in later chapters of the book.

2. Legal Philosophy and the Nature of Law: Some Initial Considerations

Should legal philosophy—or rather, as I am at pains to emphasize throughout this book—should *one part of* legal philosophy take as its task the identification and explanation of the nature of law? A significant number of legal philosophers, espousing a wide range of views on what that nature is, appear to think so:

Interpretivism is a thesis about what determines legal rights and duties, i.e. what makes it the case that the law requires what it does. As such, it is a thesis about the nature of law. These questions can be formulated in terms of the grounds of propositions of law.[1]

Essential or necessary properties of law are those properties without which law would not be law. They must be there, quite apart from space and time, wherever and whenever law exists. Thus, necessary or essential properties are at the same time universal characteristics of law. Legal philosophy *qua* enquiry into the nature of law is, therefore, an enterprise universalistic in nature.[2]

[a]s here understood, a theory of law provides an account of the nature of law. The thesis I will be defending is that a theory of law is successful if it

---

[1] N Stavropoulos, 'Interpretivist Theories of Law' in Edward N Zalta (ed), *The Stanford Encyclopedia of Philosophy* (Fall 2008 Edition) s 1 https://plato.stanford.edu/archives/fall2008/entries/law-interpretivist/. See also N Stavropoulos, 'Legal Interpretivism' in Edward N Zalta (ed), *The Stanford Encyclopedia of Philosophy* (Spring 2021 Edition) s 5 https://plato.stanford.edu/archives/spr2021/entries/law-interpretivist/; N Stavropoulos, 'The Grounds of Law: Morality and History' 7–8 https://papers.ssrn.com/sol3/papers.cfm?abstract_id2638033.
[2] R Alexy, 'On the Concept and the Nature of Law' (2008) 21 *Ratio Juris* 281, 290.

meets two criteria: First, it consists of propositions about the nature of law which are *necessarily* true, and, second, they *explain* what the law is.[3]

[the question 'What is law?'] ... reflects a philosophical effort to understand *the nature of law in general*.[4]

[a]s I intend the hypothesis, it purports to identify an essential property of law. It purports not merely to say something true or even necessarily true about law, but to say something about law's nature.[5]

What, then, are the criteria which demarcate a good or successful analytical jurisprudential theory? In short, analytical jurisprudence is concerned with explaining the nature of law by attempting to isolate and explain those features which make law into what it is.[6]

These quotations reveal some points in common: that an account of the nature of law will be general in character, and that such an account will identify and explain those properties law *must* possess in order to be law, ie those properties which make law into what it is. These features also begin to indicate that legal philosophy about the nature of law, if feasible, would hold a special place in understanding law, and would have distinctive explanatory power. It would enable us to understand what is true of law in general, and not merely in the local and temporally bound form in which we encounter it in our own society. It would enable us to understand which properties are constitutive of law, and which make it into what it is. It would enable us to separate out what is—in some sense—necessarily the case about law, ie that which *must* obtain for law to exist, from that which is *sometimes*—even frequently—the case about law, but which is dependent on some prevailing contingencies of the political, economic, cultural, and social conditions in which it develops.

Do these points commit us to the view that there is intrinsic value in understanding the nature of law for its own sake? Personally speaking, I would find no difficulty if that were so: in my view there is intrinsic value in improving our understanding of aspects of a social institution so pervasive and so central to our lives in society. In fact, however, the points made above leave it open whether understanding the nature of law is valuable for its own sake, or whether such understanding derives some, or all, of its value from its contribution to

---

[3] J Raz, 'Can There Be a Theory of Law?' in J Raz, *Between Authority and Interpretation* (OUP 2009) 17, (emphasis in original). See also J Raz, 'On the Nature of Law' ibid 91.
[4] S Shapiro, Legality (Harvard University Press 2011) 7 (emphasis in original).
[5] M Greenberg, 'The Standard Picture and Its Discontents' in L Green and B Leiter (eds), Oxford Studies in Philosophy of Law, vol I (OUP 2011) 86.
[6] J Dickson, Evaluation and Legal Theory (Hart Publishing 2001) 17.

other matters, such as shedding light on what is the appropriate attitude for us to take towards law, what we ought to do given the presence of law in our societies, or the uses to which we should and should not put law in our governance arrangements. As the discussions in Chapters 5, 7, and 8 indicate, I am firmly of the view that an understanding of the nature of law can shed light on these sorts of issues and can focus and facilitate our inquiries concerning them. Moreover, it seems to me a plausible and attractive view that understanding which features of law are contingent and can be altered and improved, and understanding which features are part-constitutive of law being law, can inform strategies for law's development and/or replacement as appropriate in various areas of our social and political lives.

It is important to note that, in claiming that legal philosophy about the nature of law—if feasible—would hold a special place in our understanding of law, I do *not* mean to suggest that other types of theoretical inquiry concerning law are less important or less interesting. As noted at the outset of this section, and as is further emphasized in Chapter 3, legal philosophy about the nature of law represents only one kind of theoretical inquiry concerning law. There is, and will continue to be, hugely important and insightful work in legal philosophy which examines various important contingent features of law (and carries with it the hope that what is revealed to be contingent can be changed and improved),[7] particular areas of law,[8] and jurisdiction-specific features of law,[9] and indeed some legal philosophers have drawn attention to the possible links between and mutual complementarities regarding accounts of certain contingent features of law, and accounts of the nature of law.[10] All that is claimed here is that an account of the nature of law possesses a distinctive explanatory power, in that it allows us to understand that which holds true of all law, and which makes law into what it is.

Of course, it is one thing to make a claim, and quite another to make good on it. The views quoted at the beginning of this section may strike some readers as 'metaphysically extravagant', and as giving legal philosophy an impossible task: to develop an account of the nature of law, wherever and

---

[7] See eg PJ Williams, The Alchemy of Race and Rights (Harvard University Press 1991). The references in this and the following three footnotes are brief indicative examples only: there is a wealth of excellent work which could be mentioned in this regard.

[8] eg J Gardner, Offences and Defences: Selected Essays in the Philosophy of Criminal Law (OUP 2007); T Khaitan, A Theory of Discrimination Law (OUP 2015).

[9] eg DM Walker, A Legal History of Scotland (W Green 1988–2004); L Farmer, Criminal Law, Tradition and Legal Order: Crime and the Genius of Scots Law, 1747 to the Present (CUP 1997).

[10] See eg M Giudice, Understanding the Nature of Law: A Case for Constructive Conceptual Explanation (Edward Elgar 2015).

whenever it is found, when, in fact, law, being a human-made social construct, simply has no such nature, and rather exhibits a variety of different features, dependent on the time, place, and culture in which it develops.[11] An objector finding such thoughts plausible could seek not so much to explain but to explain away the stances declared in the quotations above on an 'error theory' basis: these legal philosophers clearly believe that their theories contain propositions about the nature of law, ie about those properties which law must possess in order to be law, and their discourse clearly purports to assert truths about those properties, but, in fact, there are no such properties, because the kind of thing that law is renders it incapable of possessing such properties.[12]

I believe that the cogency of such objections depends on what does, and does not, need to hold in order for law to have a nature. Below, I outline certain initial considerations which are relevant to the issue of whether law has a nature that one part of legal philosophy can seek to identify and explain. As I explore these considerations, I hope to bring the notion of 'the nature of law' better into focus, and to indicate why it makes sense to regard its pursuit by legal philosophers as a feasible endeavour.

(a) The necessary/contingent distinction

For law to have a nature, and hence for it to be possible for one important part of legal philosophy to try to identify and explain it, a distinction must hold between law's necessary properties, and law's contingent properties. Moreover, it must be possible for a theory of the nature of law to identify and explain those properties of law which fall into the former category.

Two important points stemming from this should be noted here. First, this requisite does not yet claim anything about the type of necessity involved when it comes to understanding certain properties of a human-made social

---

[11] In ch 3, I critically examine the views of some legal philosophers who adopt such a stance including Brian Tamanaha, Frederick Schauer, and Kevin Walton.

[12] Error theory is most famously associated with the version of moral error theory espoused by JL Mackie, Ethics: Inventing Right and Wrong (Penguin Books 1977), but has also been used by philosophers to characterize discourse in a variety of fields, and the literature on it is voluminous. For consideration of various types or moral error theory, and the various difference arguments that can be used to support it, see eg R Joyce, The Myth of Morality (CUP 2001), especially chs 1 and 2, and R Joyce, 'Moral Anti-Realism' in Edward N Zalta (ed), *The Stanford Encyclopedia of Philosophy* (Spring 2021 Edition) https://plato.stanford.edu/archives/spr2021/entries/moral-anti-realism/. For a discussion of error theories in a variety of philosophical fields see eg C Daly and D Liggins, 'In Defence of Error Theory' (2010) 149 *Philosophical Studies* 209–30.

institution such as law. As is discussed in Chapter 3, once we consider some of the different possibilities regarding how necessity can and should be understood in this context, some of the challenges levelled at this distinction in the case of law may appear overstated or off-target.

Secondly, this requisite should render us acutely aware that we should not expect a theory of the nature of law to account for all the richness and variety that we see both within and between legal systems in the world. The reason for this should be obvious: those features of law which vary, dependent on the time, place, legal, and societal culture, and form of government in which a given legal order develops and exists, are not the features which theories of law's nature seek. This point yields two important further considerations. First, it further underlines the point that in claiming that theories of the nature of law have a distinctive explanatory role to play in our understanding of law, I am not denying, demoting, or denigrating the value of other types of inquiry, for example inquiries concerning law's myriad important contingent features, what societal conditions foster them, and what consequences follow for those administering and living under law in the societies concerned. Indeed, it is my position that in order to have a theoretically rich and well-rounded understanding of law, it is vital that we have flourishing communities of scholars investigating both law's necessary, and its contingent, properties, and doing so in a variety of ways and from different angles.[13] Secondly, as theories of the nature of law focus on those properties which law *must* possess in order to be law, this is likely to result in such theories having a relatively constrained range of phenomena to investigate and explain. This point is recognized by some legal philosophers in their work on the nature of law. For example Joseph Raz, in his essay, 'The Institutional Nature of Law', reminds us that: 'Legal philosophy has to be content with those few features which all legal systems necessarily possess.'[14] That said, having a relatively constrained range of phenomena to seek out and explain does not mean that theories of the nature of law have a simple or even finite task. Once we begin to probe those features which make law into what it is, their multi-faceted character, relevance for different aspects of our lives in law-governed societies, and puzzles within puzzles they contain, become apparent.[15]

---

[13] See further the discussion in chs 3 and 4.
[14] J Raz, 'The Institutional Nature of Law' in J Raz, The Authority of Law (2nd edn, OUP 2009) 104–105.
[15] These issues are explored further in ch 4.

(b) The sense in which law exists in our social reality

For law to have a nature that one important part of legal philosophy can attempt to identify and explain, propositions about the nature of law featuring in legal philosophers' theories must be about something which exists in our social reality and has a character independently of those legal philosophers' thoughts and beliefs about it. It is important to explore these points a little further, even at this initial stage in our inquiry, lest misunderstandings develop. We can consider the 'exists in our social reality' aspect first. In claiming that theories of the nature of law must be about something which exists in our social reality, we are not yet committing to a particular view of the character, or, we might say, the ontology, of the reality in question. Clearly, the ontology of that aspect of reality featuring law will be very different from the ontology of that aspect of reality featuring phenomena in the natural world, such as the compositional and orbital properties of the planets of the solar system. In the case of law, as the way I have put the matter already indicates, we are talking about some sort of *social* reality: about the practices, attitudes, intentions, processes, and institutions of human beings which bring legal norms and legal systems into existence, and in virtue of which those norms are modified, adjudicated upon, and followed. The issue to be considered, then, is whether it is plausible that, and what exactly needs to be the case such that, law has a nature in the sense which is relevant to, and apt for, that domain of reality to which it properly belongs. To put the matter another way: we should not assume that the standard to be met as regards whether law has a nature which exists in our social reality is the same standard as is apt in the case of the reality of entities in the natural world, and we should not assume that, because law does not have a nature *in the same sense that*, for example, Jupiter's atmosphere has a nature (for example in terms of aspects of its chemical composition), that hence law does not have a nature, period, and is not truly part of reality, appropriately understood.

Why should we not make such assumptions? One reason is that it seems odd and inappropriate to assume a 'one size fits all' approach to what is required for phenomena to be part of reality when the phenomena in question are as varied as, to pick but a few examples: law, quarks, German shepherd dogs, Irn-Bru, mobile phones, the University of Oxford, cellular RNA, chess, French new wave cinema, chrysanthemums, and lipid nanoparticles. Moreover, and as is discussed in Chapter 3, there may be a tendency on the part of some legal philosophers who doubt that law is amongst the things that can have a nature, to believe in an exaggerated dichotomy between the alleged ease of establishing that phenomena examined by the natural sciences are part of a reality that theories in that domain can correctly capture, and the alleged difficulty of establishing these things in the case of a human-made social construct such as law. Perhaps most importantly of all, given that this work is concerned with the criteria of success for understanding law, it would seem odd if not indeed perverse to decide at the outset to hold our explanandum to a standard which, given the sort of thing that it is, will be impossible for it, even in principle, to meet. Legal philosophers may have persuasive arguments supporting their challenges to the idea of law having a nature, but the route to establishing these surely cannot run via defining at the outset what would have to be the case for law to have a nature in terms of criteria which it is constitutionally incapable of satisfying.

In the characterization I gave above, I also indicated that, for law to have a nature which one part of legal philosophy can attempt to capture, our explanandum must have a character which exists 'independently of those legal philosophers' thoughts and beliefs about it'. As we know, in philosophical debates about the character of realism in various domains, the appropriate understanding of some sort of mind-independence condition is a persistent and deeply contested issue.[16] For law to have a nature which makes it into what it is, and against which our theories can be evaluated in terms of their accuracy and explanatory adequacy, then, at the very least, truths about the nature of law must hold good independently of, and not be dependent on, the fact that those truths are espoused by the legal philosophers espousing them.

However, to insist on an overly strong interpretation of a mind-independence condition, such as that for law to have a nature, that which is the case about law must hold good independently of all thoughts, beliefs, intentions, and attitudes about it, is clearly inapt in the case of a human-made social construct. Legal systems, and the norms which comprise them, are brought into existence, and maintained in existence by, inter alia, the beliefs, attitudes, intentions, and actions of those human beings who create, administer, and are subject to them. To hold that, in order for it to have a nature, that which is the case about law must hold good independently of those things that part-constitute it, is to beg the question against law having a nature from the outset, and to do so by applying to it a domain-inappropriate understanding of what is required for law to exist in our social reality.[17]

---

[16] The literature is, of course, voluminous, but for a summary of various of the issues and references to many works discussing them see eg A Miller, 'Realism' in Edward N Zalta (ed), *The Stanford Encyclopedia of Philosophy* (Winter 2021 Edition) https://plato.stanford.edu/archives/win2021/entries/realism/.

[17] Aspects of these issues are considered further in chs 3 to 6.

(c) What might tell in favour of law having a nature?

The rest of this book attempts, in various ways to further flesh out, and render plausible, a domain-apt understanding of the idea of law having a nature which one important part of legal philosophy attempts to identify and explain. Even at this initial stage in the discussion, however, there are some factors which, in my view, tell in favour of this idea. As was pointed out at the beginning of this chapter, many legal philosophers adopting a wide range of views as regards what law's nature is are committed to the view that it has some such nature. If—as is possible—they are all wrong about this, then a thorough explanation of the impossibility of law having a nature which one part of legal philosophy seeks to explain would have to explain how so many who have spent so long considering the matter have fallen into such fundamental error. Moreover, in addition to explicit statements by various legal philosophers that they regard themselves as seeking law's nature, many more legal philosophers, and works of legal philosophy, manifest commitments which are plausibly viewed as supporting aspects of the idea of law having a nature, including the idea that law forms part of social reality, and has a character which our accounts of law can capture in better and worse ways.

Law is created, maintained, developed, and applied by the attitudes, actions, beliefs, and practices of human beings. Once law has been so constituted, however, it can then exist and have a distinctive character which our theories of law can seek to explore and explain. For law to be part of our social reality in the domain-apt sense which I have begun to outline in this chapter, it must be possible that our theories of the nature of law can get things wrong as well as right about law's character. The possibility of mistake must exist as regards our attempts to understand and explain those properties which make law into what it is. Once again it is interesting to note that the acceptance of such a possibility is manifest in the work of a wide variety of legal philosophers. Many legal philosophers appear to have little trouble declaring that, and arguing to persuade their readers that, the views of other legal philosophers are mistaken, and wrong, in their understanding of law, and that their own account is more accurate, and captures and explains law's character better, and more fully.

It should be noted, however, that things are more complex, and comprise many more possibilities, than the binary picture which may come initially to our minds of a theory of law either 'getting it right' or 'getting it wrong' about law. As the discussion in this book progresses, various of the points I make should illuminate the sense in which truth is a necessary, but not sufficient, criterion of the success of a theory of the nature of law. In addition to being true, a successful theory of the nature of law must have significant, and appropriate, explanatory power; appropriate in the sense of doing adequate justice to, amongst other things: the interests and capacities of the audiences it addresses; important contemporary puzzles about law which pique our jurisprudential interest;[18] certain tensions and dualities in law;[19] the way in which law features in the self-understandings of, and practical reasoning processes of, those living under it.[20] Moreover, sometimes points of conflict between different accounts of the nature of law are best understood as disagreements about what needs to be emphasized more (or less) about some facet of law, or about the relative explanatory power of rival accounts of aspects of the nature of law, rather than as disagreements about the truth or falsity, *simpliciter*, of this or that view of law's character.[21]

With these initial considerations in mind, we can proceed to considering some interesting contemporary challenges to the idea that law has a nature which legal philosophy can attempt to identify and explain. If these challenges can be addressed successfully, then the idea of law having a nature—understood in a metaphysically modest and domain-apt way—is bolstered further.

---

[18] These points are discussed in ch 4.
[19] See ch 5.
[20] See ch 6.
[21] This point receives further attention in ch 4.

3
Legal Philosophy and the Nature of Law
Some Challenges Considered

Chapter 2 outlined some initial considerations which are relevant to the issue of whether law can be understood to have a nature which one important part of legal philosophy can attempt to identify and explain. In exploring these considerations, a domain-apt and appropriately metaphysically modest understanding of what it would be for law to have a nature began to emerge. The present chapter bolsters this understanding and explores further the character of legal philosophy about the nature of law by examining some of the challenges which have been levelled at that enterprise. The challenges in question respectively allege that legal philosophy about the nature of law is:

(1) *theoretically imperialist*
(2) guilty of *guild exclusivity*
(3) *impossible*
(4) too *abstract/neglectful of law's social character*
(5) committed to addressing *static, staple questions*.

I discuss these challenges under the above distinct headings but acknowledge that some of them are presented by their proponents—plausibly correctly—as being intertwined in various ways. I hope that by differentiating them as above, and examining each in turn, we can attain a clearer understanding of the emphasis of each challenge and can better appreciate which of them can be dealt with largely within the confines of the present chapter, and which of them demand a fuller response which emerges from the book as a whole. Challenges (1) and (2) can be addressed, and my position on them made clear, within the confines of the present chapter, and so my response to them here is relatively substantial. Challenge (3) raises extremely difficult (and fascinating) questions and puzzles regarding the possibility of developing successful accounts of law's nature. Not all of these can conclusively be put to rest, even in the book as a whole.[1] Nonetheless, various important aspects of challenge (3) are introduced and explained in the present chapter. My response to some of them is offered in the discussion below; my response to others emerges in later chapters, particularly Chapters 5 and 6. Challenges (4) and (5) are largely just identified and noted here: my response to them emerges from Chapter 4 onwards. By this chapter's close, I hope to have further fleshed out and rendered plausible an appropriately metaphysically modest and domain-apt understanding of what it is for law to have a nature that one important part of legal philosophy seeks to explain.

1. Legal Philosophy about the Nature of Law: Theoretically Imperialist?

Some challenges to legal philosophy about the nature of law claim that this enterprise is what I will term here, 'theoretically imperialist'. Such claims come in different forms of varying strength: for example, that legal philosophy about the nature of law seeks to arrogate the entire domain of theorizing about law and to supplant other jurisprudential approaches; or that legal philosophy about the nature of law seeks to establish itself as the dominant or most important approach to theorizing about law, and to demote and denigrate alternatives. Such charges can be found in various forms in the work of Frederick Schauer, Brian Tamanaha, and Roger Cotterrell.[2]

In a series of articles,[3] and in a recent book,[4] Schauer advocates a methodological approach which focuses on those features which law typically, rather

---

[1] In ch 7, s 3(a), I discuss some reasons why this is so.
[2] In each section of this chapter, I select only a few theorists' views in illustrating the character of this challenge. There are many others whose thought-provoking work could have been chosen. It should be noted that Nicola Lacey has used the terms 'intellectual imperialism' (in N Lacey, 'Philosophical Foundations of the Common Law: Social not Metaphysical' in J Horder (ed), Oxford Essays in Jurisprudence (OUP 2000) 18) and 'philosophical imperialism' (in N Lacey, 'Analytical Jurisprudence Versus Descriptive Sociology Revisited' (2006) 84 *Texas Law Review* 945, 948) in characterizing some of the pitfalls which lie in wait for legal philosophy about the nature of law. In my view, however, Lacey's criticisms primarily concern its alleged attempts to be 'self-standing', and the tendencies of some of its purveyors to turn a deaf ear to the possibility of valuable interaction between legal philosophy about the nature of law and other theoretical inquiries concerning law. This being so, I consider these aspects of Lacey's views in s 2 of this chapter.
[3] See F Schauer, 'On the Nature of the Nature of Law' (2012) 98 Archiv für Rechts- und Sozialphilosophie 457; F Schauer, 'Necessity, Importance, and the Nature of Law' in J Ferrer Beltrán, JJ Moreso, and DM Papayannis (eds), Neutrality and Theory of Law (Springer 2013); F Schauer, 'Hart's Anti-Essentialism' in L Duarte d'Almeida, J Edwards, and A Dolcetti (eds), Reading HLA Hart's The Concept of Law (Hart Publishing 2013).
[4] F Schauer, The Force of Law (Harvard University Press 2015). See especially the Preface, ch 1, ch 3 ss 4 and 5, ch 6 s 3, ch 7 s 1, and ch 11.

than necessarily, possesses. As a concomitant he casts doubt on the value of, and possibility of, legal philosophy about the nature of law, and criticizes what he regards as its overemphasis within the panoply of theoretical inquiries concerning law:

> What I do challenge is the view that conceptual analysis of the concept of law—and a conceptual analysis seeking to explain with philosophical tools the necessary or essential features of law—is the *only* worthy jurisprudential enterprise ... My target is hardly made of straw. Joseph Raz has described the analysis of features present in anything less than all possible legal systems as (mere) sociology of law, as opposed to philosophy of law.[5]

In similar vein, Tamanaha is critical of what he regards as the assumptions made by, and commitments of, theories purporting to capture law's nature:

> An account of the nature of law is, according to leading analytical jurisprudents, *the* defining characteristic of general jurisprudence ... legal philosophers of the first type [those concerned with the nature of law] reject sociological insights about what law is for being too empirical, too contingent, too parochial—not abstract and universal enough.[6]
>
> [b]eneath it all the philosopher is asserting that his intuitions about law trump others. The confident insistence by analytical jurisprudents that they have identified necessary truths about the nature of law has the effect of clothing a parochial conception of law in universalistic dress to serve as a standard for all times and places.[7]

In a somewhat gentler key, Roger Cotterrell—while making it clear that he personally supports a kind of 'distinct but mutually compatible' vision of the respective roles of the more abstract and philosophical enterprise which he terms legal philosophy, and the more concrete and empirically focused enterprise he terms jurisprudence—nonetheless cautions that:

> [w]hat usually insulates legal philosophy from systematical empirical inquiries is ultimately not the purported difficulty of the latter but a conviction that empirical research is uninteresting as compared with efforts to discover

---

[5] Schauer, 'Necessity, Importance, and the Nature of Law' (n 3) 28 (emphasis in original).
[6] B Tamanaha, 'What Is 'General' Jurisprudence? A Critique of Universalistic Claims by Philosophical Concepts of Law' (2011) 2 *Transnational Legal Theory* 287, 289–90 (emphasis in original).
[7] ibid 307.

context-free truth or to conceptualise what is essential in law, these efforts being guided by intuitions as to what is philosophically significant, or what are reliable foundations for inquiry.[8]

Albeit with some differences in the focus and the strength of their claims, these theorists all charge legal philosophy about the nature of law with 'crowding out'—by denigrating, demoting, or ignoring—other types of theorizing about law, and with having an exaggerated sense of its own scope and importance.

In considering these charges, the first point to note is that this challenge does not—at least as expressed in the quotes above—seem to cast doubt on the *possibility* of the enterprise of seeking to identify and explain the nature of law. The claim is rather that legal philosophy about the nature of law has become too big for its boots, and/or is under the mistaken impression that its boots are the only, or at any rate the only important, footwear in town. Particularly pertinent in the present context is that these objections to legal philosophy about the nature of law do not challenge that enterprise in the sense of disputing that the initial considerations discussed in Chapter 2 can hold in the case of law, such as the necessary/contingent distinction, or the idea that law—in some sense—forms part of our social reality. It is the case, however, that elsewhere in their work, Schauer and Tamanaha do at times appear to cast doubt on the very possibility of legal philosophy about the nature of law. Aspects of this challenge are discussed further in section 3 below, but we can note for now that the charge of theoretical imperialism per se is not of this character.

A second point to note is that these charges of theoretical imperialism appear to have a somewhat ad personam flavour: Schauer mentions Joseph Raz, and Tamanaha 'leading analytical jurisprudents'. But even if they are right that particular legal philosophers do or have exhibited such tendencies, this does not mean that *all* attempts to engage in legal philosophy about the nature of law *must* exhibit them, and so is not a strike against the character of such an enterprise in principle. Subscribing to the view that a useful distinction can be drawn between the enterprise of identifying and explaining those features which law must possess in order to be law, and the enterprise of ascertaining and explaining those features which law often, or typically, or characteristically, or in some socio-political circumstances, exhibits does not say anything as regards the relative importance, or value, or usefulness (however understood) of these two enterprises. Nor does it say anything about the appropriate way to understand the *relations between* these enterprises, including whether they

---

[8] R Cotterrell, 'Why Jurisprudence Is Not Legal Philosophy' (2014) 5 *Jurisprudence* 41, 50.

might be not only mutually compatible, but also complementary and mutually enhancing.

Moreover, on further examination, news of 'theoretical imperialism', even on an ad personam basis, appears to be somewhat exaggerated. Schauer identifies Raz as a particularly egregious exemplar of the tendency of legal philosophers of the nature of law to view as relatively less important, and to denigrate, other types of theorizing about law. He appears to base this view on some remarks Raz makes in his essay 'The Institutional Nature of Law':

> Since a legal theory must be true of all legal systems the identifying features by which it characterizes them must of necessity be very general and abstract. It must disregard those functions which some legal systems fulfil in some societies because of the special social, economic, or cultural conditions of those societies ... This is the difference between legal philosophy and sociology of law. The latter is concerned with the particular, the former with the necessary and universal. Sociology of law provides a wealth of detailed information and analysis of the functions of law in some particular societies. Legal philosophy has to be content with those few features which all legal systems necessarily possess.[9]

Interestingly, although I focus on Schauer's criticism here, similar points in respect of the same passage can be found in the work of several contemporary legal philosophers.[10] As has already been noted, Schauer comments on these remarks as follows: 'My target is hardly made of straw. Joseph Raz has described the analysis of features present in anything less than all possible legal systems as (mere) sociology of law, as opposed to philosophy of law.'[11] One difficulty with this comment is that the parenthetical 'mere' is entirely of Schauer's own invention. Nothing in the passage from Raz just quoted appears to state or suggest that he views sociology of law as less important or less valuable than what he variously refers to as legal theory or legal philosophy. Indeed, the passage indicates its author's view that whereas sociology of law offers us a wealth of detailed analysis, legal philosophy, by contrast, is a rather spartan and austere

---

[9] J Raz, 'The Institutional Nature of Law' in J Raz, The Authority of Law (2nd edn, OUP 2009) 104–105.
[10] See eg B Tamanaha, 'Glimmers of an Awakening within Analytical Jurisprudence' in U Baxi, C McCrudden, and A Paliwala (eds), Law's Ethical, Global and Theoretical Contexts: Essays in Honour of William Twining (CUP 2015) 357; K Walton, 'Legal Philosophy and the Social Sciences: The Potential for Complementarity' (2015) 6 Jurisprudence 231, 246; Cotterrell (n 8) 50, and also n 48; N Lacey, In Search of Criminal Responsibility: Ideas, Interests, and Institutions (OUP 2016) 192–93.
[11] Schauer, 'Necessity, Importance, and the Nature of Law' (n 3) 28.

enterprise capable of delivering truths only of a very general and abstract sort. Moreover, Raz also states explicitly elsewhere in his work that in delineating legal philosophy about the nature of law from other types of theoretical enterprises concerning law, he does not intend to denigrate those other sorts of inquiry, and that he regards the titles we give to various approaches to theorizing about law as largely a matter of terminological convenience:

> I will be using 'a theory of law' in a narrow sense, as referring to an explanation of the nature of law ... in choosing this narrow understanding of 'theory of law' I do not mean to dispute the appropriateness of other theoretical investigations about the law, some of which I dabbled in myself on other occasions, nor to deny them the title of theories of law. My choice to use the term in the narrow sense explained here is purely a matter of terminological convenience.[12]

Raz, of course, is but one legal philosopher amongst many who are interested in examining the nature of law. But that, too, supports the points I made above: even if Raz did take the disparaging view which Schauer ascribes to him—which seems false given Raz's views quoted above—this would not establish that the theoretically imperialist charge sticks against all attempts at engaging in legal philosophy about the nature of law.

For the avoidance of doubt, let me state unequivocally that the approach to legal philosophy which I advocate, although it is primarily, and certainly initially[13] concerned with identifying and explaining the nature of law, is not in the business of demoting, denigrating, or displacing any other type of theoretical inquiry concerning law. As I have already emphasized in Chapter 2, to contend that legal philosophy about the nature of law holds a distinctive place in our understanding of law is not to suggest that other types of inquiry concerning law are less important, less interesting, or less worthy of our engagement.[14] Moreover, as is demonstrated in the course of several lines of argument in this book as a whole, my own 'philosophy of legal philosophy' highlights and advocates various kinds of pluralism and diversity in legal philosophical inquiry, and welcomes opportunities for mutually enhancing complementarity between different theoretical inquiries concerning law.

---

[12] J Raz, 'Can There Be a Theory of Law' in J Raz, Between Authority and Interpretation (OUP 2009) 17.
[13] This point is discussed in chs 7 and 8.
[14] See ch 2, s 2.

2. Legal Philosophy about the Nature of Law: 'Guild Exclusivity'?

Challenges falling under this heading overlap and intertwine with those under (1) above in the views of several of those making these objections. However, there is a difference in emphasis which justifies discussing this challenge under a separate heading. The charge that legal philosophy about the nature of law indulges in what I refer to here as 'guild exclusivity' does not necessarily include a claim that this approach seeks to denigrate, demote, or supplant other types of theoretical inquiry about law. Rather, the twofold focus of the 'guild exclusivity'[15] objection is:

(a) that legal philosophy about the nature of law seeks to erect a disciplinary 'boundary fence' around a certain approach to theorizing about law, lays claim to a specific label for it—usually 'legal philosophy', but sometimes 'jurisprudence', or 'analytical jurisprudence'—and refuses to admit to its ranks anyone, and any work, not adopting that approach; and

(b) that legal philosophy about the nature of law takes the view that any enterprises classified as being outwith the 'boundary fence' are irrelevant to, and have nothing valuable to offer, legal philosophy about the nature of law.

We should note at the outset that, just as with the first challenge examined above, this line of criticism does not appear to bear directly on the very possibility of legal philosophy about the nature of law and does not appear to dispute that the initial considerations discussed in Chapter 2—regarding what would need to be the case for law to have a nature—can hold. Rather, this challenge is concerned with the character and consequences of the allegedly isolationist tendencies of one approach to theorizing about law.

In terms of point (a), the 'seeking to erect a disciplinary boundary fence' charge has been pressed by a variety of legal theorists:

> Legal philosophy's protocols divide, limit and insulate it from an outward-looking curiosity about the whole range of theoretical issues that might be raised in relation to law, and about the relevance of empirical and comparative

---

[15] It is possible the implied analogy is somewhat misplaced. Some historians argue, for example, that medieval craft guilds did not in fact exhibit all the vices commonly attributed to them: G Richardson, 'A Tale of Two Theories: Monopolies and Craft Guilds in Medieval England and Modern Imagination' (2001) 23 *Journal of the History of Economic Thought* 217.

inquiries about law.[16] Accordingly, my argument is that if legal theorists want to escape the sort of isolation or irrelevance risked by a view of jurisprudence as autonomous, they should abandon Hart's insistence that analytic philosophy is its exclusive disciplinary resource.[17] The mark of contemporary analytic jurisprudence is its intellectual isolation.[18] [a]nalytical jurists have frequently remained rather innocent of social theory and empirical social research, and have at times manifested an attitude of haughty, and not always benign, neglect towards work in these fields. Few now deny that there is a place for such inquiries, and some have insisted that it is an important place. However, they appear to have remained confident that it is a clearly different place from their own, and few show evidence of frequent visits.[19]

A perusal of these theorists' views reveals a wide range of theoretical inquiries concerning law which they respectively believe that legal philosophy about the nature of law seeks to isolate itself from, including legal sociology, comparative and empirical work, theoretical work concerning particular areas of law (sometimes termed 'special jurisprudence'), legal practice, and psychology.

The 'laying claim to a particular label, and reserving membership of that domain of inquiry for those engaged in legal philosophy about the nature of law' aspect of point (a) above emerges in particularly clear form in recent work by Schauer:

[i]n our world field definitions matter. They determine what is taught to students under this or that heading, or not at all. They influence who is or is not qualified for a position ... They influence what will be published in one journal or another, and, again, possibly not at all. Thus my attempt in The Force of Law to make clear that essentialism is contested terrain ... is an effort to avoid at the outset *the claim that any theoretical and philosophically-influenced inquiry into the character of law that does not exist within the domain of essentialism and the domain of what is necessarily true of all possible legal system in all possible worlds is simply not jurisprudence or philosophy of law at all.* The debates about essentialism are certainly worth having ... However, I do want to insist

---

[16] Cotterrell, 'Why Jurisprudence is not Legal Philosophy' (n 8) 52.
[17] Lacey, 'Analytical Jurisprudence vs Descriptive Sociology Revisited' (n 2) 948.
[18] D Priel, 'Positivism and the Separation of Law and Jurisprudence' http://digitalcommons.osgoode.yorku.ca/cgi/viewcontent.cgi?article1064&contextclpe p 1. See also D Priel, 'Is There One Right Answer to the Question of the Nature of Law?' in W Waluchow and S Sciaraffa (eds), Philosophical Foundations of the Nature of Law (OUP 2013), especially ss 4–7.
[19] M Krygier, 'The Concept of Law and Social Theory' (1982) 2 Oxford Journal of Legal Studies 155, 157. Krygier makes it clear in this article that he thinks the boundary erecting and lack of frequent visiting runs both ways between legal philosophy about the nature of law and social theory.

that these debates—including debates about the role of empirical inquiry and about the relative values of particular and general jurisprudence—should be understood as taking place within jurisprudence, and not as a ticket of admission to its domains at the outset.[20]

Immediately prior to this passage, Schauer states that he regards Joseph Raz, Jules Coleman, Scott Shapiro, and myself as making 'the claim'—which I have emphasized in the passage quoted above—that any inquiry about law which is not essentialist or concerned with what is necessarily true of all possible legal systems in all possible worlds does not count as jurisprudence or as legal philosophy at all.[21]

Do these charges stick? I am sceptical that they do. Raz, for example, as was noted above, appears to take the view that nothing much turns on what titles we give to various different approaches to theorizing about law beyond context-specific purposes such as terminological utility in the course of a particular discussion.[22] It would seem somewhat odd that a legal philosopher holding such views would be interested in policing who is, and who is not, to be properly classified as falling under one or other such approach, and in determining who is, and who is not, entitled to say they are doing philosophy of law.

For my own part, I have never held the view that only those engaged in legal philosophy about the nature of law are doing jurisprudence or legal philosophy or philosophy of law. In my book *Evaluation and Legal Theory*,[23] which Schauer references in erroneously ascribing to me the above claim, I use the term 'analytical jurisprudence' to refer to one type of theorizing about law, ie the type that I refer to in this book as legal philosophy about the nature of law.[24] In the course of so doing, I make it clear that I regard this as only one type of theorizing about law amongst many,[25] that I regard many other approaches as valuable,[26] and that I do not think much turns on the classificatory issues.[27] I also do not, as Schauer has also erroneously claimed, exclude Dworkin's work from the province of 'analytical jurisprudence', let alone jurisprudence, *tout court*.[28] Rather, I say explicitly that to do so would be very problematic, while

---

[20] F Schauer, 'A Reply to Five Friends' (2016) 29 *Ratio Juris* 343, 353 (my emphasis, to assist with the discussion that follows).
[21] ibid.
[22] See n 12 above and accompanying text.
[23] J Dickson, Evaluation and Legal Theory (Hart Publishing 2001).
[24] ibid ch 1, s (c).
[25] ibid 15–17 and text accompanying n 23.
[26] ibid.
[27] ibid 22–24.
[28] Schauer makes this claim in 'Necessity, Importance, and the Nature of Law' (n 3) 28.

mentioning that there is nonetheless some debate amongst commentators as to whether Dworkin is attempting to offer a universal account of law's nature.[29]

My views on these matters were hence set out some time ago, and, as my more recent work indicates, they have not changed:

> [i]n my view, the terms 'legal philosophy', 'philosophy of law', 'jurisprudence', and 'legal theory' are largely interchangeable, and that it is best, especially at the outset of inquiries into the character and criteria of success of our discipline, to adopt as broad a working definition of legal philosophy as possible ... by 'legal philosophy' I mean no more or less than any illuminating inquiries into and accounts of various aspects of law's character.[30]

This being so, I do not myself engage in, nor see the point of anyone engaging in, attempts to exclude from this or that disciplinary label, jurisprudential work of one kind or another.

Of course, sometimes, in some specific contexts, for some specific purpose(s), we may wish to use terms such as 'analytical jurisprudence' or 'legal philosophy about the nature of law' or 'the philosophy of law' or 'particular jurisprudence' or 'general jurisprudence' or 'jurisprudence' in particular ways, in order to express more precisely what we want to say, and to try to guard against misunderstandings regarding what we have said. As is noted above, I have done this with 'analytical jurisprudence' in *Evaluation and Legal Theory*, and with 'legal philosophy about the nature of law' in the present work. But beyond such context-specific demarcation, which should be done perspicuously, and only for good reason, such as more precisely to pin down which questions, theories, or theorists are under discussion in a particular context, I have no interest in erecting 'boundary fences' around 'legal philosophy' or 'jurisprudence', or in policing which theories and theorists are allowed entry. In this, I agree with Martin Krygier, who notes that:

> Like members of craft unions, academics are rather fond of erecting and maintaining disciplinary boundaries. Such boundaries, of course, have legitimate purposes, particularly pedagogic ones, and as indications of special skills, approaches and areas of interest ... But not all such boundaries are worth preserving, and even those that are should allow free passage where

---

[29] Dickson (n 23) 21–25.
[30] J Dickson, 'Ours is a Broad Church: Indirectly Evaluative Legal Philosophy as a Facet of Jurisprudential Inquiry' (2015) 6 *Jurisprudence* 207, 214.

appropriate. Sometimes, precisely because one has only a sketchy idea of what is happening on the other side of the fence, one caricatures it.[31]

Krygier's remarks in both this passage, and the one quoted earlier,[32] do, however, light the way towards what may be the more difficult issue in terms of the charge of 'guild exclusivity' sometimes made against legal philosophy about the nature of law. The issue in question appears in point (b) identified at the beginning of this section: that legal philosophy about the nature of law holds that other types of theoretical inquiry about law are irrelevant to it and have nothing valuable to offer it, and hence it ignores and/or inadequately engages with such types of inquiry. In my view, it is primarily *this* point which drives the concerns raised by Lacey and Krygier in the passages from their work quoted above. It has also been forcefully pressed against Raz, Shapiro, Gardner, Alexy, and myself, by Kevin Walton in his article 'Legal Philosophy and the Social Sciences: The Potential for Complementarity'.[33] Walton claims that these theorists view their subject as 'exclusively concerned with the *a priori* identification of law's essential and significant qualities'[34] and deny the possibility of any mutual benefit or complementarity arising from legal philosophy about the nature of law engaging with other types of jurisprudential inquiry.[35]

Once again, I doubt that those theorists he names hold the views that Walton ascribes to them. And I can with confidence state my own position: I do not regard our discipline—legal philosophy or jurisprudence or legal theory or the philosophy of law—as exclusively concerned with identifying law's essential qualities; I doubt that any significant part of the subject can be pursued independently of experience of the social reality of law;[36] and, as has already been mentioned, I strongly support and am open to seeking possibilities for mutual benefit and complementarity between a variety of different approaches to understanding law.[37]

Something appears to have gone wrong somewhere with respect to mutual understanding between theorists on these issues, resulting in significant misconceptions such as these. Can we, and, if so, how can we, improve this situation? It is important to begin by acknowledging that there is some truth to the complaint that legal philosophy about the nature of law has not engaged

---

[31] Krygier (n 19) 180.
[32] See n 19 above and accompanying text.
[33] Walton (n 10).
[34] ibid 245.
[35] ibid 245–49.
[36] This point is considered further in s 3(a) of this chapter.
[37] See also the discussion in chs 4 and 8.

sufficiently with other theoretical inquiries concerning law, such as to develop the possibility of productive complementarity between them. To my mind, however, and *contra* Walton, this is not due to those engaging in legal philosophy about the nature of law erroneously believing that other types of theoretical inquiry are irrelevant to theirs. Rather, I see the situation in terms of missed opportunities, most likely engendered at least in part by legal theorists of all stripes becoming more specialized as regards the issues they tackle, lacking knowledge and expertise of areas of jurisprudential research beyond their own, and sadly having neither the time nor opportunity in the conditions of contemporary academia to try to remedy this.

Nicola Lacey and Martin Krygier have, in my view, an accurate and fair-minded understanding of this situation, probably stemming in significant part from the fact that each has engaged in insightful research both in what some would classify as legal philosophy and in what some would classify as social theory and/or sociology of law. Their work exhibits considerable nuance in diagnosing the reasons behind lack of engagement between and across different approaches to theorizing about law, and highlights that often it is awareness of one's own ignorance, and/or fear of wading in to another area of research without appropriate expertise, that discourages legal theorists from stepping beyond their own research specialism to find possible complementarities with other types of research.[38] Both also acknowledge that unwillingness and/or inability to engage with other types of research emanates from both 'sides' of, for example, the alleged legal philosophy about the nature of law/sociology of law divide.[39]

I am very much in agreement with Krygier's and Lacey's views in this regard. Much more could have, and should have, been done by legal theorists to try to understand different types of inquiry concerning law, and to explore the possibilities for complementarity between them. However, and as Lacey in particular has noted, we may now be entering a more promising jurisprudential era in this regard,[40] and the fact that opportunities for complementarity have not yet adequately been explored does not mean that they cannot be explored. The wide-ranging and insightful contributions to recent volumes of essays such as *Concepts of Law: Comparative, Jurisprudential and Social Science Perspectives*,[41]

---

[38] See eg Krygier (n 19) 155–59; Lacey, 'Analytical Jurisprudence vs Descriptive Sociology Revisited' (n 2) eg at 947, 956–59, 967–69, 973–76.
[39] Krygier (n 19) 156–58, 180; Lacey, 'Analytical Jurisprudence vs Descriptive Sociology Revisited' (n 2) 947.
[40] Lacey, 'Analytical Jurisprudence vs Descriptive Sociology Revisited' (n 2) 959–60; N Lacey, 'Reflections on the Philosophy of Law' (2012) 1 *Rivista di Filosofia del Diritto* 91, 98–99.
[41] Seán Patrick Donlan and Lukas Heckendorn Urscheler (eds), Concepts of Law: Comparative, Jurisprudential and Social Science Perspectives (Ashgate 2014; Routledge 2016).

and *In Pursuit of Pluralist Jurisprudence*[42] make significant strides forward in this regard. Also of note is the increased interest shown by some legal philosophers in understanding the relations between law's necessary properties and law's contingent properties, and in using that understanding to construct well-rounded theories of law. Such an approach has found sustained and insightful expression in the work of Michael Giudice, who devotes a significant part of his book, *Understanding the Nature of Law: A Case for Constructive Conceptual Explanation*[43] to examining exactly these issues in both abstract and concrete contexts.

This being so, it is important to acknowledge that, although there is some truth to the second aspect—aspect (b)—of the 'guild exclusivity' charge, this should be tempered by a realization that there is no reason in principle why barriers to complementarity between different sorts of theoretical approaches cannot be overcome. In our attempts to overcome them, we should embrace and encourage a spirit of optimism, bolstered by some excellent work in this regard which has already emerged.

3. Legal Philosophy about the Nature of Law: Impossible?

The preceding two challenges do not contend that law cannot have a nature, or that legal philosophy about the nature of law is an enterprise which we cannot pursue successfully. The objections considered in this section, however, do call these things into question. The discussion below examines three aspects of what I term the 'impossibility' challenge, under the following headings:

(a) **Metaphysical extravagance?**
(b) **Can socially constructed entities have a nature?**
(c) **Can our concept of law successfully pick out aspects of the nature of law?**

(a) Metaphysical extravagance?

As I argued in Chapter 2, we must strive to come to an understanding of the idea of law having a nature that is appropriate to, and apt for, the kind of thing that law is. If we fail to do so and hold law to an inappropriate standard which it

---

[42] Nicole Roughan and Andrew Halpin, In Pursuit of Pluralist Jurisprudence (CUP 2017).
[43] M Giudice, Understanding the Nature of Law: A Case for Constructive Conceptual Explanation (Edward Elgar Publishing 2015), especially chs 3, 5, 7, and 9.

will inevitably fail to meet, then we stack the deck against the idea of law having a nature which one part of legal philosophy can attempt to explain from the outset, without properly exploring what that idea may, and may not, require. This being so, it is unfortunate that this very tendency—that of postulating an implausible standard which would have to be met for law to have a nature, and hence for legal philosophy about the nature of law to be possible—features significantly in the work of several theorists already encountered in this chapter.

Tamanaha, for example, contends that legal philosophy about the nature of law seeks truths about law which hold good not merely in all human societies, but in 'all possible legal systems on all possible worlds, real and imaginary, at all possible times'.[44] He further claims that proponents of legal philosophy about the nature of law unjustifiably castigate other jurisprudential approaches on the grounds that they do not seek such truths:

> It is outlandish, however, to suggest that a jurisprudential framework that encompasses multiple forms of law around the world is not universal enough because it covers only existing legal systems, failing to reach systems that do not exist. Incredibly, this cluster of views is held by some of the most prominent legal philosophers in the Anglo-American legal world.[45]

As has already been noted, Schauer regards many contemporary legal philosophers working on puzzles about the nature of law, including myself, as making the claim that:

> [a]ny theoretical and philosophically-influenced inquiry into the character of law that does not exist within the domain of essentialism and the domain of what is necessarily true of all possible legal system in all possible worlds is simply not jurisprudence or philosophy of law at all.[46]

Walton, too, adds his voice to this chorus when he criticizes much contemporary legal philosophy about the nature of law for 'engaging in an *a priori* search for law's essence'.[47]

What these theorists share is a tendency to interpret the aims, and claims, of those engaging in legal philosophy about the nature of law in what we might call a 'metaphysically heavy-duty' or even a 'metaphysically extravagant'

---

[44] Tamanaha (n 6) 290.
[45] ibid 290–91.
[46] Schauer (n 20) 353.
[47] Walton (n 10) 249.

manner: extravagant given the character of the phenomenon—law—that we are dealing with. Doing so immediately raises, and is intended by them to raise, doubts that law, and legal philosophy about the nature of law, can possibly make good on those aims and claims. Alleging that legal philosophy about the nature of law always seeks *a priori* truths immediately raises the question of whether it makes sense to think that we can have knowledge of a socially constituted and instantiated practice such as law without reference to experience of how law actually operates in society, and of how it impinges upon our practical reasoning. Claiming that legal philosophers interested in the nature of law always seek universal truths that hold not merely in human contexts but which are necessarily true in all possible worlds, immediately raises doubts that such philosophers have grasped the sense in which law is deeply rooted in the aims, functions, and limitations of governance practices in human society.

In my view, the correct approach here is not so much to engage head-on with these doubts in the form they take in the work of Tamanaha, Schauer, and Walton, as to question the interpretation of the aims and claims of legal philosophy about the nature of law that fuels them. We can begin by noting that a 'metaphysically extravagant' interpretation of what legal philosophers might mean by necessity, universality, and 'the nature of' in the context of theories about the nature of law does not sit well with various of law's social and institutional features. Law is a human-made social practice, and legal norms come into existence, remain in existence, are interpreted and applied etc. as a result of complex social and institutional practices involving the actions, beliefs, and attitudes of those who create, administer and are subject to law. Moreover, the circumstances in which law comes into being, and the governance practices it part-constitutes and supports, are deeply rooted in the character and needs of human societies at certain points in their development.

This being so it should alert us that something may have gone awry in the interpretation of the aims and claims of legal philosophy about the nature of law being offered by some of those who question the possibility of that enterprise. Perhaps, then, we should *not* jump to the conclusion that legal philosophers seeking to explain the nature of law seek to do so in some *a priori* manner without reference to experience of the social reality of law, or view them as making claims that they regard as true in all possible worlds, human or no.[48]

---

[48] NB I cannot attempt here to explore in depth what various legal philosophers who regard other legal philosophers as mounting *a priori* arguments mean by the term *a priori*, or what precisely they have in mind in critically regarding others as mounting arguments intended to be true in all possible worlds. One reason why not is that those making such claims often do not explain what they take these terms to mean, or the basis on which they interpret the aims of various other legal philosophers in the way that they do. This being so, I have attempted to render such legal philosophers' views in their own

Contra the view of some challengers, the idea of searching for law's nature does not inevitably to drive us to an understanding of that quest which is metaphysically extravagant in character. Indeed, when we examine more closely what various legal philosophers writing about the nature of law are actually doing, and how they understand what they are doing, a different picture emerges.

Michael Giudice, for example, disputes head-on the idea that legal philosophy about the nature of law is in the business of searching for either analytic, or *a priori*, truths, and devotes a chapter of his recent book to developing and defending the alternative view, that: '[t]o the extent that many of the most interesting necessity claims in jurisprudence are defensible, they are best understood and characterized... as a form of *a posteriori* necessary truth'.[49] Moreover, when Joseph Raz argues, against Hans Kelsen, that we cannot accurately determine which norms belong to one and the same legal system by looking solely to which norms belong to the same Kelsenian chain of validity, and ignoring social and political facts such as the processes by which one state can peacefully grant independence to another and the attitudes of the citizens and legal officials in those states, he does not appear to mount an argument which is *a priori* in the sense of proceeding independently of experience or observation of law's operation in our social world.[50] Indeed, given Raz's reliance in the discussion on knowledge of circumstances in human history where states peacefully grant independence to former colonies, and of the social attitudes held by both the courts and the population of each of the two independent states which emerge in such circumstances, it seems highly implausible to interpret his argument in such a manner.

In addition, Raz, in responding to criticisms that his view of law having a nature falls foul of a problematic kind of essentialism which is out of place in the case of a human-made social institution, offers the following rebuttal:

> It seems to me that Bulygin is mistaken in attributing to me a belief in essentialism. There are various things philosophers mean by essentialism. The common one is associated with the thought that some common nouns are

words wherever possible, and to give reasons why I regard aspects of their interpretation of what others are doing as implausible.

[49] Giudice, *Understanding the Nature of Law* (n 43) 90–91 (internal reference omitted) and see more generally ch 4 of that work. Giudice argues that legal philosophy should not be understood as seeking *a priori* truths about law, and that Saul Kripke's category of *a posteriori* necessary truths is useful in understanding some of the claims that legal philosophers make. For Kripke's views see S Kripke, Naming and Necessity (Blackwell 1981).
[50] See Raz, *The Authority of Law* (n 9) 127–28; J Raz, The Concept of a Legal System (2nd edn, OUP 1980) 100–109.

rigid designators, that is that the meaning of those common nouns is determined by the way reality is divided ... It has been popular to think that natural kind terms are of this kind ... No one believes that all words are natural kind words, and very few people—perhaps only Michael Moore—believe that 'the law' is a rigid designator. My discussion of the way the concept of law changes shows that I hold beliefs inconsistent with such a view.[51]

Furthermore, Leslie Green, in engaging with Schauer's recent work on methodology, notes that HLA Hart took a distinctively human, and non-metaphysically extravagant approach to the idea of necessity in his work, an approach which Green also welcomes and embraces:

[i]t is Hart who insists that 'a place must be reserved, besides definitions and ordinary statements of fact, for a third category of statements: those the truth of which is contingent on human beings and the world they live in retaining the salient characteristics which they have' ... [i]n the human sciences, as soon as we start down the dark path of things that hold true in 'all possible worlds' we hear a lot of whistling to keep up courage, since we do not have a secure grasp of which worlds are possible. To the extent that Schauer is on Hart's side here, I am on Schauer's. What is 'humanly necessary' is as important to jurisprudence as what is 'strictly' (conceptually, metaphysically, nomically) necessary.[52]

As these examples show, several legal philosophers engaged in identifying and explaining law's nature espouse a considerably more metaphysically modest understanding of what is involved in so doing than is attributed to them by Tamanaha, Schauer, and Walton. I also support taking an appropriately metaphysically modest view of legal philosophy about the nature of law. Given the points made above about law's human-made and societally situated character, such a view seems plausible, sensible, and well supported.

Is an appropriately metaphysically modest understanding of what we are doing when we engage in legal philosophy about the nature of law compatible with the initial considerations discussed in Chapter 2? In my view: yes.

---

[51] J Raz, 'Theories and Concepts: Responding to Alexy and Bulygin' in Una Discusion Sobre la Teoria del Derecho (Marcial Pons 2007) (in Spanish) 118; also available (in English) at http://sites.google.com/site/josephnraz/theory%26concepts. See also B Bix, 'Raz on Necessity' (2003) 22 Law and Philosophy, 537.
[52] L Green, 'The Forces of Law: Duty, Coercion, and Power' (2016) 29(2) Ratio Juris 164, 177. The internal quotation is from HLA Hart, The Concept of Law (3rd edn, OUP 2012) with a Postscript edited by PA Bulloch and J Raz, and with an Introduction and Notes by L Green 199–200.

Contending that a necessary/contingent distinction must hold, differentiating those properties which law must possess in order to be law from those properties which it may or may not possess and still remain law, does not, of itself, commit us to a particular interpretation of the sort of necessity involved. The views of Giudice, Raz, and Green noted above also support this view, and begin to indicate some alternative possibilities in this regard. Furthermore, as is discussed in sub-section (b) below, adopting a metaphysically modest understanding of what it is for law to have a nature does not appear to threaten the idea of law being part of our social reality, so long as we adopt an appropriately 'domain-apt' interpretation of this idea.

(b) Can socially constructed entities have a nature?

We can work our way into the challenge falling under this heading by considering a comparison frequently made, and a contrast frequently drawn, between natural kinds, such as gold or water, and socially constructed entities, such as law:

> [w]hatever the status of essentialist understandings of concepts like triangle and gold, such understandings may be inappropriate for the concept of law in the same way they may be inappropriate for concepts like art.[53] Artefact concepts, even simple ones like 'chair,' are notoriously resistant to analyses in terms of their essential attributes, both because they are hostage to changing human ends and purposes, and because they cannot be individuated by their natural properties—unlike say natural phenomena like 'water', which just is H2O.[54]

We should readily acknowledge that the character of those aspects of reality picked out by concepts such as water and gold differs from the character of those aspects of reality picked out by the concept of law, and that this affects the criteria for the correct application of those concepts to that reality. It is

---

[53] Schauer, 'On the Nature of the Nature of Law' (n 3) 466 (internal references omitted).
[54] B Leiter, 'The Demarcation Problem in Jurisprudence: A New Case for Scepticism' (2011) *31 Oxford Journal of Legal Studies* 663, 666 (internal reference omitted). It should be noted that I use these quotations from Schauer and Leiter to introduce the relevant issues, rather than to attribute to them precise stances on these issues, or to examine the extent to which their views can or cannot be reconciled with mine. These theorists' views in this regard are nuanced and have changed somewhat over time. See eg Schauer (n 20) s 2; B Leiter, 'Legal Positivism about the Artifact Law: A Retrospective Assessment' in L Burazin, K Himma, and C Roversi (eds), Law as an Artifact (OUP 2018).

important to emphasize, however, that we should resist any temptation to overstate or exaggerate those differences, from either direction.

As I have already outlined in Chapter 2, and as will be explored further in Chapters 5 and 6, it is vital to note that, although the 'social reality' that the concept of law picks out is different from the 'natural world reality' picked out by concepts such as water and gold, this does not mean that the latter two concepts do pick out aspects of reality to which our understanding is answerable, while the former does not. The way we think of, speak of, reason about, and plan our social lives in terms of law indicates that we take its social reality very seriously indeed, and know that it is, in the relevant sense, independent of our thoughts and beliefs about it.

For example, suppose I go on holiday to Scotland and I believe that, as Scotland is part of the same state (ie the United Kingdom) as England (where I live), that hence the law in Scotland on the legal limit of blood alcohol allowed for driving is the same as in England, ie 80 milligrams of alcohol per 100 millilitres of blood.[55] Suppose, too, that from past experience I know that, in my case, if I drink two small glasses of wine, and wait for one hour after finishing the second one, I will have less than 80 mg of alcohol per 100 ml of blood. I do this during my holiday in Scotland, then drive from the pub to the holiday cottage I have rented. If I am stopped by the police and they determine, on administering the relevant tests to me, that my blood alcohol level is 60 mg of alcohol per 100 ml of blood, they may charge me with driving a motor vehicle with alcohol concentration above the prescribed limit, because, contrary to my belief, in Scotland the relevant legal limit is not 80 mg per 100 ml of blood, but was reduced in 2014 to 50 mg of alcohol per 100 ml of blood.[56] Suppose, further, that I explain the situation to the police officers with reference to my belief about the prescribed limit in Scotland, and supplement my submission to them by revealing that I am a legal philosopher by profession, and that I also believe and have published work arguing that it is in the nature of law that, on any given issue, law must determine the normative situation of citizens of the same state in the same situation so that the legal norms that apply to them do not differ. If they do appear to differ, I further contend, such legal norms cannot fully or properly[57] be regarded as law (assume I am a United Kingdom citizen—there is no separate Scottish or English citizenship in the United Kingdom as things stand).

---

[55] Road Traffic Act 1988, ss 5, 11.
[56] By Regulation 2 of the Road Traffic Act 1988 (Prescribed Limit) (Scotland) Regulations 2014.
[57] I discuss further what such a claim might mean in chs 5 and 6.

As should be obvious, my (false) belief about the content of the legal norm governing alcohol limits when driving in Scotland, and my (false) belief about the nature of law will cut no ice with the police officers dealing with my situation and will not prevent me from being charged with driving while above the prescribed alcohol limit. My beliefs about what the law, and about what the nature of law, require in the situation, are one thing; the social reality of what is actually required of me according to law, and of what is required in order for a norm to count as law, is quite another.

Of course, what the law in Scotland, or anywhere else, requires on this or that topic, and that there is law at all, with certain characteristics which make it into what it is, and certain identification conditions which determine the normative situation of those subject to it, is not strongly independent of all the beliefs, thoughts, attitudes, and actions, of all the persons who create, administer, apply, and are subject to the law. Law is a human-made social institution, and is part-constituted by, and maintained in existence by, just those things. But once it has been so constituted, then the fact that it exists, and that it has certain characteristics, and requires certain things of us, is a matter regarding which I may have true beliefs, or, as in the example above, I may have false beliefs. Although ultimately constituted by social attitudes and practices, once law has been created it has a social reality to it which is, in the sense just outlined, independent of my beliefs about it. Moreover, that social reality has important consequences, and exerts significant effects on my life as a member of law-governed society.

In the situation outlined in my example, I might find myself with a criminal record, subject to a fine, and/or without a driving licence as a result of my actions stemming from my incorrect beliefs about the content of the relevant legal norms and about the nature of law. These factors may, in turn, affect my current and future employment status, and/or my ability to hold certain offices. If I reflect on the situation after the fact, I should realize that I have reasoned incorrectly about the content and the character of the law and that, in order successfully to use law to guide my conduct in future I must come to a better understanding of these matters.

We hence have good reason, in considering and deliberating about how to live our lives in law-governed societies, to understand and take due notice of the social reality of law's existence. It is important to realize that our beliefs about the character of law and about what law requires of us may be mistaken, and that significant and in some situations even life-altering consequences may ensue if we are found to have broken the law. It is in this sense that law is properly understood as being a part of our social reality—a reality which our theories of law can characterize in more, or less, accurate and explanatorily adequate ways.

A second point is also important in resisting the temptation to overstate the differences between certain concepts in the natural sciences, and concepts which feature in the philosophy of law. There is a tendency on the part of some of those who work in the social sciences and in the humanities to assume that concepts in the natural sciences unproblematically and objectively 'carve nature at its joints'.[58] According to this line of thought, in the natural sciences that which a concept picks out has a determinate and discoverable nature, the properties of which dictate correct use of the concept. However, even a brief consideration of some relevant work in the philosophy of science indicates that this is an outsider's view, and reveals that, in fact, things are much more problematic, complex, and deeply contested as regards the character of concepts in the natural sciences and the way in which those concepts individuate, and apply to, aspects of natural reality.

For example, in a series of publications, philosopher of science and of language Joseph LaPorte has mounted challenges to certain aspects of semantic theories such as those championed by Saul Kripke and Hilary Putnam according to which the correct extension of natural kind terms is determined by those microstructural properties necessarily possessed and shared by those entities to which the natural kind term refers.[59] LaPorte refers to 'Kripke-Putnam semantics' as offering a 'discovery picture' of the alleged essences of natural kind terms, and notes that: 'In the broader philosophical community it has become the received view; it is commonly taken for granted by philosophers who have occasion to mention natural kinds in various discourses about related topics.'[60]

LaPorte, however, casts significant doubt on whether this discovery picture can indeed hold true in the case of several concepts in the chemical and biological sciences, such as whales, rodents, water, jade, and topaz, and offers an alternative picture of how, and to which properties of things, natural kinds refer. Although he arguably retains a revised notion of certain natural kinds having essences in some relevant sense, LaPorte argues that the Kripke-Putnam view overstates the relevance of microstructural properties in determining the reference of natural kind terms. John Dupré, a

---

[58] This metaphor is usually traced back to Plato's *Phaedrus*, at 265c–266c.
[59] See eg J LaPorte, 'Chemical Kind Term Reference and the Discovery of Essence' (1996) *30 Noûs* 112; J LaPorte, 'Essential Membership' (1997) *64 Philosophy of Science* 96; J LaPorte, Natural Kinds and Conceptual Change (CUP 2004).
[60] LaPorte, 'Chemical Kind Term Reference and the Discovery of Essence (n 59) 112.

philosopher of science with a focus on the philosophy of biology, goes further: he contends that the Kripke-Putnam semantic theory does not hold in the case of several concepts in biology, rejects wholesale the notion of such natural kinds having unifying essences, and believes that LaPorte's philosophical commitments should also lead LaPorte to abandoning more of essentialism about natural kinds than he does.[61]

As such examples highlight, it is important to keep in mind that, even in the domain of natural kinds, things are much more complex and contested than they initially may seem.[62] We should be wary of positions which contend that an obvious and rigid dichotomy holds wherein natural kinds unproblematically have essential properties waiting to be discovered by our best scientific theories, but social constructs, such as law, do not. Some of the doubts about the possibility of law having a nature which legal philosophy can attempt to identify and explain may stem from a false picture of the character and the extent of the contrast between natural kinds on the one hand, and social constructs such as law, on the other. Even in the natural sciences, it is neither an unproblematic nor uncontested matter that natural kind concepts refer to entities with essential properties waiting to be discovered. Moreover, law does constitute an important part of the social reality in law-governed societies. That social reality outstrips the beliefs that individuals subject to law hold in respect of it, and can have significant and pervasive consequences on the lives of those whom it affects.

(c) Can our concept of law successfully pick out aspects of the nature of law?

Another challenge to the possibility of legal philosophy about the nature of law proceeds from a consideration of the character of our *concept* of law, and of the relations between our concept of law, and aspects of the nature of law which that concept picks out. This challenge assumes different forms in the work of different theorists but can be introduced by considering aspects of the views of Liam Murphy and of Brian Leiter.

---

[61] See eg J Dupré, 'Natural Kinds and Biological Taxa' (1981) 90 *The Philosophical Review* 66; J Dupré, The Disorder of Things: Metaphysical Foundations of the Disunity of Science (Harvard UP 1993); and, on LaPorte, J Dupré, 'Review of Joseph LaPorte, *Natural Kinds and Conceptual Change*' (2004) *Notre Dame Philosophical Reviews* http://ndpr.nd.edu/news/natural-kinds-and-conceptual-change/.

[62] For further discussion see eg JK Campbell, M O' Rourke, and MH Slater (eds), Carving Nature at Its Joints: Natural Kinds in Metaphysics and Science (MIT Press 2011).

Liam Murphy has written thoughtfully and insightfully about methodology in legal philosophy during the last two decades, and his views on various issues have evolved subtly during that time. In his early work in this area, Murphy made two main claims which are relevant to the issue of whether our concept of law can successfully pick out aspects of the nature of law: one negative, the other positive:

(1) our concept of law is partly, but significantly, indeterminate and contested, such that no amount of reflection upon it will yield agreement on certain issues, such as the issue at stake between legal positivists and Ronald Dworkin regarding whether, and, if so, in what sense, moral and political considerations play a role in identifying propositions of law (the negative point), and

(2) that, given (1), a distinctive methodology can and should be used in legal philosophy to operate where leeway exists owing to indeterminacy in our concept of law—a methodology which Murphy originally referred to as a 'practical-political' argument, and, in later work, as an 'instrumental argument'—according to which we should adopt whichever view of the character of law leads to better moral and political consequences (the positive point).[63]

At this stage in the development of his views, Murphy also believed that his approach yielded the conclusion that legal positivism's social thesis, and more particularly, the 'exclusive legal positivist' form it assumes in Joseph Raz's explanation of the 'sources thesis',[64] was the best position to take on the issue of how to identify propositions of law, as it was less likely than the alternatives to lead to a certain kind of 'quietism': an insufficiently critical and overly compliant attitude towards the state and its legal directives.[65]

In later work on this topic, however, Murphy somewhat modified point (1) above, and significantly modified point (2). As regards (2), Murphy's

---

[63] See L Murphy, 'The Political Question of the Concept of Law' in J Coleman (ed), Hart's Postscript: Essays on the Postscript to The Concept of Law (OUP 2001), and L Murphy, 'Concepts of Law' (2005) 30 *Australian Journal of Legal Philosophy* 1.

[64] On the sources thesis see J Raz, 'Legal Positivism and the Sources of Law' in J Raz, The Authority of Law (2nd edn, OUP 2009) ch 3.

[65] Murphy, 'The Political Question of the Concept of Law' (n 63) 389-97; Murphy, 'Concepts of Law' (n 63) 10-15. During the time that he espoused these views, some legal philosophers criticized Murphy's view on the grounds that his methodological approach appeared to involve a problematic sort of wishful thinking, as it appeared to claim that law has certain features-eg that propositions of law can be identified by looking solely to social sources—because it would be better and more desirable to view it as having those features. See eg W Waluchow, Inclusive Legal Positivism (Clarendon Press 1994) 88-95; J Dickson, Evaluation and Legal Theory (Hart Publishing 2001), ch 5.

later view is that the particular 'practical-political' or 'instrumental' argument he formerly adopted with regard to (2) cannot work, and indeed that all such arguments will be problematic, owing to the fact that there are so many variables in terms both of the number of different possible beneficial instrumental effects, and/or desirable moral and political consequences which would need to be factored into an overall calculus of which view of law would be better, and the fact that the overall calculus of what are the most desirable consequences would itself be highly dependent on varying societal circumstances.[66]

The modification to (1) is more subtle, and harder to pin down. Murphy appears, however, to have moved in the direction of rejecting his earlier position that indeterminacy in, and disagreement regarding, certain aspects of our *concept* of law indicates that there is no fact of the matter about what *law* is really like:

> I am not arguing that there is no truth of the matter about the nature of law. What I believe is that the disagreement in this case is stark and fundamental, and does not seem to connect sufficiently to other matters we care about, or at least not in the right way, to make substantive argument possible.[67]

> [d]isagreement about the grounds of law runs so deep and is so tenacious that we frequently have no option but to say that on one not unreasonable understanding of the nature of law, the content of law is such and such, but that on another, it is something else. Of course I haven't proved that this standoff is permanent; there's no claim that greater convergence is impossible ... Though I have said that the versions of this approach offered by Raz ... and Dworkin ... are unsuccessful, I certainly haven't shown that no version of this approach will succeed.[68]

If I am correct in my reading of this shift in Murphy's views as regards point (1) above, then his later position, as compared with his earlier views, appears to endorse more of a distinction between our *concept of law* on the one hand, which is, as regards certain features of law, deeply contested and unlikely to yield one determinate view of those features, and *the actual nature of law* on the other, ie that aspect of reality which our concept of law picks out, regarding

---

[66] See L Murphy, 'Better to See Law This Way' (2008) 83 *NYU Law Review* 1088, especially s III; L Murphy, What Makes Law: an Introduction to the Philosophy of Law (CUP 2014) ch 6, especially 73–76.
[67] Murphy, *What Makes Law* (n 66) 88.
[68] ibid 102.

which there may indeed be facts of the matter. On this understanding of Murphy's views, the problem with successfully engaging in legal philosophy about the nature of law lies with the fact that we can only understand the nature of law via our concept of law, and that our concept of law is so contested and disputed that it is highly unlikely that we can grasp accurately the nature of law via that concept.

This shift in stance may also indicate that Murphy's later position has certain things in common with some of the views held by Brian Leiter in his thought-provoking work in jurisprudential methodology. At points in Leiter's work—although, as I discuss in Chapter 6, he may later have modified his stance in this regard[69]—he accepted that a form of what he referred to as 'modest conceptual analysis' has an important role to play in legal philosophy. Leiter's view of 'modest conceptual analysis' can be gleaned from the way he contrasts it with the 'immodest' conceptual analysis he rejects. The latter, according to Leiter, claims that analysing the way that we talk about, use, and apply our concepts will yield knowledge not merely of those concepts themselves, but of what the world is like, i.e. of aspects of the reality that those concepts pick out. In the case of law, 'immodest conceptual analysis' would hence yield knowledge about the nature of law: it would be able to identify and explain those properties which law must possess in order to be law, and which make it into what it is.[70] By contrast, 'modest' conceptual analysis: '[i]lluminates our concepts—our *talk* as it were—not the referent we might have intended to understand'.[71]

The view that legal philosophy can and should engage in modest but not immodest conceptual analysis has some interesting implications for the work of some proponents of legal philosophy about the nature of law. Of note in the context of the discussion in this and the preceding chapter is that the 'modest conceptual analysis' that Leiter outlines will not, it seems, deliver what some legal philosophers have explicitly thought they were after, ie an account of the nature of law, of those properties which make law into what it is. Instead, such analysis will deliver an understanding only of our concepts, and will be 'ethnographically relative' in character, yielding conclusions only about what some relevant 'we', 'round here' understand as law.[72]

---

[69] See ch 6, s 2.
[70] See B Leiter, Naturalizing Jurisprudence: Essays on American Legal Realism and Naturalism in Legal Philosophy (OUP 2007) 175–99.
[71] ibid 197 (emphasis in original).
[72] ibid 196–99. The above exposition of Leiter's views draws on J Dickson, 'On Naturalizing Jurisprudence: Some Comments on Brian Leiter's View of What Jurisprudence Should Become' (2011) 30 *Law and Philosophy* 477, s III.

In my view, Murphy's and Leiter's views on these issues share some points in common, even as they also differ in their interpretation of those points and their consequences. In particular:

(i) at certain points in their work, both espouse an understanding of the relation between our concept of law and the nature of law which allows for significant separation between the two; and
(ii) partly as a result of the understanding in (i), both hold that there are serious difficulties as regards legal philosophy about the nature of law being able to succeed in its self-appointed task.

Laying out aspects of the views of Murphy and Leiter relevant to the challenge under discussion in this sub-section brings better into focus the contention that legal philosophy about the nature of law has a difficult, and perhaps impossible, task, because, at best, we can gain understanding only of our concept of law, rather than of the nature of law itself. My response to this contention is primarily to be found in Chapter 6, and comes in the form of developing and defending my own view of the role which our self-understandings in terms of the concept of law play in constructing a successful theory of law's nature.

4. Legal Philosophy about the Nature of Law: Too Abstract/Neglectful of Law's Social Character?

Another charge sometimes levelled at legal philosophy about the nature of law is that it is too abstract in character, a vice which is alleged to result in a lack of connection to the concrete realities of law as it operates in society. This charge has been laid by several of the legal philosophers whose views have been discussed in this chapter:

> Current legal philosophy's focus is not on juristic experience in all its practical complexity, ethical ambiguity and contextual specificity, but on abstract problems defined by philosophical interest.[73]
>
> Legal philosophy, then ... is engaged in theorising social phenomena which have a "real" existence, and to the contours of which the philosophical account is hence in some sense answerable. It follows that legal philosophers have to be concerned with 'law' not just in a conceptual or doctrinal sense,

---

[73] Cotterrell (n 8) 52.

but also in the sense of a dynamic social practice which is interpreted and enforced, with decisive effects on individuals, groups and the social order.[74]

[t]he richer the characterization of law's social basis—its institutional forms, its various types of rules, its role, and its functions—the less plausible is any theoretical claim to universality.[75]

In these passages, Cotterrell and Lacey delineate what they regard as a problematic divide which both believe needs to be bridged, but—in their view—the attempted bridging of which reveals tensions amongst various goals of legal philosophical inquiry. The divide in question is between understanding law in the abstract by means of a 'conceptual' theory of law seeking universal truths on the one hand, and a richer characterization of law as a social practice in its concrete and dynamic complexity on the other. Both contend that this divide can and should be bridged by legal philosophy about the nature of law doing more to appreciate, build on, and integrate into its theoretical accounts, insights about law drawn from inquiries into law in its social context. But both also highlight an alleged tension between legal philosophy about the nature of law doing this successfully, and such legal philosophy maintaining what they regard as its claims to universality.

While there are some valuable points to take from this challenge, it is also misleading to an extent, because, in some important respects, the divide on which it is premised is false. As I indicated in the introduction to this chapter, this challenge is largely just identified and noted here as my response to it emerges in the discussion from Chapter 4 onwards. Some ways in which the divide upon which this challenge is premised is false are considered in Chapter 4; others are discussed in Chapters 5 and 6. The thrust of my views on this issue is that legal philosophy about the nature of law can only be successful when it characterizes law accurately and adequately as a social phenomenon and as a social practice, and when it helps us to understand law as it already exists in our societies, and in our societal self-understanding. Moreover, as is particularly discussed in Chapter 4, the possibilities that exist for pluralism and diversity in the questions and issues addressed by legal philosophy mean that many different areas of law as a social practice can and should be explored, and that the exploration may require or be enhanced by certain sorts of experience of law in its social context.

---

[74] Lacey (n 40) 103.
[75] Lacey, 'Analytical Jurisprudence vs Descriptive Sociology Revisited' (n 2) 957.

5. Legal Philosophy about the Nature of Law: Static, Staple Questions?

A final criticism sometimes made of legal philosophy about the nature of law is that it is problematically static in character. In its search for *the* nature of law, this line of thought runs, this type of legal philosophy inevitably seeks correct, once and for all answers to unchanging, staple questions regarding law's nature.[76] To this criticism some commentators are inclined to add the thought that, as legal philosophy about the nature of law has been addressing the same static, staple questions for quite some time, should we not expect some progress to have occurred and/or some definite answers to have emerged by now?[77]

In my view, these lines of thought rest on some misunderstandings about the character of legal philosophy, including legal philosophy about the nature of law. The misunderstandings are problematic as they can lead to an impoverished view of the opportunities for diversity and development in the questions, puzzles, and tasks of legal philosophy. Much of Chapter 4 is concerned with exploring these issues.

6. Conclusion: A Metaphysically Modest and Domain-apt Understanding of Legal Philosophy about the Nature of Law

Where does the discussion in this chapter leave us, as regards the idea that one important part of legal philosophy seeks to identify and explain aspects of law's nature? My hope is that it leaves us with a more nuanced, and hence stronger, stance than at its outset, as regards what is, and what is not, involved in embracing this idea. As I have sought to make clear, legal philosophy about the nature of law is but one part of legal philosophy and is just one valuable approach amongst many to theorizing about law. Although, when successful, it has distinctive explanatory power in its ability to help us understand that which makes law into what it is, this does not connote that it is intellectually or otherwise superior to, or that it seeks to demote, denigrate, or imperialistically crowd out, other sorts of legal philosophy. Legal philosophy about the nature

---

[76] See eg M Krygier, 'Reply to Patrick Emerton' (2014) *39 Australian Journal of Legal Philosophy* 176, 186, K Rundle, 'Reply to Patrick Emerton' (2014) *39 Australian Journal of Legal Philosophy* 189, 195, and the discussion in ch 4.

[77] This thought hovers over the discussion of methodology in legal philosophy in B Leiter, 'The Demarcation Problem in Jurisprudence: A New Case for Scepticism' (2011) *31 Oxford Journal of Legal Studies* 663.

of law should be open to, and be willing to explore, various potential complementarities which may exist between its own approach to theorizing about law, and other approaches, including those which feature empirical and sociological studies about law, and those which investigate law's contingent, rather than necessary, features. Legal philosophy about the nature of law should acknowledge that work remains to be done to explore what it is and is not committed to holding about the nature of law, and, in my view, should adopt as metaphysically modest a view as possible of what it is for law to have a nature. It should reject, and remain robust in the face of, excessively polarized comparisons and contrasts between the natural sciences and the social sciences which attempt too quickly to dismiss it as a possibility. Legal philosophy about the nature of law should stand by the view that law forms one important aspect of our social reality and is something about which our theories of law can be more, or less, accurate, and more, or less, explanatorily rich. It should also be alive to the issues involved in understanding the relations between our concept of law, and the nature of law, and to the role of legal philosophy in evaluating and taking a stance on our self-understandings in terms of law. Legal philosophy about the nature of law should emphasize that it is not overly abstract or insufficiently connected to the social realities of law as it operates in people's lives in law-governed societies. And it should both exemplify, and champion, an approach to understanding law wherein the questions of legal philosophy multiply, diversify, change, and innovate. Such an approach will ensure that we adopt an appropriately modest, and domain-apt understanding of what it is for law to have a nature, and what it is for theorists to seek to explain it, while also emphasizing the diverse and dynamic character of legal philosophical inquiry.

4
The Questions of Legal Philosophy
Diversity, Development, and Distribution of Emphasis

> May it not be that we have made too much of conviction as an ultimate goal? ... May it not be the greater merit of questions that they lead not to answers but to new questions, and the new questions to others, and they to others yet?[1]

1. Introduction: The Questions of Legal Philosophy

The focus of this chapter lies not with the answers legal philosophers offer to questions concerning law's nature, but with the diversity of and developments in the questions they ask, and the leeway they have in selecting which questions to address and how to address them. I argue that there is room for significant, and welcome, 'question pluralism' within legal philosophy about the nature of law, and that we should embrace the fact that the many and varied questions legal philosophers address are shaped by and responsive to the time and context in which they arise.

As I have argued in Chapters 2 and 3, however, the philosophy of legal philosophy I champion is committed to the idea that the task of one important part of our discipline is to identify and explain the nature of law (understood in a metaphysically modest and domain-apt manner). To some, this may immediately sound perplexing: how can the questions of legal philosophy be plural, various, arise in and change over time, yet the answers to those questions be about the *nature* of law—those properties which all law possesses, and which make it into what it is? Navigating this puzzle is the task of the present chapter. The voyage around it reveals several ways not so much to solve it as to *dissolve* it, revealing the puzzle to be more apparent than real. I examine what drives the diversity of and developments in the questions legal philosophers address

---

[1] John Ciardi, Manner of Speaking (Rutgers University Press 1972) 85–86.

Elucidating Law. Julie Dickson, Oxford University Press. © Julie Dickson 2022.
DOI: 10.1093/oso/9780198727767.003.0004

and consider some senses in which theorists exercise choice as regards what to explain, how to explain it, and what to emphasize in their explanations. The discussion also begins to illuminate some important issues regarding the explanatory power of, and constraints upon, theories of law, aspects of which are explored further in later chapters.

2. Two Roles for Choice in Theory Construction in Legal Philosophy

In discussing elucidating law in Chapter 1 I noted that: 'law is a multi-faceted and complex phenomenon, different aspects of which can be illuminated from different theoretical directions, at different times, and for different reasons. Accordingly, the questions of legal philosophy are various, diverse, arise in and change over time, and its quest is never-ending'.[2]

But what exactly is meant by different aspects of something being illuminated from different directions at different times and for different reasons? And how much choice do legal philosophers have in deciding to illuminate one facet of law rather than another, and in one way rather than another? We can begin to explore these issues by drawing a distinction—possibly somewhat permeable, but in my view useful nonetheless—between two different roles for choice, or for selectivity, in theory construction in legal philosophy. I term these *subject-matter selectivity* and *distribution of emphasis selectivity* and briefly outline them below before exploring each in greater detail in sections 3 and 4, respectively.

Subject-matter selectivity first. To construct successful theories of law, legal philosophers must select the aspect, or aspects, of their subject matter that they wish to focus upon, and then, within that selection, further choose which puzzles and questions to address in respect of that aspect, or those aspects, of law. No theory of law can be comprehensive in the sense of focusing on *all* of the properties comprising law's nature, and on *all* of the puzzles which those properties might give rise to. Any such attempt would be overwhelmed by the voluminous issues, questions, and topics to be addressed, and would run a high risk of failing to offer a focused and cogent account of *any* facet of law, in its attempt to address all of them. In the words of John Finnis, it would be less a theory of law, and more a '[v]ast rubbish heap of miscellaneous facts described in a multitude of incommensurable terminologies'.[3] Moreover, as is discussed

---

[2] See ch 1, s 2, point (ii).
[3] J Finnis, Natural Law and Natural Rights (1st edn, OUP 1980; 2nd edn, OUP 2011) 17.

further in this chapter, the importance of some aspects of law's character, and the importance of some of the puzzles concerning them, may only come to light at certain points in time, or in response to particular interests and concerns. Attempting a comprehensive account of all of law's properties and of all the possible puzzles which could arise in respect of them would result in a haphazard wild goose chase.

Examples of legal philosophers selecting facets of law to focus on, and selecting specific puzzles within those facets, abound. To mention just three contemporary examples, we can think of Timothy Endicott's focus on the topic of law and language, and on the specific puzzles within that topic concerning vagueness, in his book *Vagueness in Law*,[4] Nicole Roughan's focus on the authority of the law, and on the puzzles concerning the character and legitimation of law's authority generated by a transnational legal world featuring multiple competing such authorities in her book *Authorities*,[5] and Maris Köpcke's focus on legal validity, and on puzzles concerning its purpose or point in the circumstances of moral under-determination and moral disagreement in *Legal Validity: The Fabric of Justice*.[6]

The second role for choice in constructing theories of law[7] I term here *distribution of emphasis selectivity*.[8] This notion is more difficult to pin down and, indeed, there may be some overlap between this sort of selectivity and subject-matter selectivity. To make an initial attempt at demarcating distribution of emphasis selectivity: it concerns not so much *what* legal philosophers choose to focus on, as is the case with subject-matter selectivity, but rather *how* they explain what they choose to explain, with particular focus on how, and why, legal philosophers choose to foreground and emphasize certain things over others in their explanations of law. To what extent do legal philosophers have leeway in selecting what is foregrounded and emphasized in their theories, and what is left in the background, and what effect do their choices have on their theories' explanatory power? What constraints might be incumbent upon legal philosophers as they exercise whatever leeway they have in these matters?

---

[4] TAO Endicott, Vagueness in Law (OUP 2000).
[5] N Roughan, Authorities: Conflicts, Cooperation, and Transnational Legal Theory (OUP 2013).
[6] M Köpcke, Legal Validity: The Fabric of Justice (Hart Publishing 2019).
[7] Note that there may be other roles for choice in theory construction in legal philosophy beyond the two which I focus on here.
[8] I borrow the term 'distribution of emphasis' from Richard Ashcraft in his reinterpretation of the work of John Locke, especially in R Ashcraft, Locke's Two Treatises of Government (original edn, Allen & Unwin 1987; edn from which the pagination referred to here is drawn: Routledge 2010) *passim*, but see especially at 3, 14, 233, 235. This term resonated with me when I first encountered it and seemed to capture something I wanted to explore in the philosophy of legal philosophy. But it is very much my own take on this idea which is presented here; it is only the term that I borrow from Ashcraft's illuminating and thoughtful work.

3. Subject-matter Selectivity in Legal Philosophy

Towards the end of Chapter 3,[9] I noted that legal philosophy about the nature of law is sometimes criticized as being problematically static in character. In its search for *the* nature of law this line of thought runs, it inevitably seeks correct, once and for all answers to unchanging staple questions regarding law's nature. As Martin Krygier puts it:

> Staples of legal philosophy are built around universal answers to single questions: what *is* law? what *is* the relationship between law and morality, between law and coercion, law and politics, law and reason? and so on. Typically such questions are posed as though a single universal answer is appropriate to each of them: for John Austin, law is the command of a sovereign, for HLA Hart it is a system of two types of rules.[10]

Brian Leiter has also claimed that legal philosophers have been primarily focused on the same puzzle—how to distinguish between the normative guidance systems of law and of morality—for some 200 years, and that for the last century or so, this 'demarcation problem', as Leiter terms it, has been *the* dominant issue in the field.[11]

The view of legal philosophy about the nature of law as addressing static, staple questions, and as perhaps being 'stuck' in a fruitless loop of trying to answer them, is very much at odds with my own view of the questions, puzzles, and developments of our discipline. If the 'addressing static, staple questions' view were correct, it would indicate a fixed, and finite, goal for legal philosophy about the nature of law: the aim of this enterprise would be to give conclusive, correct answers to unchanging questions, and, were theorists to be successful in this regard, legal philosophy about the nature of law would have completed its task, and its inquiries could cease. Moreover, if we were *not* successful at giving such answers to the supposedly perennial questions of legal philosophy, then we might rightly wonder whether something is wrong with our discipline

---

[9] See ch 3, s 5.
[10] M Krygier, 'Reply to Patrick Emerton' (2014) 39 *Australian Journal of Legal Philosophy* 176, 186 (emphasis in original). This sentiment is echoed by Kristen Rundle in a 'Reply' piece in the same journal edition from which the above quote from Krygier is taken: Rundle is also at pains to reject, both on her own behalf, and as regards her interpretation of Lon Fuller, what she sees as the 'universal answers to staple questions' approach; see K Rundle, 'Reply to Patrick Emerton' (2014) 39 *Australian Journal of Legal Philosophy* 189, 195.
[11] B Leiter, 'The Demarcation Problem in Jurisprudence: A New Case for Scepticism' (2011) 31 *Oxford Journal of Legal Studies* 663, 664.

or its proponents, that despite centuries of puzzling over the same questions, no significant progress was being made.[12]

My own view is that the landscape of legal philosophy is pluralistic in character, open to the possibility of, and the value of, many different and changing lines of inquiry concerning law's character, and open to exploring mutual complementarities between such lines of inquiry. Contemporary legal philosophy features a huge variety of work on diverse topics. Moreover, despite a rich array of accounts, views, answers to questions, and responses to puzzles, legal philosophy about the nature of law seems neither to have ceased, nor to have fallen into despair that no progress has been made. This begins to light the way toward a more nuanced view of the questions of legal philosophy. Those questions are not static, staple, fixed givens. Rather, they are pluralistic, fluid, and arise in and vary over time, in response to changes as regards which topics we find interesting, and which issues we find puzzling within those topics.

This brings us back to the question raised in the introduction to this chapter: how can the questions of legal philosophy be plural, various, arise in and change over time, yet the answers to those questions be about the *nature* of law—those properties which all law possesses, and which make it into what it is? The first point to note in this regard is that even brief reflection on law's character indicates that it is a complex and multi-faceted phenomenon. Given, for example, its institutional complexities, and the intricate character of relations amongst its norms and between its norms and other normative requirements we encounter in our lives, it should strike us as highly plausible that law may possess numerous properties which mark it out as distinctive, and which make it into what it is. Moreover, it is also plausible that each of those properties which make law into what it is can be examined from different angles, in response to different puzzles and questions which strike us as interesting at any given time. The character of law hence supports pluralism as regards jurisprudential accounts of it: different theories of law can and do investigate different sets and sub-sets of those plausibly numerous properties which comprise law's nature and do so in multiple ways driven by changes in our sense of puzzlement with respect to those properties. Accordingly, legal philosophers must, and have ample and welcome opportunity to, exercise subject-matter selectivity in settling on just *some* questions and puzzles to focus on in their work.

---

[12] This possibility is raised by Brian Leiter in 'The Demarcation Problem in Jurisprudence' (n 11) 669–71, in the course of advocating that legal philosophy abandon trying to solve 'the demarcation problem', ie how to distinguish between the normative guidance systems of law and of morality (ibid 677).

A range of examples can assist in further illuminating subject-matter selectivity, and in exploring those factors guiding legal philosophers as they make the choices that it involves: choices regarding which aspect(s) of their subject matter to focus upon, and then further choices concerning which puzzles about those aspects of law to address. With respect to selecting which aspect(s) of law's nature to work on, often theorists make such choices in a reactive manner, by choosing to work on features of law which they believe have been neglected, under-explained, or poorly explained in accounts of law preceding theirs. Redressing such neglect, and correcting errors of either emphasis or substance in other theorists' accounts can be a strong driving force in motivating legal philosophers to work on a particular topic.

For HLA Hart, for example, it was John Austin's failure to do proper justice to the role of rules in law, and to how those rules are used to guide conduct, which provided the impetus for his criticisms of the command theory approach, and for the development of his alternative account: that the key to understanding legal systems lay in the union of primary and secondary rules, and in the attitudes towards and actions in terms of those rules held and undertaken by those who guide their conduct by them.[13] For Ronald Dworkin, it was HLA Hart's neglect of how legal materials are used to generate and to justify propositions of law in the argumentative and contested context of adjudication proceedings which prompted him to develop his powerful account of these facets of law, from which an entire legal, political, and moral theory eventually grew.[14] The wish to displace an erroneous orthodoxy can also shape the direction of theorists' work. In early writings, Dworkin was drawn to consider certain facets of law by the fact that those facets were, in his view, inadequately explained in what he referred to as 'the ruling theory of law'.[15] Recent work by Nicos Stavropoulos and by Mark Greenberg, challenging what they term 'the orthodox view'[16] and 'the standard picture',[17] respectively, appears similarly motivated.

---

[13] See eg HLA Hart, The Concept of Law (3rd edn, OUP 2012) with a Postscript edited by PA Bulloch and J Raz, and with an Introduction and Notes by L Green chs 1–4.
[14] See eg R Dworkin, Taking Rights Seriously (Harvard University Press 1978); Law's Empire (Fontana Press 1986); R Dworkin, Justice in Robes (Belknap Press 2006); R Dworkin, Justice for Hedgehogs (Belknap Press 2011).
[15] Dworkin, Taking Rights Seriously (n 14) Introduction.
[16] See N Stavropoulos, 'Obligations, Interpretivism and the Legal Point of View' in A Marmor (ed), The Routledge Companion to Philosophy of Law (Routledge 2012), passim.
[17] See M Greenberg, 'The Standard Picture and Its Discontents' in L Green and B Leiter (eds), Oxford Studies in Philosophy of Law, vol 1 (OUP 2011) passim. I engage with aspects of Stavropoulos' and Greenberg's work in ch 6.

Sometimes, certain aspects of law's nature come more acutely into focus, and strike us as in need of examination, not in response to the work of present and past legal philosophers, but because of shifts of focus and interest in neighbouring or cognate disciplines. For example, a resurgence of interest in Wittgenstein's rule-following remarks amongst philosophers of language and philosophers of mind in the latter decades of the twentieth century[18] was taken up by the legal philosophical community in the 1990s. Many legal theorists at that time became interested in and began to address questions concerning the possibility of rule-following and the role of interpretation in grasping the meaning of rules, influenced by the movement of this intellectual current from philosophy of language and philosophy of mind, into philosophy of law.[19]

These examples indicate some of the reasons why jurisprudential attention shifts from one property or set of properties comprising law's nature, to another such property or set of properties. As regards changes in what legal philosophers find puzzling about one and the same aspect of law, we can consider the topic of law's authority. In the early 1970s, the puzzle for Robert Paul Wolff was whether law possessing legitimate authority could be compatible with our duties of moral autonomy and of rationality.[20] Some four decades later, however, the puzzle about authority for Nicole Roughan shifted to how we should understand the character, and justification conditions, of law's authority in a transnational legal world featuring multiple competing such authorities.[21]

This latter example also indicates that sometimes changes in society, and in legal and political governance arrangements—such as the rise and proliferation of intra-, trans-, supra- and international legal regulation—influence both which aspects of law legal philosophers choose to focus on, and what they perceive as puzzling about them. Roughan's focus lies with how we should understand legal authorities in the context of such developments. Some of my own work, prompted by these same societal changes, has instead focused on the

---

[18] The work on this topic is voluminous but see eg GP Baker and PMS Hacker, Scepticism, Rules and Language (Blackwell 1984); GP Baker and PMS Hacker, Wittgenstein: Rules, Grammar and Necessity, vol 2 of an Analytical Commentary on the Philosophical Investigations (Blackwell 1985); S Holtzman and C Leich (eds), Wittgenstein: To Follow a Rule (Routledge & Kegan Paul 1981); S Kripke, Wittgenstein on Rules and Private Language: An Elementary Exposition (Blackwell 1982); J McDowell, 'Wittgenstein on Following a Rule' (1984) 58 *Synthèse* 325; J McDowell, 'Meaning and Intentionality in Wittgenstein's Later Philosophy' (1992) 17(1) *Midwest Studies in Philosophy* 40.
[19] See eg A Marmor, *Interpretation and Legal Theory* (1st edn, OUP 1992; 2nd rev edn, Hart Publishing 2005); B Bix, *Law, Language, and Legal Determinacy* (OUP 1993); DM Patterson (ed), *Wittgenstein and Legal Theory* (Westview Press 1992); GA Smith, 'Wittgenstein and the Sceptical Fallacy' (1990) 3 *Canadian Journal of Law and Jurisprudence* 155; M Stone, 'Focusing the Law: What Legal Interpretation Is Not' in A Marmor (ed), *Law and Interpretation* (OUP 1995).
[20] RP Wolff, In Defense of Anarchism (Harper & Row 1970). Wolff's conclusion, of course, was that it could not.
[21] Roughan (n 5).

concept of a legal system, and whether it is still of use in understanding intra-, trans-, supra- and international legal phenomena.[22]

More generally, the drifting in and out of jurisprudential fashion over the years of work on the concept of a legal system furnishes us with another example illustrating what guides legal philosophers in exercising subject-matter selectivity. The late 1960s and early to mid-1970s witnessed a flurry of legal philosophical interest in questions surrounding the identity of legal systems and their continuity through time. For some legal philosophers, this interest was prompted by puzzles generated by the journey to political independence taken by certain former British colonies.[23] Others looked not beyond but within the United Kingdom, keen to explore the sense in which the Scots have their own legal system without their own state, the relations between the Scottish legal system and the Articles and Acts of Union, and the role Scots law plays in expressing and shaping national identity, including national political identity.[24] Others still seemed less concerned with solving particular post-colonial or post-Union puzzles, but, perhaps influenced by the intellectual interest which such issues generated, attempted to develop aspects of their general accounts of the nature of law specifically in relation to questions concerning the identity and continuity of legal systems.[25]

Once these societal issues and the intense state of academic activity they generated ran their course, however, legal philosophers' interest in the theory of legal systems waned dramatically, with little writing explicitly on this topic emerging from the late 1970s onwards. It is only relatively recently that new life has been breathed into this topic by the rapid growth of and increasing interest in intra- trans-, supra-, and international governance arrangements. This time round, the focus is not so much on how to think about states ceding territories

---

[22] See eg J Dickson, 'How Many Legal Systems? Some Puzzles Regarding the Identity Conditions of, and Relations Between, Legal Systems in the European Union' (2008) 2 Problema 9 https://revistas.juridicas.unam.mx/index.php/filosofia-derecho/issue/view/371; J Dickson, 'The Idea of a Legal System: Between the Real and the Ideal' in N Walker (ed), MacCormick's Scotland (Edinburgh UP 2012); J Dickson, 'Towards a Theory of European Union Legal Systems' in J Dickson and P Eleftheriadis (ed), Philosophical Foundations of European Union Law (OUP 2012).
[23] See eg AM Honoré, 'Reflections on Revolutions' (1967) 2 Irish Jurist 268; JM Eekelaar, 'Rhodesia: the Abdication of Constitutionalism' (1969) 32 Modern Law Review 19; JM Eekelaar, 'Principles of Revolutionary Legality' in AWB Simpson (ed), Oxford Essays in Jurisprudence (Clarendon Press 1973); JW Harris, 'When and Why Does the Grundnorm Change?' (1971) 29 Cambridge Law Journal 103.
[24] See eg G Maher, 'The Identity of the Scottish Legal System' [1977] Juridical Review 21; N MacCormick, 'Does the United Kingdom Have a Constitution? Reflections on MacCormick v. Lord Advocate (1978) 29 Northern Ireland Legal Quarterly 1.
[25] See eg JM Finnis, 'Revolutions and Continuity of Law' in AWB Simpson (ed), Oxford Essays in Jurisprudence (Clarendon Press 1973); J Raz, The Concept of a Legal System (1st edn, OUP 1970; 2nd edn, OUP 1980).

which then go on to become independent states with separate legal systems, but rather on puzzles stemming from the legal and other consequences of the coming together of formerly more independent polities in larger units of regional or global cooperation, and the relations between those larger units and their constituent parts.[26] In the case of the European Union, the revival of interest in the theory of legal systems plausibly stems in part from the strong claims that this polity, and especially the Court of Justice of the European Union, consistently makes on its own behalf: that EU law is much more than a series of intergovernmental agreements between states, and that it represents 'a new legal order',[27] and has 'created its own legal system'.[28] These claims have prompted some legal philosophers to focus on whether and to what extent they are true, what would render them true (or false), and hence whether we should understand supra-national law, and the relations between supra-national law and national law, in terms of the concept of a legal system.[29]

These examples illustrate change, and some of the factors which drive and influence change, in: (i) the features of law that legal philosophers choose to focus on, and (ii) the puzzles about any given feature of law which they decide to address. In Chapter 3, in seeking to rebut charges that legal philosophy about the nature of law is theoretically imperialist as regards other approaches to understanding law, and/or seeks to erect boundary fences around itself and deny that other approaches have any relevance for it,[30] I championed a view of legal philosophy that is instead pluralistic in character, which welcomes a variety of theoretical approaches to understanding law, and is open to seeking out and developing complementarities between legal philosophy about the nature of law and other ways of understanding law. The present discussion both cements and adds to that pluralistic vision, making it clear that I am committed to these same desiderata also *within* legal philosophy about the nature of law.

Contra the criticism noted at the outset of this section, then, legal philosophy about the nature of law does not have a static goal, and does not aim to

---

[26] See in addition to those works cited in note 22 above: C Richmond, 'Preserving the Identity Crisis: Autonomy, System and Sovereignty in European Law' (1997) 16 *Law and Philosophy* 377; I Weyland, 'The Application of Kelsen's Theory of the Legal System to European Community Law: The Supremacy Puzzle Resolved' (2002) 21 Law and Philosophy 1; Roughan (n 5); and the essays in J Dickson and P Eleftheriadis (eds), Philosophical Foundations of European Union Law (OUP 2012).
[27] Case 26/62 *Van Gend en Loos* [1963] ECR 1, 12.
[28] Case 6/64 *Costa v ENEL* [1964] ECR 585, 593.
[29] See eg Dickson, 'How Many Legal Systems?' (n 22); Dickson, 'Towards a Theory of European Union Legal Systems' (n 22); K Culver and M Giudice, Legality's Borders: An Essay in General Jurisprudence (OUP 2010); K Culver and M Giudice, 'Not a System but an Order: An Inter-Institutional View of European Union Law' in J Dickson and P Eleftheriadis (eds), Philosophical Foundations of European Union Law (OUP 2012).
[30] See ch 3, ss 1 and 2.

offer single, conclusive answers to unchanging questions, which, once correctly given, would signal the end of such inquiry. Rather, in the ways illustrated by the examples above, the inquiries of legal philosophy about the nature of law are multiple, proliferating, open-ended, and ongoing, so long as there are legal philosophers who find such matters interesting and can find an audience for their work. Moreover, as some of the examples discussed in this section also reveal, some properties of law, and some puzzles about some properties of law, may not even reveal themselves to us, or strike us with sufficient force to spur investigation of them, until certain points in time, prompted by certain changes and developments in society. This being so, even when legal philosophers do succeed in understanding aspects of law's nature, this is highly unlikely to result in a progressive narrowing, or termination of jurisprudential inquiry.

The vision of legal philosophy about the nature of law emerging from the discussion above should also prompt us to consider anew what counts as progress within it. As we are not tackling the same unchanging questions throughout the history of the discipline, then we should not expect progress always or only to come in the form of better and better answers to some perennial set of questions. In my view, two models of progress in legal philosophical inquiry suggest themselves, both of which have value.

Sometimes, in respect of some issues, we may be able convincingly to argue that a linear kind of progress has occurred, wherein a given feature of law is explained in a better and more apt way than previously, superseding earlier, less explanatorily powerful explanations of that feature of law. A plausible example of this is HLA Hart's point that legal norms, in order to be understood adequately, must be understood—to some extent, and in some sense—from the internal point of view of those who administer, are subject to, and who guide their conduct by those norms.[31] This point is widely accepted amongst legal philosophers as having superseded those aspects of earlier command theories of law which attempted to reduce normative legal phenomena to conjunctions of, and/or predictions of conjunctions of factual phenomena. Although Hart's insight in this regard is subject to significant differences in interpretation as to, for example, what is, and what is not, involved in achieving such an internal understanding of legal norms, the idea that some such internal understanding is vital in understanding certain aspects of law adequately, is accepted in a wide range of legal philosophical work.[32]

---

[31] See Hart (n 13) chs 3–6.
[32] See eg Finnis (n 3) ch 1; Dworkin, *Law's Empire* (n 14) 49–65 and *passim*. This point resurfaces in s 4(c) of this chapter.

Although sometimes progress may take a linear form, a second sort of progress in legal philosophical inquiry is also possible: progress in the direction of greater, and richer, pluralism in the avenues of inquiry. Working on existing puzzles about aspects of law may result in a deeper understanding of them, and of what, precisely, puzzles us about them. This deeper understanding opens up and lights the way toward a range of further, and possibly different, future inquiries. Changes in social, legal and political life inaugurate discussion of new issues unimagined by preceding generations of legal philosophers. Intellectual currents from cognate disciplines flow into and enrich the pluralistic delta of jurisprudential inquiry. This being so, we should not assume that there is something wrong with our discipline when, after generations of inquiry, we do not always detect a linear sort of progress towards better and better answers to the same set of questions. Innovation and diversification in the questions that we ask, and a richer understanding of that which puzzles us, and of why the puzzles matter, are also markers of the progress we make.

None of the points discussed so far poses a threat to the possibility of successfully engaging in legal philosophy about the nature of law. The examples of legal philosophers' work discussed in this section are all inquiries concerning the nature of law which presuppose that there is a difference between law's necessary properties and its contingent properties. All conceive of their task as being to identify and adequately explain aspects of the character of something which exists in our social reality, and hold themselves to standards of correctness regarding the accounts they offer, acknowledging that their theories can be wrong as well as right, and can offer better or worse explanations of law's character and of what makes it into what it is.

In considering legal philosophers' exercise of subject-matter selectivity, an interesting question remains: how constrained or otherwise are theorists when they make choices of the sort discussed above? In my view we are, and should view ourselves and others as, very little constrained in this regard. We should follow our intellectual interests wherever they rise and flow, and for whatever reasons grip us. Clearly, there are situations where choosing to work on certain topics might be helpful in terms of fitting in with the research agenda of one's department or university, getting invited to conferences, or being asked to do media appearances and other forms of public engagement. These, however, are pragmatic constraints and, though they can flow from very real pressures, they vary according to and are dependent on how important to us certain kinds of fitting in or certain sorts of recognition are. In terms purely of our intellectual interests, and our many and various reasons why those interests form and are sustained, my instinct is that we should encourage rich diversity in intellectual work and follow our intellectual interests down whichever avenues they lead us. The main 'risk' in being thus unconstrained may be that some of our work will seem boring, or otherwise unappealing, to others. But as we do not know in advance which avenues will in themselves be, or will lead on to others which will be, captivating and engaging for ourselves and our various readers, it seems a risk worth running.

4. Distribution of Emphasis Selectivity in Legal Philosophy

As I mentioned in section 2, distribution of emphasis selectivity is more difficult to pin down than the subject-matter selectivity just discussed. In my view, however, this kind of selectivity concerns not *what* legal philosophers pick as their topics or puzzles, but *how they go about explaining* what they choose to explain, with particular focus on how, and why, legal philosophers choose to foreground and emphasize certain things over others in their explanations of law's nature, shaped by their views of the explanatory power which their accounts will possess as a result. In the discussion which follows, I explore several different facets of, and possible consequences of, distribution of emphasis selectivity, thereby bringing this idea better into focus.

(a) Audience-dependence

One facet of distribution of emphasis selectivity arises from the fact that all explanations, interpretations, and accounts of phenomena, including legal phenomena, are audience-dependent, and their success audience-relative. As both theorists and teachers we make choices about the way in which we explain things, which partly depend on what the explanation is trying to achieve, and who it is seeking to inform and/or convince. For example, an explanation of Ronald Dworkin's ideas of constructive interpretation and his 'one right answer' thesis aimed at promoting self-reflection amongst judges with no prior philosophical training or exposure to legal philosophical literature on adjudication, might focus to a considerable extent on the case law where, according to Dworkin, the constructive interpretation method can be found, and its operation illustrated. The explanation could then proceed to invite the judges to reflect on whether they think this is something that they do, or that they should do, in cases they have adjudicated upon in the past, and/or in the context of hypothetical case law scenarios reflecting the kinds of issues they might be asked to adjudicate in future. By way of contrast, an explanation of Dworkinian constructive interpretation and the 'one right answer' thesis offered to an audience of political and moral philosophers, with no prior legal training or exposure to case law, might emphasize and foreground issues regarding the status in terms of their truth and objectivity of the propositions of law claimed by Dworkin to emerge from the process of constructive interpretation, explain Dworkin's own attempts to elide all issues concerning the meta-ethical status of those propositions, and then invite the moral and political philosophers to reflect on these matters in relation to their own work on, and/or other philosophers' work on the character of moral reasoning, and the meta-ethical status of moral propositions.[33]

Might it be that this does not so much exemplify distribution of emphasis selectivity, as that aspect of subject-matter selectivity which is concerned with differences in what is found puzzling as regards a given topic? Perhaps,[34] but in my view this understanding would not properly capture the kind of pluralism in explanation which the example evinces. For both audiences, the topic—Dworkinian constructive interpretation and its one right answer thesis—are the same. Moreover, that which puzzles each audience about those topics could also be the same—to extend the example further, we can imagine both the judges, and the moral and political philosophers, to be puzzled by whether, and, if so, how, Dworkinian constructive interpretation can yield one right answer for reasoners faced with multiple and conflicting factors bearing on what ought to be done, and how it could justify that one right answer. Both ways of explaining outlined could take the relevant audiences to deeper consideration of and understanding of these same points, albeit via different routes. The variation in the explanations hence does not seem to lie with a difference of topic, or a difference as regards what is puzzling about that topic. Rather, the variation responds to differences in the audience to whom the explanation is given, especially differences in their prior knowledge and training, and in what they want to get out of the explanation concerned. Often, when we try to explain something, we do and should start from that which a given audience is likely to find familiar, and seek explanatory examples, analogies, and comparisons involving phenomena which that audience has already encountered and understands reasonably well.

---

[33] For Dworkin's views on the relevant issues see those works referred to in n 14 above, especially *Law's Empire* and *Justice for Hedgehogs*, and see also R Dworkin, 'Objectivity and Truth: You'd Better Believe It' (1996) 25 *Philosophy and Public Affairs* 87.

[34] As I mentioned in s 2, there may be some overlap and/or permeability between the two categories. Nonetheless, I regard the distinction as tenable and helpful in the present discussion.

The example thus also reveals that explanations, in addition to being audience-dependent, can also be, in certain sense, 'route-dependent'. In the example, each audience can best be helped to deepen their understanding of the same puzzle within the same topic by the respective explanations they are given each having its own distinctive starting point and explanatory route. The resulting variation in the way the explanations unfold stems from the fact that, when we seek to understand something ourselves, or to explain it to others, we must work with and give due attention to where we already are in our knowledge of the phenomenon in question, and of cognate phenomena, and must start from where we are and build bridges to further understanding from there.

However, to hold that the phenomenon of audience-dependence can require successful explanations to take different routes is not to claim that each audience can never come to understand the explanation given to the other. In terms of the example above, given sufficient time, willingness, and assistance, there is no reason in principle why at least some of the judges on the one hand, and some of the moral and political philosophers on the other, cannot come to understand the puzzle and the topic from the starting point, and via the explanatory route offered to the other group. Such understanding may also further illuminate from a different angle, and so enrich, the understanding they have previously attained.

(b) Experience-sensitive engagement with features of law

A second facet of distribution of emphasis selectivity involves the idea that the shape, and explanatory power, of an account of law might vary dependent not on who the audience is, but, in a certain sense, on who the theorist is, and on the sensitivities and concomitant capacities for understanding they possess. According to this line of thought, sometimes, a certain feature of law, or a certain issue involving law, may strike a theorist as particularly salient and in need of illumination owing to certain experiences of law's character and operation that they have had, or have come to learn about and intimately understand. Importantly, explanations of features of law which theorists offer in such circumstances plausibly have a distinctive character, and proceed in a distinctive way, owing to that theorist's experience-sensitive engagement with the relevant aspects of law's operation. Some examples can assist in unpacking this idea further.

In my view, this phenomenon of 'experience-sensitive engagement' can arise across a broad spectrum of work in legal philosophy. On first consideration it may most readily spring to mind in the context of certain strands of work in feminist legal theory and in critical race theory.[35] Many legal scholars working in these areas have argued that certain features of law, and the consequences of its workings on the lives of those it affects, are more likely to be noticed, and to be understood with appropriate depth and sensitivity, by those who have experienced first-hand certain aspects of law's operation (and, sometimes, by those who have worked with those who have experienced first-hand certain aspects of law's operation, including in the capacity of acting as their legal representatives).[36] Persons who have been sexually assaulted, and have then been aggressively questioned on their sexual history in cross-examination during their attacker's trial, plausibly have a distinctive and particularly sensitive understanding of the character and effect of the legal rules on evidence and on criminal procedure which shape such experiences.[37] Those who have experienced, or who have worked very closely with those who have experienced, domestic violence, plausibly can identify and understand certain thoughts, attitudes, and behaviours in this area that may be less readily noticed and understood by those without the relevant experiences. Plausibly, they can also understand the effects on individuals and their children of the law's shortcomings in dealing with certain aspects of domestic violence in a layered and nuanced way that may be extremely difficult to grasp for those without the relevant experience.[38]

Sometimes, persons who have had such experiences are, or become, legal theorists. On other occasions, those who are legal theorists with an interest in these areas work with, come to understand, and be the voice of, those who have had such experiences. The experience which the theorist has, or has access to, opens the door to the possibility of a distinctive understanding. In such cases, it seems to me highly plausible that certain features of law, and the character and consequences of their operation on individuals, are more fully, and subtly, knowable, and, perhaps in some situations, are only adequately knowable, by

---

[35] These are, of course, vast, varied, and richly insightful areas of legal scholarship, and I readily admit my relative lack of expertise as regards them. Moreover, I am aware that I can barely scratch their surface in noting some themes and examples for the purposes of the present discussion. Nonetheless, I believe that these areas of scholarship furnish us with resonant and plausible examples of the phenomenon I seek to explain above. I hope to explore further some of the issues raised in this sub-section in my next project, on the possibility and potential of content-independence in law—see further n 53 below.

[36] See eg C Mackinnon, Towards a Feminist Theory of the State (Harvard University Press 1989) especially ch 6: 'Method and Politics'; PJ Williams, The Alchemy of Race and Rights (Harvard University Press 1991) 3 and *passim*.

[37] See eg A Konradi, Taking the Stand: Rape Survivors and the Prosecution of Rapists (Greenwood 2007); O Smith, 'Sexual History Evidence in Rape Trials' in O Smith, Rape Trials in England and Wales (Palgrave Macmillan 2018).

[38] See eg RE Dobash and RP Dobash (eds), Rethinking Violence Against Women (Sage Publications 1998) especially chs 1 and 2; MM Dempsey, Prosecuting Domestic Violence: A Philosophical Analysis (OUP 2009).

those who have—in various senses—experience of them. True propositions about law which emerge from experience-sensitive engagement with features of law, and which feature in a theoretical account of law, can be termed experience-sensitive truths about features of law.[39]

There are several strands to this idea. Two have already been highlighted: (i) that having had, or having had certain sorts of access to, certain experiences of law's operation can make one more likely to notice and be interested in certain features of law which may go unnoticed by many others, and (ii) that having had, or having had certain sorts of access to, certain experiences can yield a distinctive, and, perhaps in some cases, an otherwise unavailable understanding of and insight into those features of law (which may in turn lead to distinctive ideas about how to manage and improve aspects of law's operation).

Are (i) and (ii) examples of what I have termed 'distribution of emphasis selectivity'? In terms of the distinction drawn between subject-matter selectivity and distribution of emphasis selectivity, I can see a possible case for classifying (i) as an example of the former, and it may well be that some aspects of (i) do fall under this head. However, I view (i) as including not only situations where certain experiences of law draw theorists to work on this rather than that topic, or this rather than that puzzle, but also situations where those theorists appreciate and understand the relevance and importance of aspects of the topic or the puzzle in a distinctive way, and hence foreground and emphasize those aspects of the topic or the puzzle in a distinctive manner in developing their accounts of law. (ii) seems clearly to be an example of distribution of emphasis selectivity, given that it involves explaining certain features of law in a distinctive way, and foregrounding and emphasizing certain things over others in the explanation one gives.

A third strand of thought—which I would likewise classify as an example of distribution of emphasis selectivity—flows from the idea of experience-sensitive truths about features of law: that in order appropriately and effectively to communicate such truths, including to those who have not had, or not had certain sorts of access to, the experiences in question, theorists may need to turn to, or indeed to partly invent, novel methods and means of explanation. This thought finds expression in the work of some legal scholars working in, for example, feminist legal theory and critical race theory, in the form of employing a 'narrative' or 'story-telling' method to supplement, and sometimes to replace,

---

[39] Although the examples I give concern significantly negative experiences of aspects of law's operation, it could also be the case that positive and/or empowering such experiences could also lead to a distinctive understanding yielding experience-sensitive truths about features of law.

more traditional modes of explanation often found in academic discourse.[40] Part of the rationale for using such methods is that they are a more effective way, and perhaps sometimes the only effective way, of bringing home to those who lack the relevant experiences what it is like to be on the receiving end of certain aspects of law's operation. Narrative or storytelling methods can grab our attention, engage our faculties of empathy and compassion, and stimulate our moral imagination, leading to better understanding of certain features of law that we might otherwise struggle to understand adequately.

The discussion so far reveals significant and ample opportunities for pluralism and diversity in theorizing about law stemming from differences in how theorists choose to distribute emphasis in their theories in focusing on and bringing to light experience-sensitive truths about law. However, this may not yet demonstrate such opportunities in the case of legal philosophy about the *nature of law*. Why not? Because a considerable proportion of the work featuring in the discussion in this sub-section involves theorists highlighting the operation of, and deepening our understanding of, features of law which are held to be contingent rather than necessary. Indeed, many instances of scholarship exploring the challenges faced by individuals on the receiving end of certain problematic aspects of law's operation focus strongly on the possibilities for improvement and reform of law,[41] a project which would make little sense if the scholars concerned believed those features they focus on to be part of law's nature, without which it would not be law.[42]

However, although many of the examples of theoretical work involving experience-sensitive engagement with features of law considered thus far do focus on contingent features of law, there seems no reason in principle why accounts of the nature of law could not feature experience-sensitive truths concerning law's necessary properties. For example, suppose that Leslie Green is correct that it is a necessary property of law that it is morally risky in certain

---

[40] The literature is voluminous but see eg D Bell, And We Are Not Saved: The Elusive Quest for Racial Justice (Basic Books 1987); R Delgado, 'Storytelling for Oppositionists and Others: A Plea for Narrative' (1989) 87 Michigan Law Review 2411; Williams (n 36) *passim*; P Ewick and S Silbey, 'Subversive Stories and Hegemonic Tales: Towards a Sociology of Narrative' (1995) 29 *Law and Society Review* 197; DG Solorzano and TJ Yosso, 'Critical Race Methodology: Counter-story Telling as an Analytical Framework for Education' (2002) 8 *Qualitative Inquiry* 23.

[41] See various of the works referred to in nn 36–38 above and eg A Dworkin and CA MacKinnon, Pornography and Civil Rights: A New Day for Women's Equality (Organizing Against Pornography 1988).

[42] Certain strands of radically critical thinking about law, perhaps especially those influenced by the works of Marx, Engels, and Pashukanis, do contend that various problematic aspects of law are part of law's nature, and hence that the revolutionary transformation of society they advocate must involve a turn away from legal regulation. For a thoughtful discussion of this issue and its associated literature which ultimately rejects this line of thought see C Sypnowich, The Concept of Socialist Law (Clarendon Press 1992).

ways.[43] Green claims that, because legal systems are necessarily institutionalized normative systems administered and enforced by a professional class of legal officials, law, *by its nature*, always and inevitably runs the moral risk of becoming distant from the communities it regulates, such that those communities become alienated from the law in terms of its creation, administration and enforcement by legal officials, and regard it not as 'their law' but as something remote, imposed on them from without.[44]

The character and significance of this moral risk, and the reasons why it is inherent in law's nature, might plausibly be noticed, and understood in a particularly acute and distinctive manner by legal philosophers who have had, or have come intimately to understand those who have had, the experience of being part of a community which is alienated from the law that is applied to it. Such an understanding could stem from, for example, the experience of being part of a demographic which is disproportionately subject to police 'stop and search' powers,[45] or being part of a demographic which is subject to legal directives concerning important aspects of their council housing which they correctly perceive as operating upon them from without, with scant regard for their input and concerns, and impervious to their attempted challenges.[46] Although some of the experiences prompting reflection and insight into an aspect of law's nature might be contingent, as in the examples above, the standing moral risk of law becoming alienated from the community it applies to due to its scale and the need for a professional class of legal officials to administer it, in Green's view and in mine, is part of law's nature. It thus strikes me as highly plausible that an understanding of aspects of law's nature can be experience-sensitive, and can be distinctively highlighted, explored, and subject to critical analysis by those with access to certain experiences of it.

It is the case, however, that in discussing experience-sensitive engagement with features of law, I had no trouble pointing to a wide range of existing theoretical accounts as examples in the case of such engagement with *contingent*

---

[43] I believe that he is.
[44] See L Green, 'Positivism and the Inseparability of Law and Morals' (2008) *83 New York University Law Review* 1035, s IV; L Green, *Introduction* to HLA Hart (n 15) xxix–xxx.
[45] See eg the discussion in N Bland, P Quinton, and T Miller 'The Impact of Stops and Searches on Crime and the Community' (Home Office, Policing and Reducing Crime Unit 2000) https://www.westmidlands-pcc.gov.uk/media/237972/prs127_the_impact_of_stops_and_searches_on_crime_and_the_community.pdf and in F Qureshi, 'The Impact of Extended Police Stop and Search Powers under the UK Criminal Justice Act 2003' (2007) *30 Policing: An International Journal of Police Strategies and Management* 466.
[46] See eg T Shildrick, 'Lessons from Grenfell: Poverty Propaganda, Stigma and Class Power' (2018) *66 The Sociological Review* 783; D Foster, 'The Way Residents and Tenants Are Treated Is a Stain on Modern Britain' *The Guardian* (18 August 18 2017) https://www.theguardian.com/housing-network/2017/aug/18/social-housing-residents-tenants-badly-treated-grenfell-ledbury-modern-britain; Grenfell: The Untold Story *Channel 4 TV* Grenfell: The Untold Story–All 4 (channel4.com).

features of law, but that when it came to considering this phenomenon in the context of aspects of law's nature, I had to resort instead to offering a *possible* outline of a *possible* account that *could* be developed, albeit drawing on insights which I regard as readily available in existing work. Is this difference significant? Importantly, does it indicate that experience-sensitive engagement with features comprising law's *nature* is less likely than in the case of contingent features of law, or that theoretical accounts featuring such engagement may be rare, or even unattainable, in the case of legal philosophy about the nature of law?[47] My view is that these conclusions are not warranted, because the current situation can be explained, and because I hope that in future, I and others can contribute to exploring and using the idea of experience-sensitive engagement with aspects of law's nature in our work in legal philosophy.

The explanation first: I suspect that, unfortunately, there do not seem to be many examples of legal philosophy about the nature of law drawing on the idea of experience-sensitive engagement with features of law due to a relative lack of mutual understanding and of engagement between legal philosophy about the nature of law and approaches such as feminist legal theory or critical race theory which have emphasized aspects of experience-sensitive engagement with features of law. Although as I argued in Chapter 3,[48] and as is a running theme throughout this book, I believe that legal philosophy about the nature of law can and should be open to exploring complementarities between its approach to theorizing about law, and other sorts of theoretical approaches, not enough of this has occurred to date. But that there has not yet been enough such interaction does not mean that there cannot be in future. Moreover, in my view, those interested in exploring issues surrounding the idea of experience-sensitive truths about aspects of the nature of law will find waiting for them a range of rich and nuanced ideas from which they can draw. One example which particularly captures my interest will have to suffice here. In 'The Pain of Word Bondage', Patricia Williams tells the tale of the very different approaches taken by her on the one hand, and by a white, male colleague on the other, to seeking out and signing a formal lease on the respective apartments they rented at the time they taught a contract law class together.[49] Williams reports that she sought, and signed, after lengthy and precise negotiations,

---

[47] I am grateful to Max Etchemendy for raising this thoughtful and challenging point during a wonderfully exploratory discussion on two draft chapters of this book at the Law and Philosophy Workshop, University of Chicago, in February 2021. I would like to extend my thanks to Brian Leiter, Max, and the graduate students in that seminar for their helpful comments.
[48] See ch 3, s 2.
[49] PJ Williams, 'The Pain of Word Bondage' in PJ Williams, The Alchemy of Race and Rights (Harvard UP 1991) ch 8.

a detailed, formal, legally operative lease, whereas her white, male colleague wanted to dispense with the formality of such a lease, and rented an apartment on an extremely informal basis merely by handing over a deposit in cash to strangers after a handshake.[50] Williams' analysis of the reasons for this difference is extremely nuanced, but one aspect of it is that she suspects that her experiences as a black woman, including her experiences of how law operates in respect of certain demographic groups in US society, resulted in her having a view of the importance, character, and consequences of aspects of law's formalities that were not shared by her colleague, arguably due to his very different experiences. As the discussion progresses, Williams draws out from these insights a hypothesis about a difference in attitudes towards legal rights held by 'the white left'[51] (the male colleague is a founding member of the Critical Legal Studies movement, and Williams draws out a certain antipathy within CLS towards legal rights) and by black members of US society respectively.[52] Although I cannot discuss the details of the argument here, it strikes me that some of it concerns features of law which are part of what make law into what it is, rather than features which are contingent in character: features such as law's validity, enforceability, formality, and its ability to foster arms-length transactions by means of these features. Moreover, Williams notices, highlights, and explains aspects of these features of law drawing heavily on her experience as a black woman in US society, rendering this, in my terminology, an example of experience-sensitive engagement with features of law which are part of what makes it into what it is.[53]

Two final points should be noted about experience-sensitive truths about law, and the opportunities for pluralism and diversity in legal philosophy which they engender. First of all, it is vital to grasp that what I have referred to here as experience-sensitive truths about law are still truths about law and can be evaluated in terms of their accuracy and explanatory power. There is no suggestion in anything discussed in this sub-section that truths about law which are noticed, highlighted, and explained in a distinctive and nuanced manner by those with experience-dependent access to those truths are thereby rendered problematically subjective in character. If—to use a well-worn example by

---

[50] ibid 146–48.
[51] ibid 152.
[52] ibid *passim*, but especially at 148–54, and 159–65.
[53] Much more remains to be said about this thought-provoking, and, to my mind, highly plausible example of experience-sensitive engagement with aspects of law's nature. I hope to explore the points it raises further in future work, including in J Dickson, *Content-Independence: Possibility and Potential* (currently under contract with Cambridge University Press as part of the 'Cambridge Elements' series in Law).

means of analogy—indigenous peoples of the Arctic region have reason to, and are in a position to, notice, highlight, explain and use multiple and nuanced categorizations of snow and ice which are not known to or used by populations living elsewhere on the planet, this does not mean that these multiple and nuanced categorizations do not pick out real features of the world, or that they are mere subjective impressions or projections. On the contrary, Arctic peoples' experience-sensitive, distinctive, and nuanced understanding of differences between multiple types of snow and ice have most likely developed precisely *because* they pick out real features of the world which are of crucial importance to many aspects of their economic and social lives, in the conditions in which those lives are lived.[54]

Secondly, the above discussion of the opportunities within legal philosophy to highlight and explore experience-sensitive truths about law should readily indicate the tenor of my response to the charge, outlined in Chapter 3, that legal philosophy about the nature of law is overly abstract, and is neglectful of insights and truths regarding law's character as it actually functions in society.[55] *Contra* that charge, legal philosophy about the nature of law can feature, and is likely to have considerable explanatory power when it does feature, insights afforded to legal philosophers as a result of their deep immersion in, and profound understanding of, law as it actually operates in concrete social contexts, and at the sharp end, in and between communities, in our law-governed societies.

(c) Choices about where to start and concerning sufficient explanatory depth given the question addressed

A further issue raising intriguing questions about the degree to which legal philosophers can exercise choice is that of 'where to start' in constructing an account of law's nature. Can legal philosophers choose, and, if so, to what extent can they choose, which features of law and which questions about those features of law, to investigate *first* in their inquiries into law's nature? Some legal philosophers explicitly couch aspects of their methodological stance in terms of issues concerning 'where to start' and have reached a variety of conclusions

---

[54] I am aware that this example is controversial but maintain that the point it reveals is illuminating when considered in the present context. For recent empirically focused research relevant to this issue see I Krupnik and others (eds), SIKU: Knowing Our Ice: Documenting Inuit Sea Ice Knowledge and Use (Springer 2010).

[55] See ch 3, s 4. Further responses to this challenge feature in chs 5 and 6.

on those issues. John Finnis, for example, has claimed that accounts of law's nature will falter if they do not make what he regards as the correct choice in this regard, namely that they should proceed: '[f]rom the starting point of the one hundred percent normative question, what should I decide to do and, equivalently, what kind of person should I resolve or allow myself to be'.[56]

John Gardner on the other hand, views the matter differently, contending that: '[o]ne can in principle begin one's investigations with any aspect of the nature of law so long as one does not attempt to open up everything else at the same time'.[57] My own stance on this issue is developed in Chapter 5, where I discuss the need to approach understanding law with an 'attitude of due wariness', and in Chapters 7 and 8, where I discuss the point and value of what I refer to as 'staged inquiry' in understanding law's nature.[58]

Another interesting issue concerns the extent to which legal philosophers have leeway to decide the point at which their account of some aspect of law has sufficient explanatory depth given the question they are addressing. Consider, for example, the debate surrounding the need for, and the proper characterization of, the internal point of view in understanding legal norms. HLA Hart famously took to task the command theories of Jeremy Bentham and John Austin for reducing to predictions of fact, and hence failing adequately to explain, the internal point of view of those being guided by and following legal rules.[59] Much of Hart's criticism of Austin on this issue in *The Concept of Law* proceeds not by exposing Austin's treatment of legal commands as false,[60] but by emphasizing that it is explanatorily inadequate in failing to account for a vital dimension of the social life under law of those subject to it.[61] The tenor of Hart's criticism here is that Austin has failed to grapple with and explain rule-following in the manner, depth, and from the perspective it demands. In Hart's view, Austin is not free to decide to offer an explanation of legal norms, and of their operation on those subject to law, which reduces them to conjunctions of facts.

---

[56] J Finnis, 'Law and What I Truly Should Decide' (2003) 48 *American Journal of Jurisprudence* 107, 115. See also J Finnis, 'What Is the Philosophy of Law?' (2014) 59 *American Journal of Jurisprudence* 133; G Webber, 'Asking Why in the Study of Human Affairs' (2015) 60 *American Journal of Jurisprudence* 51.

[57] J Gardner, 'Nearly Natural Law' in J Gardner, Law as a Leap of Faith (OUP 2012) 167. It is interesting to note that Gardner altered his position on this issue, having formerly believed that where legal philosophers start, and the order in which they pursue various inquiries, does matter. See ibid 167, n 28 for a brief history of Gardner's views in this regard.

[58] I also explore this issue with respect to Gardner's views in J Dickson, 'Does It Matter Where We Start? Some Remarks on Some Remarks by John Gardner on the Methodology of Legal Philosophy' (2019) 19 *Jerusalem Review of Legal Studies* 71.

[59] Hart (n 13) chs 2–6.

[60] To be sure, *some* of Hart's arguments are designed to expose aspects of Austin's theory as false.

[61] Hart (n 13) 90.

Hart's point has been accepted—albeit subject to significantly different interpretations—in a wide range of subsequent theories about the nature of law.[62] Some legal philosophers who accept it, however, have mounted what can be viewed as a kind of 'tu quoque' or perhaps 'hoist by one's own petard' sort of argument against Hart. John Finnis, for example, accuses Hart himself of offering an account which lacks sufficient explanatory depth as regards the character and role of the internal point of view in understanding legal norms and what it is to be guided by them:

> Rather obviously, this position of Hart and Raz is unstable and unsatisfactory. As against Austin and Kelsen they have sharply differentiated the 'internal' or 'legal' point of view from the point of view of those who merely acquiesce in the law and who do so only because, when, and to the extent that they fear the punishments that will follow non-acquiescence. But both theorists firmly refuse to differentiate further. They recognize that the 'internal' or 'legal' viewpoint, as they describe it, is an amalgam of very different viewpoints.[63]

According to Finnis, legal philosophers should go further than this in the sense that they should differentiate between central and peripheral cases of the internal point of view itself,[64] and should reach the conclusion that: 'If there is a point of view in which legal obligation is treated as at least presumptively a moral obligation ... then such a viewpoint will constitute the central case of the legal viewpoint.'[65] Hart's response to this is along the lines that: (1) by not singling out one variant of the internal point of view as primary, he is being true to the fact that, in the messy realities of human institutionalized normative systems, many people do not, and need not, take that particular attitude towards rules they follow or even administer, and (2) he does not need to differentiate further between variants of the internal point of view, nor to prioritize any one of these in order to answer the question which he has taken as his task at the relevant point in *The Concept of Law*, namely, what are the minimum conditions necessary and sufficient for the existence of a legal system?[66] In Hart's view, given the question he sets out to answer at that point in his work, he has done enough to render his explanation sufficiently explanatorily powerful as an answer to it.

---

[62] See n 32 above and accompanying discussion.
[63] Finnis (n 3) 12.
[64] ibid 13–14.
[65] ibid 14.
[66] See Hart (n 13) chs 5, 6, and 9, especially at 105–17 and 203.

Finnis, however, maintains that Hart is *not* at liberty to regard himself as having done enough to explain the phenomena he aims to explain, and is not at liberty to demarcate in the way that he does which questions legal philosophers need, and need not, answer, in explaining law's nature. This stance stems, in part, from Finnis' view that the important issues about the nature of law cannot be adequately engaged with let alone answered if we take Hart's 'minimum conditions necessary and sufficient for the existence of a legal system' as our central question. It also emanates from standing claims in Finnis' work that schools of thought in legal philosophy other than Finnis' own, legal positivism chief amongst them: (i) attempt artificially and somewhat arbitrarily to truncate the ambit of legal philosophy so that it properly addresses only certain questions concerning law as social fact, and (ii) insist on 'hiving off' to other disciplines or sub-disciplines, such as political philosophy or ethics, the truly important issues about law's character such as whether, when, and why it has moral authority over us and its directives create reasons for action.[67]

Who has the better of these arguments? To what extent do legal philosophers have leeway in deciding the appropriate level of explanatory depth of aspects of their theories? My own view on these issues is developed in Chapters 5 to 8.

(d) Not everything that looks like disagreement is disagreement

The aspects of distribution of emphasis selectivity considered in subsections (a) to (c) above further highlight the scope for pluralism and diversity in legal philosophical inquiry. Reflecting upon them can also yield valuable insights for our understanding of disagreements and rivalries between theories of law. The main point I want to emphasize here is that, although *some* of the choices legal philosophers make regarding distribution of emphasis do indicate and result in genuine disagreements between their accounts of aspects of law's nature, others do not: not everything that looks like disagreement is disagreement.

Consider, for example, the phenomenon of audience-dependence discussed in sub-section (a) above. The pluralism and diversity flowing from this facet of distribution of emphasis selectivity is considerable and may lead to the appearance of disagreement between audience-dependent alternative explanations of the same thing, when in fact no such disagreement exists. As the example

---

[67] Finnis (n 3) ch 1; Finnis, 'Law and What I Truly Should Decide' (n 56); Finnis, 'What Is the Philosophy of Law?' (n 56).

I gave indicated, alternative explanations of Dworkin's account of constructive interpretation in law could appear very different from one another upon first encounter, and this might give some the false impression that those explanations contain conflicting propositions concerning their explanandum.

Furthermore, in the case of theories featuring experience-sensitive truths about aspects of law, in principle, there need be no disagreement between, or rivalry between, for example, an account of law which explores the standing moral risk of law becoming distant from the communities it regulates, and an account exploring law's claims to moral authority and the conditions—if any— under which such claims are justified. Both accounts can reveal truths about law and both can reveal such truths about aspects of law's nature. The properties that make law into what it is are likely to be numerous enough for each account to be capable of holding true of different facets of law, such that one could espouse both without finding oneself committed to any conflicting propositions about law's character.[68]

Different views concerning where to start and about sufficient explanatory depth are perhaps more likely to yield genuine disagreements between theories of law. Even here, however, this is not necessarily the case. If John Gardner is correct that we can start anywhere in our investigations into law's nature, so long as we do not try to open up and investigate everything at once, then theories of law which look very different on first sight, because they start in very different places—for example, a theory which starts with law's moral aims on the one hand, and a theory which starts with law's structural and institutional properties on the other—may not actually be in disagreement. Different decisions theorists make regarding when and why their accounts of law have sufficient explanatory depth given the questions they are addressing, however, may well reveal genuine, rather than merely apparent, disagreement. In the examples outlined in sub-section (c) concerning Hart's criticisms of Austin, and, in turn, Finnis' criticisms of Hart, in each case the legal philosopher doing the criticizing is asserting that the theory criticized is not explanatorily adequate or powerful enough: it has not yet reached a level of explanation of the explanandum in the terms in which it requires to be explained. A disagreement as to whether a given explanation of some X truly grasps and explains the nature of

---

[68] Of course, it is also possible for a particular account of law's standing moral risk of becoming alienated from those it governs to take a stance on aspects of law's nature that *is* incompatible with a particular theory of law's authority. But this possibility is not different in kind from the potential for disagreement between any two accounts of law, including between two different accounts of law's authority. There is no extra, or special, risk of disagreement between theories on the basis that one theory makes more use of experience-sensitive engagement with features of law than the other.

that X in the way its character requires is likely to be a genuine disagreement, and rival theories of law featuring such disagreements are likely to contain conflicting propositions about law's nature.

(e) Explanatory power and constraints on distribution of emphasis selectivity

Finally, we come to the issue of the existence and character of constraints incumbent on legal philosophers as they exercise distribution of emphasis selectivity.[69] My view is that there are significantly more constraints on distribution of emphasis selectivity than on subject-matter selectivity. In the case of subject-matter selectivity, as I advocated at the end of section 3 of this chapter, we should encourage rich diversity in intellectual work and follow our intellectual interests down whichever avenues they lead us. Things are somewhat different, however, with distribution of emphasis selectivity, although the extent of the difference will vary depending on which facet of distribution of emphasis selectivity we are concerned with. Constraints on distribution of emphasis selectivity are tied to the explanatory power of the resulting account of law: legal philosophers are constrained to the degree that making certain choices over others will improve the explanatory power of their theories.

Audience-dependence, in my view, does generate significant constraints on legal philosophers exercising distribution of emphasis selectivity. An explanation of something is successful when it facilitates understanding of that something to some relevant audience. Who the audience are and what understanding they already possess of the phenomena in question or cognate phenomena supply the relevant constraints. As was discussed in sub-section (a) above, these constraints may guide the theorist offering an explanation towards different materials, different examples, different orders, and directions of explanation, depending on the audience at whom the explanation is aimed.

In the case of experience-sensitive engagement with features of law, in my view it is important to hold that no legal philosopher is constrained to the point where they *must* engage in a certain way with certain features of law because they happen to have, or to have access to, a given experience or range of experiences. As discussed in sub-section (b) above, the possibility of such

---

[69] Given the focus of the discussion in the present chapter, this section is necessarily brief. In different ways, however, each of the remaining four chapters of this book address various of the constraints which, in my view, are important to observe if we are to develop a successful philosophy of legal philosophy.

engagement should be viewed as an *opportunity* for noticing things that others may overlook, and for explaining things in a distinctive and nuanced way. Should those who lack certain experiences steer clear of addressing aspects of law's operation where it is plausible that experience-sensitive engagement may result in a deeper understanding? I suspect that there can be no context-independent answer. As legal philosophers we should be sensitive to our various strengths and weaknesses as regards our ability to understand and explain certain phenomena and should be humble in attempting to explain matters where our lack of experience of may affect that understanding. But it is important to remember, too, that one valuable opportunity afforded us in intellectual work is to broaden and deepen our understanding by building intellectual bridges from the understanding we already have, to new areas which we have understood less fully hitherto. This being so, reading about, and reflecting on, experience-sensitive engagement with features of law in the work of others and in the reality of how law is encountered by various groups in society, can provide us with fresh insights into and improved understanding of those matters, and may shepherd our own work in novel directions.

Regarding 'where to start': the correct view of the constraints incumbent on legal philosophers will be dependent on the correctness of their stance on the methodological issue of whether it matters where we start in our accounts of law's nature. If Finnis is correct, for example, then legal philosophers are very constrained in this regard, and a failure to start where he claims we should start will result in an explanatorily inadequate theory. By contrast, if Gardner is correct, then there appear to be very few constraints on where to start.[70]

Decisions concerning sufficient explanatory depth—ie when a legal philosopher has done enough to explain some aspect of law in a way appropriate to the character of the explanandum—are significantly constrained by the explanatory power of the resulting theory. For example, as was outlined in subsection (c) above, Hart contends that the command theorists were not free to decide that their accounts of law had sufficient explanatory depth without explaining what it is to follow and be guided by a rule from the internal point of view; Finnis contends in turn that Hart's account, though an improvement on the command theories which preceded it, is itself in error as regards the explanatory depth required to understand legal norms' role in guiding human conduct.[71]

---

[70] See the discussion in s 4 (c) above. My own view emerges in chs 5, 7, and 8.
[71] Finnis (n 3) ch 1 12–15. I offer my own view regarding various constraints on a successful theory of law generated by the distinctive character of law in chs 5–8.

5. Conclusion

Where do the various discussions in this chapter leave us? Hopefully with a better understanding of the various senses in which there is significant scope for pluralism, diversity, and development in the questions of legal philosophy, including legal philosophy about the nature of law. *Contra* various of the criticisms of it discussed in Chapter 3, legal philosophy about the nature of law is not problematically static or focused only on one narrow sub-set of staple questions about law's character in a manner that leads it to be imperialist about and/or dismissive regarding a wide variety of other theoretical inquiries about law. It is also my hope that, with the character of, scope of, and opportunities for pluralism and diversity within legal philosophy about the nature of law better understood, at least some of the needless and wasteful misunderstandings between, and false oppositions involving, this enterprise and other sorts of theoretical inquiries about law may be dissolved.

5
Approaching Law

A Constraining Duality and an Attitude of Due Wariness

'Ca' canny but ca' awa' …'[1]

1. Introduction: Towards Indirectly Evaluative Legal Philosophy

This chapter, and the three which follow it, develop and defend my 'philosophy of legal philosophy': indirectly evaluative legal philosophy. As I noted in Chapter 1, indirectly evaluative legal philosophy (IELP) can be thought of, in metaphorical terms, as the species of legal philosophy which I particularly champion within the more general genus of elucidating law.[2]

Chapters 5 to 8 focus on different aspects of IELP. The discussions in these chapters are complementary, and mutually supporting. Taken together, they explain and defend my view of various constraints incumbent on legal philosophers as they attempt to explain aspects of law's nature. As a schematic map of the territory to be traversed may prove helpful, IELP can be summarized as comprising the following six tenets:[3]

---

[1] Scots phrase or saying meaning 'go carefully, but go', 'proceed warily/with caution, but proceed', which also features on the coat of arms of the town of Kirkintilloch, located to the north-east of Glasgow, Scotland. For origins and usage (both historical and contemporary) see eg http://www.dsl.ac.uk/entry/snd/ca_canny; http://www.dsl.ac.uk/entry/snd/sndns651; https://www.edlc.co.uk/heritage-arts/local-history/towns-and-villages/kirkintilloch-coat-arms; http://www.heraldscotland.com/opinion/16117711.Herald_View__Edinburgh_needs_to_ca____canny_with_its_tartan_blush/.

[2] See the discussion in ch 1, s 4.

[3] In some previous work, I have outlined IELP in five rather than six main tenets: see eg J Dickson, 'Ours Is a Broad Church: Indirectly Evaluative Legal Philosophy as a Facet of Jurisprudential Inquiry' (2015) 6 *Jurisprudence* 207; J Dickson, 'Why General Jurisprudence Is Interesting' (2017) 49 *Crítica: Revista Hispanoamericana de Filosofía* 11. There has been no change in the substance of my views: the division of issues outlined above has merely been altered slightly to reflect the structure of this book.

Elucidating Law. Julie Dickson, Oxford University Press. © Julie Dickson 2022.
DOI: 10.1093/oso/9780198727767.003.0005

Tenet 1: IELP seeks to identify and explain significant, important, and illuminating aspects of the nature of law, and to consider what it is for law to have a nature, and how truths about its nature are to be ascertained.

Tenet 2: IELP seeks to understand and be sensitive to the ways in which the questions of legal philosophy are multiple, diverse, and arise in and change over time.

Tenet 3: In approaching law, IELP respects the constraints stemming from an important duality running through law between its social character and its normative character and advocates adopting what can be termed an 'attitude of due wariness' as the outset of jurisprudential inquiries.

Tenet 4: IELP aims adequately to account for, explain the relevance of, and respect the constraints imposed by the self-understandings—in terms of the concept of law and related concepts—of those who create, administer, and are subject to the law.

Tenet 5: IELP embraces what can be termed 'the value of staged inquiry' and contends that understanding law's nature should proceed by investigating certain of law's properties before others. In particular, IELP advocates understanding law's nature by postponing and, in a certain sense, limiting the role of moral evaluation in our theories of law, until certain questions have been addressed.

Tenet 6: IELP has a role to play in engendering and facilitating moral and other evaluation, criticism, and reform of law, tasks which are a vital part of legal philosophy, and which have significant relations of continuity and of complementarity with the task of identifying and explaining law's nature.

As the above summary of IELP indicates, there are many interesting miles to cover on the road ahead. Moreover, it will also be apparent that some of the territory has already been visited: aspects of tenets 1 and 2, for example, are discussed in Chapters 2–4. Although this is so, the issues featuring in tenets 1 and 2 are revisited in the course of examining other aspects of IELP, and a more fully rounded understanding and defence of all six tenets of this approach will emerge over the coming chapters.

The present chapter is primarily concerned with how—according to the IELP approach—legal philosophers ought to approach, and begin to get to grips with, their subject matter. The discussion seeks to elucidate some important constraints to be observed and proposes that a particular theoretical attitude or theoretical orientation should be adopted at the outset of legal philosophical inquiries. The chapter is hence particularly concerned with tenet 3 of IELP, although the discussion also reinforces my stance on certain aspects of tenet 1, and so builds on the discussions in Chapters 2 and 3 of what it is for law to have a nature. Section 2 below outlines a key duality between law's social character and its normative character, which, as I go on to argue in section 3, imposes significant constraints on a successful theory of law, and hence influences how legal philosophers ought to approach their explanandum. In section 4, I offer and critically analyse an example of an account of law that does not do adequate justice to each aspect of this key duality, in order further to illustrate the constraints I have in mind. In section 5, I argue that various aspects of law's character—including the need to do adequate justice to the duality running through law identified earlier in the chapter—justify legal philosophers adopting a particular theoretical attitude, or theoretical orientation, at the outset of their inquiries. I term this orientation 'an attitude of due wariness' and seek to show how its adoption is both justified and helpful. By the chapter's close, I aim to have explored and defended several important aspects of IELP's manner of approaching law, and these are drawn together in the concluding section.

Before embarking on this discussion, at this juncture in the book it is important to note the following point. In speaking in this chapter and the three which follow it of certain constraints that I view as being incumbent on legal philosophers as they strive to identify and explain aspects of law's nature, and in exploring how those constraints shape the methodological approach—IELP—that I champion, I do *not* view the constraints in question as being purely methodological in character, or as being driven primarily by theoretical and meta-theoretical considerations influencing theory construction in the social sciences in general. Rather, and as should become clear over the remaining chapters, I view these methodological constraints as being driven by aspects of the specific character of legal philosophers' explanandum—ie by the character of law itself and its actualization in our law-governed societies. In other words, and as I have sought to explain in previous work,[4] I view questions of methodology and questions of substance in legal philosophy as being intricately linked. I say more about this issue and its relevance for IELP in Chapter 7, but it is important to mention it now in order to give a more contextualized picture of what, in my view, drives the methodological constraints that I regard as incumbent on legal philosophers as they seek to identify and explain law's nature. My

---

[4] See J Dickson, Evaluation and Legal Theory (Hart Publishing 2001) ch 1, s B.

stance in this regard should also become progressively clearer as the discussions in this chapter, and the three which follow, proceed.

2. An Important Duality: Law's Social and Normative Nature

Those who live in law-governed societies are aware that law is created, modified, applied, and enforced by social and institutional practices and processes. Such awareness is widespread and need not be implausibly complex or convoluted in character. We are aware that institutions such as parliaments and courts exist, and that their activities can create, change, and decide disputes regarding the law. We know that people who are employed by government departments and agencies are authorized to give advice on, and to apply, rules relating to everyday matters such as paying the right amount of tax, receiving welfare benefits, attaining a licence to drive various types of vehicle, obtaining a passport. We also know that someone found to have broken the law can be subject to visits from the police, requirements to pay fines, and, in the most serious cases, to deprivation of liberty in social institutions such as prisons and young offenders' institutions. Moreover, not merely knowledge of, but direct or indirect (eg via the experiences of family, friends, and colleagues) experience of at least some of these social and institutional aspects of law is an inevitable part of life in law-governed societies. One does not have to be involved with law in a professional capacity to know that its institutions and processes, and the actions of its officials, are woven through many aspects of our lives in society. Those who are involved with law in a professional capacity of course have a more focused and acute understanding of the practices, processes, and institutions on which law's operation rests.

These commonplace understandings are important. They tell us that law has, and is correctly perceived by those living under it to have, a social reality to it, comprising those social facts and institutional processes by means of which it is created, modified, applied, and enforced. Moreover, those social facts and institutional processes have significant effects across myriad areas of our lives, and over the whole course of our lives. This facet of law is vitally important. We ignore or underplay it at our peril, as several of the discussions in this and in subsequent chapters reveal.

All this said, however, the social reality of law—its existence as an actualized social practice having pervasive effects on the lives of those subject to it—is but one side of an important duality running through it. Both aspects of this duality must be accorded importance, and be accounted for and explained, in understanding law's character.

The 'other side' of this duality is law as a normative phenomenon. 'Normative' is a slippery term in legal philosophy, in part because it can appropriately be used in framing a variety of different but related questions that we might want to ask of law. Such questions might usefully be divided into three categories:[5]

(1) questions concerning the meaning of normative statements or of normative language, eg 'How should we interpret statements of the form "according to law, X ought to ϕ"?'; 'Can such statements be reduced to combinations of facts and/ or to statements about other people's beliefs?'; 'Does "ought" mean the same thing in legal and moral contexts?';
(2) questions concerning the character of the claims that law makes, eg 'Does law claim to be morally binding and to provide reasons for action which operate in a distinctive way in our practical reasoning?';
(3) questions concerning whether and under what conditions law truly is morally binding and truly does provide moral reasons for action of a certain kind, and whether and to what extent it successfully achieves certain moral aims and realizes certain moral values.

While all of these questions concerning law's normativity are important, it is for the most part aspects of those issues in categories (2) and (3) that I focus on here and in later chapters. Some might take the view that only those issues in category (3) truly concern the normative side of the duality running through law, and that issues in category (2) are more appropriately thought of as concerning the interpretation of certain social facts comprising law's claims. However, as emerges from the discussions in this chapter and those which follow, the issues in (2) and (3) are linked in various important ways that are relevant to the philosophy of legal philosophy that I seek to develop and defend.

To understand law well, we need to understand what it is trying to be and to bring about, and how it is taken by those who accept its claims. When we are faced with a legal directive, we are faced with something that makes a claim over us, that states a view of what we truly ought to do, and which does not accept as a reason for not acting according to it that we, or anyone else, hold a different view of what we ought to do. Attempting to understand and do adequate justice to these features of law opens up further issues: whether and under

---

[5] I am grateful to Brian Leiter for this clarifying suggestion.

what conditions law's claims to state what truly ought to be done could be true; which values law aspires to, and in light of which it should be judged; whether law has, and whether it succeeds in realizing, a moral purpose or aim.

Law exists both as institutional practice and social fact, and as a normative, reason-giving, and value-aspiring phenomenon. Doing adequate justice to each aspect of this key duality, and to the relations between them, is vitally important in developing a successful theory of law.[6]

3. Law's Duality in Indirectly Evaluative Legal Philosophy

Why is this so? The answer emerges over the course of the discussions in the present chapter and the three which follow it. However, we can begin by noting that, as I have argued previously, the job of the legal philosopher is not to home in on and explain just any old truths about features of law. Rather, and as is discussed in depth in Chapter 7, legal philosophers must make judgements which are—in a certain sense—evaluative judgements of what is significant and important to focus on, in constructing theories of law.[7]

Law's dual character as both social fact and normative phenomenon is one such important and significant feature about it. Its significance lies in the effects which law has in our lives as a consequence of it. As was mentioned towards the end of section 2, when we are faced with the law, we are faced with something that makes a normative claim over us, that states a view of what we truly ought to do, and which does not accept as a reason for not acting according to it that we, or anyone else, hold a different view of what ought to be done. These features, when combined with the social reality of law—including the fact that it can be applied to us and enforced against us in concrete social processes capable of having a deep-reaching effect on our lives—make it a powerful, important, and pervasive phenomenon in society.

Each aspect of the duality also influences how, methodologically speaking, we should approach law. Law's normative character is important in furnishing us with important standards which law holds itself out as meeting, and in

---

[6] Note that there may be other important dualities running through law that legal philosophers might fruitfully explore. My claim is only that this duality is central to understanding law and plays a key role in explaining the methodological position I espouse in this book.

[7] I have discussed these points in Dickson (n 4), especially chs 2–4. See also J Dickson, 'Methodology in Jurisprudence: A Critical Survey' (2004) 10 *Legal Theory* 117; J Dickson, 'Legal Positivism: Contemporary Debates' in A Marmor (ed), The Routledge Companion to Philosophy of Law (Routledge 2012). In the present work, in addition to the discussion above see also the conclusion to this chapter, ch 4, and ch 7.

terms of which it ought to be judged.[8] Moreover, and returning to the other aspect of the duality, one reason why it is vital to identify those standards law should be judged by, and to engage in critical scrutiny of law, is because of the far-reaching and large-scale effects that it can have as a result of its social and institutional character. Law can require certain courses of conduct from vast numbers of people in societies, and can effect a significant degree of compliance with its directives due to various of its social and institutional features, such as having courts and executive officers of the law to implement, apply, and enforce it. This being so, where law operates, the stakes are high as regards its impact on the lives of those living under it. It is vital that such a powerful phenomenon be properly evaluated and subject to critical scrutiny in terms of its ability to make good on those normative claims that it makes.

IELP seeks to do justice to both law's social, and normative, character. Each aspect of this duality should be given due standing in a theoretical account of law, and one side of the duality should not be inappropriately promoted, or demoted, at the expense of the other. Moreover, the relations between each aspect of the duality, and the relevance of these relations to understanding law are also vital matters for a theory of law to address. These factors place important constraints on a successful theory of the nature of law. IELP seeks to observe these constraints in various ways: by rejecting accounts of law which fail to grant appropriate weight to each aspect of law's duality;[9] by adopting an attitude of due wariness towards law's normative claims;[10] by doing adequate justice to the self-understandings of those living under law and respecting the limits of revisionism as regards those understandings;[11] by highlighting relations of continuity and complementarity between accounts of what law *must* be in order to be law, and accounts of what law ought to be.[12]

This last point raises some further questions as regards how this key duality of law plays out in IELP. IELP claims that, in order to understand law, it is necessary to understand its *nature*, ie those properties which make it into what it is, and without which it would not be law. This being so, it might be tempting to think that only inquiries into one aspect of the duality of law—law as a social fact—properly belong to this enterprise, on the reasoning that law's other aspect—its normative claims and what, if anything, could render

---

[8] There may be other important criteria by which law should be judged, in addition to those stemming from the standards that it itself purports to meet. I discuss these issues further in ch 8.
[9] See the discussion in the remainder of this section and in s 4.
[10] See s 5 of the current chapter.
[11] This issue is discussed in ch 6.
[12] See chs 7 and 8.

them true—would be the subject of inquiries concerning what law ought to be, rather than what it must be, in order to be law. According to this line of thought, as law can fail to be as it ought to be and yet still be law, the normative aspect of law's character must fall to be considered in inquiries into law's contingent properties rather than inquiries into law's nature.

Although tempting, as it stands the above line of thought is misleading in several respects. First of all, certain aspects of law's normative character, such as the character of the *claims* that it makes, including, arguably, claims that it possesses legitimate authority over us, generates reasons for action of a certain sort, and morally ought to be obeyed, are plausibly part of law's nature.[13] Secondly, it is possible that at least some of the standards by which law ought to be judged are so because of law's nature, even if successfully attaining those standards is not part of law's nature. One example of a legal philosopher who espouses such a position is Joseph Raz, who contends that law has a specific moral task to perform arising out of its character as a structure of authority,[14] namely: '[t]o secure a situation whereby moral goals which, given the current social situation in the country whose law it is, would be unlikely to be achieved without it, and whose achievement by the law is not counter-productive, are realised'.[15]

Raz views the fulfilment of this moral task as something which law, in virtue of its nature, ought to achieve, and hence sets an important standard by which, in virtue of its nature, law ought to be judged. By way of contrast, Raz also contends that there are other things that law ought to be and to do—such as being a worthy object of identification and respect[16]—which do *not* arise from its nature. Although he contends that law has a moral task to perform as part of its nature, Raz maintains that law which fails in this moral task remains law nonetheless.[17]

These points reveal some senses in which aspects of law's normative character seem plausibly to have a place within investigations into law's nature. Moreover, my own view is that questions concerning those standards law ought to be held to, what would have to be the case in order for it to meet them, and whether and to what extent certain legal systems do meet them, form a vitally important part of jurisprudential inquiry. Some of those questions will concern aspects of law's nature, but others will not, and will rather involve

---

[13] These points are discussed at greater length in ch 7.
[14] J Raz, 'About Morality and the Nature of Law' (2003) 48 *American Journal of Jurisprudence* 1.
[15] ibid 12 (emphasis in original).
[16] ibid 14.
[17] ibid 10–15. This issue is discussed further in the next section, and in ch 7.

inquiries into some of law's contingent properties: properties that it may have and ought to have, but which are not part of its nature. As I emphasized in Chapters 2 and 3, inquiries into aspects of law's nature are but one important sort of jurisprudential inquiry amongst many valuable others. Furthermore, even in the case of questions about law's normative character which do not fall within inquiries into law's nature, our understanding of them and ability to answer them can be focused and advanced by conducting inquiries into aspects of law's nature in an appropriate way, according to certain precepts, and while observing certain constraints.[18]

4. Failing to Do Justice to the Duality: An Example Considered

I contended in sections 2 and 3 that each facet of the social fact/normative phenomenon duality of law should be given appropriate recognition in a theory of law's nature, and that one aspect of the duality should not be inappropriately promoted, or demoted, at the expense of the other. This section considers an example to illustrate this point, and to illuminate further the methodological constraints that flow from the importance of properly doing justice to each aspect of law's dual character.

The example hails from a certain aspect of the work of John Finnis. At various points in his writings, Finnis claims that his distinctive take on a natural law position recognizes and does justice to both facets of the duality of law discussed above.[19] In terms of his recognition of law's social fact character, Finnis states that:

[h]uman law is artefact and artifice, and not a conclusion from moral premises[20]

[w]hy deny that the facts which are referred to as 'human positing' - custom, legislation, judgments—can all be identified by lawyerly historical methods, without 'moral argument'?[21]

---

[18] See further the discussion in chs 6–8.
[19] I have discussed some of these points previously, eg in Dickson, 'Legal Positivism' (n 7) and in J Dickson, 'Law and Its Theory: A Question of Priorities' in RP George and J Keown (eds), Reason, Morality and Law: The Jurisprudence of John Finnis (OUP 2013).
[20] J Finnis, 'The Truth in Legal Positivism' in R George (ed), The Autonomy of Law: Essays on Legal Positivism (OUP 1996) 205.
[21] ibid.

As regards understanding law as a normative phenomenon, Finnis attempts throughout his general theory of law to address questions concerning the conditions under which law's claims to generate reasons for action are justified, and whether law has an overall normative point or value.[22] Indeed, not only does he address these questions, but it would not be an exaggeration to say his view of law is largely characterized by the distinctive answers which he gives to them: that law's overall normative point is reasonably to resolve coordination problems for the sake of societal common good, thus allowing citizens successfully to pursue the basic goods in their lives,[23] and that law generates reasons for action and morally ought to be obeyed when and for the reason that it achieves that normative point.[24]

Moreover, Finnis sometimes explicitly claims that he seeks to do adequate justice to both these facets of law within his version of natural law theory:

> Natural law theory accepts that law can be considered and spoken of *both* as a sheer social fact of power and practice, *and* as a set of reasons for action that can be and often are sound as reasons and therefore normative for reasonable people addressed by them.[25]
>
> In short: a natural law theory of (the nature of) law seeks both to give an account of the facticity of law and to answer questions that remain central to understanding law ... these further questions (which 'legal positivism does not aspire to answer') are: What kinds of things could possibly count as the merits of law? What role should law play in adjudication? What claim has law on our obedience? What laws should we have? And should we have law at all?[26]

Finnis, then, appears to endorse the point that legal philosophers need to do adequate justice to both law's social, and normative, aspects, and to be

---

[22] These issues are discussed at more points in Finnis' work than could possibly be referenced here. However, the declaration of intent contained in the opening sentences of *Natural Law and Natural Rights* makes the point well enough: 'There are human goods that can be secured only through the institutions of human law, and requirements of practical reasonableness that only those institutions can satisfy. It is the object of this book to identify those goods, and those requirements of practical reasonableness, and thus to show how and on what conditions such institutions are justified.' J Finnis, Natural Law and Natural Rights, (2nd edn, Clarendon Press 2011) 3.
[23] ibid *passim*; but see especially chs VI, IX, and X.
[24] ibid especially chs XI, XII. For the sake of brevity in exposition, I do not consider the possible complexities arising from Finnis' views on 'collateral obligation' to obey the law see Finnis (n 22) 354–62, 365, 367, 476.
[25] J Finnis, 'Natural Law Theories' in Edward N Zalta (ed), *The Stanford Encyclopedia of Philosophy* (Summer 2020 Edition), Introduction (emphasis in original) https://plato.stanford.edu/archives/sum2020/entries/natural-law-theories/.
[26] ibid.

committed to doing so in his own account. However, when we examine how this apparent commitment plays out in certain aspects of his position, a picture emerges in which Finnis' declared aim does not come to well-balanced fruition, for he inappropriately promotes one side of law's dual character at the expense of the other.

This point is brought keenly into focus when we consider Finnis' view of how we should understand instances of legal systems which meet the relevant social fact criteria for counting them as law (for example, they consist of norms of a practised system emanating from the social institutions of that system and meeting its intra-systemic tests for legal validity), but which fail in terms of fulfilling law's normative point or value (those norms, and the system of which they are a part, do not coordinate for the common good, or perhaps even coordinate in order to produce morally bad outcomes). According to Finnis, although there is a certain sense in which such systems, and the norms which constitute them, can still be law,[27] he emphasizes that they are also to be regarded—depending on his chosen turn of phrase—as not really law,[28] less than fully law,[29] law only in a secondary, watered down, non-central, or distorted sense,[30] or, simply, not law.[31] In terms of the facets comprising law's dual character, then, the social fact properties of law seem less central to law's nature, less central to its being law, for Finnis, than its ability successfully to realize what he regards as law's overall normative point or value.

This begins to reveal the sense in which Finnis' account of law, despite his claims to the contrary, does not in fact do adequate justice to both aspects of law's duality. The point is further underscored by a remark he makes in his article, 'Law and What I Truly Should Decide' in response to a challenge by Joseph Raz as to why, according to Finnis, law should be regarded as not really or fully law when it is bad, whereas novels or paintings or people still remain novels or paintings or people even when they are bad. Finnis' response to Raz runs as follows:

> On the occasion of the Lecture, Joseph Raz asked why law should be thought to be like argument, medicine or contracts, rather than like novels or paintings, or people, that are still novels or paintings, or people, even if they are

---

[27] Finnis (n 22) ch XII.4; see also Finnis (n 25).
[28] Finnis (n 22) 277–78.
[29] ibid 279.
[30] Finnis (n 25) s 4.
[31] J Finnis, 'Law and What I Truly Should Decide' (2003) 48 *American Journal of Jurisprudence* 107, 114.

bad. One answer is that, like argument, medicines, and contracts, *law has a focused and normative point to which everything else about it is properly to be regarded as subordinate*. Novels and paintings, on the other hand, can have incompatible points, e.g. to entertain or arouse (like kitsch or porn) or to tell a truth with artistry. People exist in the natural order as living substances even if they are not functioning adequately or at all in the orders of logic and thought, deliberation, and/or exercises of skill.[32]

This quote—especially that part of it which I have italicized—provides further evidence that Finnis' understanding of law places considerable emphasis on one facet of law's dual character—its normative point or value—and demotes, and fails to place proper emphasis on, the other facet—law's social facticity. Those features of law which comprise the social fact aspect of its nature—such as consisting of norms meeting intra-systemic tests of legal validity which are created, recognized, applied, and enforced by legal officials and institutions— are regarded by Finnis as subordinate qualities of law, and law that exhibits those qualities, but that does not instantiate law's overall normative point or value is seen as a watered down or secondary kind of law (when it is seen as law at all). Law's 'focused and normative point'—its moral task of reasonably resolving coordination problems for the common good—is hence what Finnis regards as most important to its being law.

This promotion of law's normative point or value and concomitant demotion of its social fact properties as regards what constitutes it as law, is problematic, and significantly undermines Finnis' claims that his version of natural law theory can adequately account for law's dual character. As was discussed at the outset of section 2, law has an important social reality to it which plays a significant role in the lives of those in law-governed societies. Legal systems are institutionalized normative systems in which inter-related norms are created, modified, applied, and enforced by legal institutions and officials such as legislatures, courts and tribunals, the police, and other executive agencies. In any jurisdiction governed by law, some such institutions exist and they and the norms they generate and apply have a deep and pervasive impact on the social reality of those living in the society in question. People fall under the jurisdiction of the legislature, courts, and other legal institutions, are subject to their norms, stand liable to have them forcefully applied to them by legal officials in case of non-compliance, and know and view as important these characteristics of law. Moreover, these features of law, and their impact on the lives of

---

[32] ibid 114, n 9 (emphasis added).

those living under it, persist irrespective of whether law successfully realizes any moral point or value that it may have. Law on the one hand, and people on the other, are hence not disanalogous in the way that Finnis claims in the quotation above in which he responds to Raz's question. Although the social reality of law is very different in character from the biological reality of people, both persist even when those entities fail to live up to the standards they ought to, and both are properties of considerable importance in demarcating those entities' character and making them into what they are. In the case of law, those social fact properties are important because law's social and institutional character plays a deep and pervasive role in people's lives, irrespective of whether or not it successfully achieves any normative point it may have, and because those living under law regard those social features of law as important and significant.[33] Law's social facticity must hence be granted its proper place in our understanding of law, if we are to understand it successfully. It is not something to be regarded as subordinate to other of law's properties and hence significantly demoted in our explanatory accounts of what law is, resulting in the view Finnis advocates wherein law, despite possessing those social fact properties, and despite being applied to and enforced against people, is rendered not fully law, not really law, or just not law[34] when it fails to achieve its normative point. In endorsing and indeed highlighting this demotion in his own understanding of law, Finnis' account fails in its claim to be capable of doing appropriate justice to both facets of law's dual character.

5. Approaching Law: An Attitude of Due Wariness

The duality running through law discussed above is one important constraint which a successful theory of the nature of law should observe, and which should influence how legal philosophers approach law in embarking on their inquiries. This section discusses another such constraining and influencing factor: that legal philosophers ought to approach theorizing about law with what I refer to as an 'attitude of due wariness'. As is explored further below, the core of such an attitude involves being appropriately cautious as regards the claims that law makes, and the manner in which law presents itself, in order to facilitate understanding it without prematurely ascribing certain qualities to it.

---

[33] For further discussion of this issue see Dickson (n 4), especially at 59–60, 120–21, and 139–43. I return to this point in the conclusion to this chapter and discuss it in more depth in chs 6 and 7.
[34] See those works of Finnis referenced in nn 28–31 above for his various formulations of this point.

But what could justify the adoption of an attitude of due wariness, or, for that matter, the adoption of any sort of attitude towards law at the outset of legal philosophers' inquiries? Should we not strive to approach our subject matter in an even-handed manner, in order to give ourselves the best chance of understanding it accurately? My answer is that we should indeed strive to approach our subject matter in an even-handed manner, and that adopting an attitude of due wariness towards law can facilitate, rather than undermine, our efforts to do so.

As was discussed in section 2 above, one facet of an important duality running through law is law's normative character. Law makes a normative claim over us in telling us what we ought to do. It holds itself out as having the authority to do so and does not accept as a reason for not acting according to its directives that we, or anyone else, hold a different view of what ought to be done. Law also claims for itself the right to authorize the use of coercion against those who do not comply with its view of what ought to be done.[35] These aspects of law indicate that it does not approach us in a neutral manner; rather, it comes at us claiming to state what truly ought to be done and claiming that it is justified in so doing. Law hence presents itself as a good and justified phenomenon which ought to be understood as such, and ought to be obeyed on the terms in which it presents itself. This being so, the adoption of an attitude of due wariness as we approach law can function as a helpful 'push back' or corrective given the non-neutral manner in which law approaches us. Moreover, I think of this attitude as one which both persons living under law and facing its normative claims, and legal philosophers analysing law and seeking to understand it (including seeking to understand its normative claims) are justified in adopting. Given the aims of this book, however, it is the latter perspective—that of legal philosophers—that I primarily focus on here.

But what do I mean, exactly, by a helpful 'push back' or corrective? Let me begin by saying what I do *not* mean in this regard. I do not mean that, because law approaches us with an insistence that it is good and justified and ought to obeyed, that we should 'push back' by adopting an attitude at the outset of our investigations into its character which holds that it is *not* any of those things. Adopting an attitude of due wariness towards law does not mean occupying a starting point where we assume that law is bad, or unjustified, or not to obeyed, and it does not mean starting with presumptions to this effect and claiming that law must somehow rebut them in order to establish itself as being as it

---

[35] For an excellent discussion of this point see G Lamond, 'Coercion and the Nature of Law' (2001) 7 *Legal Theory* 35.

claims to be. Rather, I am using wariness in the sense of a trait of being watchful or cautious, and hence, in the current context, of not being too quick to accept at face value and trust the claims law makes for itself. An attitude of due wariness thus has much in common with the instruction in the Scots phrase with which this chapter opened: 'Ca' canny but ca' awa' ...'[36]

Why might it be helpful for legal philosophers to adopt such an attitude in approaching law? In my view: because it facilitates them having some 'cognitive breathing space' wherein they can pause for thought and consideration in the face of law's powerful normative claims and its manner of self-presentation. Such pausing for thought, I contend, improves our chances of understanding law and its claims in a clear-sighted and cool-headed manner, and ameliorates the risks of prematurely accepting law's claims as true.[37]

It is especially important to approach law in this manner because of (i) the powerful and compelling character of law's normative claims, (ii) the seriousness of the consequences of attributing to law qualities which it claims to but may not in fact possess, and (iii) the need—for the sake of elucidating law accurately—to counter the tendencies of some legal philosophers who are too quick to assume that law can and does make good on its claims, and are too willing to gloss over evidence to the contrary in the form of the social reality of law. I return to (i) and (ii) below, but some discussion relevant to (iii) has already been offered in section 4 above, where I argued that John Finnis' work exhibits a tendency to demote, and hence to fail to do adequate justice to, the social fact aspect of law. Finnis is too ready to regard genuinely as law only that which succeeds in its normative claims, and which realizes what he regards as law's normative point or value. Hence, he deems instances of law which fail in those respects to be not really law, not fully law, not a central case of law, or, simply, not law.[38] Moreover, according to Finnis, when we approach law—as citizens or as legal philosophers—we should view it as presumptively morally obligatory.[39] As I explore further below, adopting such an attitude runs certain serious standing risks. Finnis is also not the only legal philosopher to exhibit such tendencies. In Chapter 6 I consider aspects of the views of Mark Greenberg and of Nicos Stavropoulos and contend that they also appear too ready to conclude that law is that which succeeds in its normative claims, and too ready to classify as not law phenomena which do not so succeed.[40]

---

[36] See n 1 and accompanying quotation.
[37] In addition to the discussion in the remainder of this section, I also address issues relevant to this point in ch 7.
[38] See nn 28–31 above and accompanying discussion.
[39] Finnis (n 22) 14–15, 325–46, 354–59.
[40] See ch 6, especially s 3.

As regards (i)—that it is important to approach law with an attitude of due wariness because of the powerful and compelling character of law's normative claims—as has already been noted, one important sense in which law's normative claims are powerful is in terms of the effect they purport to have, and are intended to have, in our practical rationality. Law claims that it has authority to mandate certain courses of conduct, and requires us to set aside what would otherwise be our own views of what we ought to do, and instead do as law says. In addition to this, it is important to register the compelling *manner* in which law makes these normative claims, and the symbolic, linguistic, and even architectural tactics and techniques it deploys in its attempts to convince us of their truth. Law approaches us in a magisterial and monumental manner. It characteristically uses archaic and convoluted terminology, phraseology, and forms of address largely impenetrable to those not extensively educated in its ways. Its most public face is frequently shown in grand imposing buildings decorated with symbols of justice and proclamations of high virtue. Its adjudicative institutions employ distinctive and often hierarchical settings, procedures, and etiquette. They are staffed by learned and sometimes bewigged-and-gowned judges and lawyers using terms of art and turns of phrase more likely to confuse than to clarify what is happening to the very people it is happening to.[41] Its associated nomenclature—'Ministry of Justice', 'Royal Courts of Justice', etc.—proclaims not only the importance of law's domain, but also its august credentials within that domain: ministries and courts of justice appear by their very name to be holding themselves out not merely as aspiring to, but as delivering, justice. Such features of law's operation create and sustain a powerful impression that law is to be venerated and obeyed, and that law's normative claims over us are true. Law approaches us in a manner liable to convince us *not* to weigh things up for ourselves or to exercise critical judgement over the judgement of the law, but to do as law says, because it says so, and because it knows best. Given that these are enduring features of its character, it is conducive to understanding law as it is, not merely as it claims to be, if we approach it with an attitude of due wariness. Doing so can assist us in seeing beyond law's magisterial aura, and enables us to pause for thought and to consider in a coolheaded manner which, if any, of its claims are true.

---

[41] Some of these aspects of law are thoughtfully discussed in works such as L Mulcahy, Legal Architecture: Justice, Due Process and the Place of Law (Routledge 2011); J Resnik, D Curtis, and A Tait, 'Constructing Courts: Architecture, the Ideology of Judging, and the Public Sphere' in A Wagner and R Sherwin (eds), Law, Culture and Visual Studies (Springer 2014); L Farmer, 'Trials' in A Sarat, M Anderson, and CO Frank (eds), Law and the Humanities: An Introduction (CUP 2009); L Solan, J Ainsworth, and R Shuy (eds), Speaking of Language and Law: Conversations on the Work of Peter Tiersma (OUP 2015).

But what of point (ii) mentioned above: the seriousness of the consequences of attributing to law qualities which it inevitably claims but may not in fact possess? My contention is that this point makes it even more important for legal philosophers to adopt an attitude of due wariness, because it highlights the sense in which the stakes are very high when we approach law and face its normative claims. Law regulates matters of considerable moral and other importance to us, and regards itself as justified in so doing. It claims to state what truly ought to be done, and demands that we put aside our own views of what ought to be done, and do as law requires. But human history stands witness to the fact that these claims are not always true and furnishes us with many instances where law regulates matters of deep moral importance and significance in a repugnant way. Law has part-constituted, and helped to support and maintain, regulatory schemas and regimes which have discriminated against and ruined the life chances of many of those living under it. Law has been used to curtail and remove civil, political, and even human rights from some of those subject to it, and so has facilitated abhorrent discriminatory agendas. Examples sadly abound: the nineteenth and twentieth century 'Jim Crow laws' in the United States,[42] the apartheid-constituting-and-supporting legal directives of the 1948 to 1994 South African governments,[43] and the continuing criminalization, and other discriminatory treatment, of homosexuality in many states[44] being just a few. Moreover, when law and its officials get things wrong, and fall into moral and other error, the consequences for us and for our societies are far more serious than when an individual makes mistakes in judgement and/or in action. Law operates on a mass scale, applying itself compulsorily to large swathes of a state's population. It characteristically comes with the back-up of the full panoply of state coercion. Errors perpetuated by a social institution on this scale and with this character have the capacity to be wide-ranging, far-reaching, and to have deep and sometimes catastrophic effects on the life chances of those living under it. None of this is to ignore the fact that law can be—and often is—an instrument of tremendous social and personal good; it is merely to remind

---

[42] For thoughtful discussion of this period see eg MJ Klarman, From Jim Crow to Civil Rights: The Supreme Court and the Struggle for Racial Equality (OUP 2004); JC Cobb, The Brown Decision, Jim Crow, and Southern Identity (University of Georgia Press 2005).

[43] See eg W Beinart and S Dubow, Segregation and Apartheid in Twentieth Century South Africa (Routledge 1995); NL Clark and WH Worger, South Africa: The Rise and Fall of Apartheid (3rd edn, Routledge 2016).

[44] The ILGA (the International Lesbian, Gay, Bisexual, Trans and Intersex Association) 'State Sponsored Homophobia' annual report provides a comprehensive overview of the situation: L Ramon Mendos and others, State-Sponsored Homophobia 2020: Global Legislation Overview Update (ILGA, December 2020) https://ilga.org/downloads/ILGA_World_State_Sponsored_Homophobia_report_global_legislation_overview_update_December_2020.pdf. I return to this example in ch 6.

ourselves of its—and our—possible darker sides. A great deal of human misery has been caused by morally misguided and/or abhorrent law, and it is thus vital to remind ourselves that when law approaches us with its normative claims, we should be wary of too readily viewing those claims as true.

These points further bolster the point that it is both helpful and justified for legal philosophers to adopt an attitude of due wariness when approaching law. This attitude is an important element within the IELP approach that I champion. Moreover, in the broader context of our discipline it is interesting to note that an awareness of the importance of aspects of this attitude and of those considerations that support it echoes down through a certain tradition in legal philosophy which places significant emphasis on law's social fact properties in understanding its nature.

Jeremy Bentham, for example, espoused a strong commitment not to take law at its self-presented face value. He believed that law 'shews itself in a mask'[45] and that it is the job of those seeking to understand it to remove that mask, and hence to 'draw aside that curtain of mystery which fiction and formality have spread so extensively over the Law'.[46] In both his writings on particular areas of law, and his approach to constructing a general theory of law, Bentham was wary of law, and sought to strip away the cloak of moral veneration which he believed Blackstone and others had draped around it, in order that we might see clearly, and in the cold light of day, its character, and what exactly it was asking of us. Only then, with such a cool-headed and unromanticized understanding of law in mind, would we be able effectively to undertake the vital task of evaluating and reforming it, with social progress as our lodestar.[47]

HLA Hart followed in Bentham's wake as regards this methodological course.[48] He reminded us of the dangers of being too ready to take law at face value and to regard it as being morally obligatory. No matter how august its normative claims, Hart counsels us to be circumspect about what law asks of us, and to think always for ourselves whether we ought to obey it:

> What surely is most needed in order to make men clear-sighted in confronting the official abuse of power, is that they should preserve the sense that the certification of something as legally valid is not conclusive of the question

---

[45] JH Burns and HLA Hart (eds), The Collected Works of Jeremy Bentham: A Comment on the Commentaries and A Fragment on Government (OUP 1977) 12e.
[46] ibid.
[47] For discussion of these issues see HLA Hart, 'The Demystification of the Law', essay I in HLA Hart, Essays on Bentham (Clarendon Press 1982).
[48] Of course, Hart did not follow in Bentham's wake in other matters regarding, for example, the role of coercion in law, or the character of legal normativity.

of obedience, and that, however great the aura of majesty or authority which the official system may have, its demands must in the end be submitted to a moral scrutiny.[49]

That Hart stood inheritor to these methodological aspects of Bentham's position is also noted by Joseph Raz. Raz views both Bentham and Hart as members of an important tradition in legal philosophy, a tradition which emphasizes aspects of law's social reality, and highlights aspects of law's character as social fact:

> H. L. A. Hart is heir and torch-bearer of a great tradition in the philosophy of law which is realist and unromantic in outlook ... His analysis of the concept of law is part of the enterprise of demythologizing the law, of instilling rational critical attitudes to it ... His essays on 'Bentham and the Demystification of the Law' and on 'The Nightmare and the Noble Dream' showed him to be consciously sharing the Benthamite sense of the excessive veneration in which the law is held in common-law countries, and its deleterious moral consequences. His fear that in recent years legal theory has lurched back in that direction, and his view that a major part of its role is to lay the conceptual foundation for a cool and potentially critical assessment of the law are evident.[50]

Moreover, aspects of Raz's own work exhibit affinities with these themes, including some of his views on jurisprudential methodology[51] and on whether there is a moral obligation to obey the law:

> There are risks, moral and other, in uncritical acceptance of authority. Too often in the past, the fallibility of human judgment has led to submission to authority from a misguided sense of duty where this was a morally reprehensible attitude.[52]

As these points indicate, the approach to understanding law that I advocate in this chapter finds kinship with the views of some other legal philosophers who,

---

[49] HLA Hart, The Concept of Law (3rd edn, OUP 2012) 210.
[50] Joseph Raz, 'Authority, Law, and Morality' in J Raz, Ethics in the Public Domain: Essays in the Morality of Law and Politics (Clarendon Press 1995) 210.
[51] See eg J Raz, 'The Morality of Obedience' (1985) 83 Michigan Law Review 732, especially s I; Raz (n 50); Raz (n 14). I return to some of these works in chs 7 and 8.
[52] J Raz, 'The Obligation to Obey: Revision and Tradition' in J Raz, Ethics in the Public Domain: Essays in the Morality of Law and Politics (Clarendon Press 1995) 351.

in Raz's words, take their place in 'a great tradition in the philosophy of law which is realist and unromantic in outlook'.[53]

6. Conclusion: Further Towards Indirectly Evaluative Legal Philosophy

But what is the 'great tradition' referred to by Raz? It may be tempting to think that it goes by the name 'legal positivism', and certainly Bentham, Hart, and Raz have all been associated with this school of thought. However, as several legal philosophers have noted, this term may conceal more than it reveals, and may be of dubious accuracy and determinacy.[54] Moreover, even insofar as it remains helpful to use the category 'legal positivism' for certain purposes, and to classify certain aspects of the work of Bentham, Hart, and Raz as falling within it, each of these theorists has a very different take on what are often held to be legal positivism's central concerns, such as the conditions of legal validity.[55]

This being so, it seems more accurate and illuminating simply to say that these theorists are part of a tradition in legal philosophy which places significant emphasis on law as a social fact, and which insists that we approach law with a wary and circumspect eye. This tradition counsels that we should not be too ready to take law at its self-proclaimed face value and to accept its claims as true, and that we must always subject its normative claims to our own moral and critical scrutiny. It is sensitive to the fact that law presents its claims in compelling and magisterial ways and emphasizes that it is part of the role of legal philosophy to strip away the cloak of claimed and/or perceived veneration which surrounds law, in order to facilitate seeing it as it is. This tradition emphasizes that in deciding how we should respond to law, and whether we should act according to its requirements, we should remember that the stakes are high, and that faulty judgement can lead to serious moral errors with large-scale, grave consequences. The affinities with the approach to legal philosophy which I champion—IELP—should be clear, and are evident in two important aspects of IELP which I have focused on in this chapter: the need to do justice

---

[53] See n 50 above and accompanying text.
[54] See eg J Raz, 'The Argument from Injustice, or How not to Reply to Legal Positivism' in G. Pavlakos (ed), Law, Rights and Discourse: The Legal Philosophy of Robert Alexy (Hart Publishing 2007) 17, 35; N MacCormick, Institutions of Law: An Essay in Legal Theory (OUP 2007) 278; J Gardner, 'Legal Positivism: 5½ Myths', (2001) 46 American Journal of Jurisprudence 199.
[55] For an overview see L Green and T Adams, 'Legal Positivism' in Edward N Zalta (ed), The Stanford Encyclopedia of Philosophy (Winter 2019 Edition) https://plato.stanford.edu/archives/win2019/entries/legal-positivism/; Dickson, 'Legal Positivism' (n 7).

to the duality of law as both social fact and as normative phenomenon; and the contention that it is helpful and justified for legal philosophers to adopt an attitude of due wariness in approaching law.

IELP hence also stands in the line of descent of the great tradition in legal philosophy which is unromantic in outlook. And indeed it shares still more with it, because the tradition in question did not seek to focus on law as social fact, and on identifying and explaining those features which make law into what it is, solely for the sake of that explanatory enterprise. As I discussed in sections 2 and 3 above, legal philosophers must do justice to law as a normative phenomenon as well, in terms of advancing our understanding of the character of the normative claims law makes, the conditions, if any, under which they might be justified, and the standards to which law ought to aspire, and in light of which it should be judged. Theorists in the tradition discussed above wholeheartedly embrace this point, and address such issues in their work.[56] In Hart's words, theorists such as Bentham were: '[n]ot dry analysts fiddling with verbal distinctions ... but ... the vanguard of a movement which laboured with passionate intensity and much success to bring about a better society and better laws'.[57]

Moreover, it is not merely that such theorists (1) happen to be interested in what law ought to be, and in how we ought to think and act in light of it, in addition to (2) being committed to seeing law as it is, in the cold light of day, resisting temptations to romanticize it. Rather, their view is that (2) significantly shapes and advances their inquiries into the issues mentioned in (1), and that (2) is a vital precursor to well-focused and clear-sighted inquiries into those matters in (1).[58]

This point is also of vital importance in IELP. IELP is committed to what I refer to as the value of staged inquiry.[59] In constructing accounts of law, legal philosophers must make evaluative judgements in selecting features of law which are important and significant to explain, and in supporting their arguments regarding the character and operation of those features. I contend, however, that legal philosophers can and should make such evaluative judgements without yet taking a view on whether those features of law render law morally good or bad, or whether they weigh for or against law's directives being

---

[56] This point is explored in chs 7 and 8.
[57] HLA Hart, 'Positivism and the Separation of Law and Morals' in HLA Hart, Essays in Jurisprudence and Philosophy (Clarendon Press 1983) 52.
[58] This point is discussed in depth in chs 7 and 8, but see eg Raz (n 51), especially s I; HLA Hart, 'Postscript' to HLA Hart, The Concept of Law (3rd edn, OUP 2012) s I.
[59] This important issue is discussed in depth in chs 7 and 8.

reason-giving and morally obligatory. Judgements of importance and significance made at the earlier stage of inquiry are evaluative judgements, and they contribute to, and help to advance, later inquiries into law's moral worth, value, and obligatoriness. But they help us to reach those later inquiries indirectly, and by featuring in a series of staged inquiries along the relevant route.

6
Self-understandings and the Limits of Revisionism

1. Self-understandings Introduced

Chapter 5 began to explore the character of indirectly evaluative legal philosophy (IELP) by considering certain constraints—constraints relating to an important duality in law, and to the appropriate attitude to adopt in approaching law—that I argue are incumbent on legal philosophers attempting to identify and explain law's nature. This chapter considers another such constraint that arises from the fact that the concept of law and related concepts have a distinctive character in that they feature in various ways in the self-understandings of those living their lives in law-governed societies. The discussion which follows hence explores tenet four of indirectly evaluative legal philosophy (IELP): IELP aims adequately to account for, explain the relevance of, and respect the constraints imposed by, the self-understandings of those who create, administer, and are subject to law.[1] Claims regarding the importance of how those living under law think of it, and think of their lives in terms of it, are frequently made in one form or another by a variety of legal philosophers. But, although frequently made, such claims are not always clearly explained or understood. One aim of this chapter is to try to improve this situation. What does it mean for the concept of law, and related concepts, to have a distinctive character because they feature in the self-understandings of those living under law? It means that those living under law refer to, use, and frame things in terms of, the concept of law (and related concepts) when they talk about, think about, and engage with aspects of their lives in society. It also means that such self-understandings are commonplace and widespread, and feature, albeit with varying degrees of explicitness and specificity, in the social lives both of legal professionals who create, administer, and advise on the law, and of non-legally expert persons living their lives under law.

---

[1] See ch 5, s 1.

Elucidating Law. Julie Dickson, Oxford University Press. © Julie Dickson 2022.
DOI: 10.1093/oso/9780198727767.003.0006

In Chapter 5, I gave some examples of such self-understandings in discussing the need for theories of law to account sufficiently for the social fact aspect of law's nature.[2] I noted that people living in law-governed societies are aware that institutions such as parliaments and courts exist, and that their activities create, change, and decide disputes regarding the law. People also know that law is compulsory and obligatory, and that, as a result, someone found to have broken the law of their society can be subject to visits from the police, requirements to pay fines, and, in the most serious cases, to deprivation of liberty. Moreover, people think about, talk about, and act according to their beliefs about, issues such as whether something is against the law or not, whether something should be against the law or not, whether law operates in an even-handed and fair manner or whether it treats different groups and different communities differently, whether we should always obey all laws or whether, for example, we should follow the requirements of our religion, or of the social code of the community we have grown up in, when these conflict with what law requires. In what sense are these to be regarded as *self*-understandings? In the sense that they are attempts by polities and by the individuals within them to understand aspects of their own social and political lives and their own social and political organizational arrangements in terms of law.

I am far from alone in noting the existence and ubiquity of such phenomena. Legal philosophers espousing a range of views on law's character make frequent reference in their theories to the existence of, and the significance of, how those who administer and/or are subject to law think about it, and understand aspects of their lives in terms of it:

> The concept of law is part of our culture and of our cultural traditions. It plays a role in the way in which ordinary people as well as the legal profession understand their own and other people's actions. It is part of the way they 'conceptualize' social reality ... unlike concepts like 'mass' or 'electron', 'the law' is a concept used by people to understand themselves.[3]

> We will study formal legal argument from the judge's viewpoint ... Citizens and politicians and law teachers also worry and argue about what the law is ... But the structure of judicial argument is typically more explicit, and judicial reasoning has an influence over other forms of legal discourse that is not fully reciprocal.[4]

---

[2] See ch 5, s 2.
[3] Joseph Raz, 'Authority, Law, and Morality' in J Raz, Ethics in the Public Domain (OUP 1994) 237.
[4] R Dworkin, Law's Empire (Fontana Press 1986) 14–15.

> Rules conferring private powers must, if they are to be understood, be looked at from the point of view of those who exercise them ... Such power-conferring rules are thought of, spoken of, and used in social life differently from rules which impose duties.[5]
>
> [these thoughts] about *our* law certainly warrant a theory of *law*, a general account of what ... has indeed existed ... in virtually every human community of which we are aware, and has been and is manifested in the translatable language, that is, the self-understanding and thus the concepts, of every such community.[6]

These quotations bring to the fore several important issues. First, they highlight the fact that self-understandings in terms of law feature in how both non-legally expert individuals living their lives under law, and legal professionals and legal officials, understand aspects of their lives and of the social reality around them. In the case of non-legally expert laypersons, it is important to realize that such self-understandings need not be implausibly complex or overly intellectualized in character. Many of the relevant understandings may be implicit, and may require extrapolation from various of the thoughts, beliefs, attitudes, and actions of those living under law.[7] By contrast, the self-understandings of legal professionals may characteristically be much more explicit and exact.[8]

Secondly, these quotations begin to indicate what I intend by referring to 'the concept of law, and related concepts'. Some of the passages focus on self-understandings in terms of the concept of law *in toto*, whereas others focus on self-understandings in terms of what we might think of as aspects of the concept of law, or sub-concepts which reveal understanding of aspects of the concept of law, or concepts related to the concept of law. The quotations above from Raz and Finnis are plausibly understood as the former; Dworkin's focus on the character of legal argument, and Hart's claims regarding the self-understandings of users of power-conferring rules, seem to be examples of the latter. In my view, both self-understandings in terms of the concept of law, *in toto*, and self-understandings in terms of sub-concepts of the concept of law, or concepts related to the concept of law, are relevant, important, and exert a constraining force on successful theories of law's nature. As the discussion

---

[5] HLA Hart, The Concept of Law (3rd edn, OUP 2012) 41.
[6] J Finnis, 'Law and What I Truly Should Decide' (2003) 48 *American Journal of Jurisprudence* 107, 113 (emphasis in original).
[7] This point receives further attention in s 2.
[8] Ronald Dworkin makes this point in the quotation referenced in n 4 above.

proceeds, I will at times use the phrase 'self-understandings in terms of the concept of law' to refer collectively to all these sorts of self-understandings.

Thirdly, the quotations begin to reveal (and further aspects of their authors' theories confirm) that different legal philosophers make different, and often contested, claims about the content of the self-understandings they draw on in constructing their theories. For example: Dworkin claims that judges understand themselves to be reasoning to the required one right answer in adjudicating cases; Finnis contends that reasonable persons living under law understand it to have an overall valuable purpose or point which is essential for a flourishing community. Other legal philosophers reject these points, and instead attempt to highlight alternative self-understandings in terms of aspects of the concept of law in the course of constructing their theories of law.

Finally, although the quotations alone do not yet reveal this, it should be noted that legal philosophers take significantly different stances on what legal philosophers should do with the self-understandings in terms of law that they identify, and on how constraining or otherwise they regard such self-understandings as being. This point is explored further in the remainder of this chapter.

2. Self-understandings as Constraints on Successful Theories of Law I: What to Do with Them and Why

Self-understandings in terms of the concept of law and related concepts feature in the work of a range of legal philosophers. But noting this does not yet address the questions which lie at the core of this chapter: what should legal philosophers do with those self-understandings, and what constraints, if any, do they place on successful theories of law?

My view is that the self-understandings of those who create, administer, and are subject to the law are important 'data points' which a successful theory of law must sufficiently take into consideration and do adequate justice to. They impose significant constraints on a successful theory of law because of their relation to both the explanandum of legal philosophy—law—and to certain of the criteria of success of theories of the nature of law. My argumentative strategy in support of this stance is two-pronged. In the remainder of the current section, I seek to clarify the character of self-understandings in terms of the concept of law and related concepts, and to address some concerns about according them a central role in our theories of law. In section 3, I complement these points by considering some jurisprudential views which differ significantly from mine

108 SELF-UNDERSTANDINGS AND THE LIMITS OF REVISIONISM

in that they do not accord such a central, or such a constraining, role to self-understandings in terms of law in their theories. As a result, the accounts in question regard themselves as free to be significantly revisionist as regards how law is thought of, spoken of, and used by those who create, administer, and live under it. I seek to demonstrate that such theories run a standing and serious risk of misidentifying and mischaracterizing vitally important aspects of their explanandum, and that this counts strongly against such theories when we come to evaluate their success.

(a) Two concerns noted

Two concerns regularly appear in works expressing reservations about according a central and significantly constraining role in theories of law to self-understandings in terms of the concept of law and related concepts:

(1) the self-understandings in question are too indeterminate, and/or too inchoate, and/or too divided, to do the job required of them;
(2) even to the extent that the self-understandings in question are or might become determinate enough to yield a common view, focusing on our self-understandings in terms of the concept of law is problematically limiting in that it will not yield an understanding of what law itself is really like. Rather, such a focus will yield only an understanding of what our understanding of law is like: it will not take us 'all the way' to the nature of that which the concept of law picks out, ie the nature of law itself.[9]

The first concern—that the self-understandings in question are too indeterminate/inchoate/divided to do the job required of them—obviously assumes something, or some things, about the job required of them. I return to this point in sub-section (b) below. This concern is evident from the following passages from the work of Liam Murphy and Nicos Stavropoulos:

---

[9] I have rendered (1) in several alternatives, because it appears in a variety of forms in the literature. Regarding both (1) and (2), it should be noted that while I give examples of theorists raising each of these concerns, it is not my aim to offer an exegesis of any theorist's stance, nor to home in on a particular version of each concern to serve as interlocutor. Rather, I aim to show that the concerns above feature in a range of works concerning jurisprudential methodology, and then move in sub-ss (b) and (c) to address them.

[p]eople in general disagree about the conceptual question just raised. This disagreement will survive, I believe, abstract reflection about the very idea of law. If this is right, then Hart and Dworkin's disagreement about the concept of law cannot be adjudicated by any philosophical investigation into what we already share by way of a concept of law.[10]

[d]isagreement about the grounds of law runs so deep and is so tenacious that we frequently have no option but to say that on one not unreasonable understanding of the nature of law, the content of law is such and such, but than on another, it is something else ... the persistent disagreement does not come from case-by-case differences in judgements about how to apply various generally accepted criteria to particular cases, but rather from disagreement about what those criteria are.[11]

The formal approach to the explanation of promising supposes that there exists some determinate and complete common tacit conception. The version defended by Raz supposes that it includes a clause that discriminates between the action having such an effect on a promisor's other circumstances that the promisor comes to have an obligation ... and the action's being itself the reason to perform ...

I suggest that such discrimination is too demanding to be part of a common conception of promising. Besides, even if it's not unreasonably demanding, chances are we are likely to find evidence of both sides of the distinction in common reflection.[12]

As for the second concern, an illustration of it can be found at one stage in Brian Leiter's thinking on this issue (although, as is noted in sub-section (c) below, in more recent work, Leiter's views may have altered significantly):

But the Razian approach, I fear, may confuse the central jurisprudential question—what is law?—with a different question, namely, what role does the folk concept of 'law' play in the self-understanding of agents? ... Armchair

---

[10] L Murphy, 'The Political Question of the Concept of Law' in J Coleman (ed), Hart's Postscript: Essays on the Postscript to the Concept of Law (OUP 2001) 372 (internal footnote reference omitted). The discussion in this chapter builds on the account of Murphy's views offered in ch 3, s 3(c).

[11] L Murphy, What Makes Law: An Introduction to the Philosophy of Law (CUP 2014) 102. Murphy emphasizes that his views on the character and intractability of disagreements over the grounds of law do not extend to all other features of law. See ibid 5, and ch 8.

[12] N Stavropoulos, 'Obligations, Interpretivism and the Legal Point of View' in A Marmor (ed), The Routledge Companion to Philosophy of Law (Routledge 2012) 84–85. Although Stavropoulos is talking about promising in this passage, throughout the article from which it is taken he uses the concept of promising to demonstrate an analogy with the concept of legal obligation, holding that the same considerations apply to both: see ibid 19–28.

sociology about people's self-understandings may or may not be reliable when it comes to finding out what law is essentially like.[13]

Mark Greenberg and Nicos Stavropoulos also appear to share this concern:

> Another reason that one might recommend moving away from conceptual analysis of ordinary nontechnical concepts is that our ordinary classifications tend not to carve the world in explanatorily deep ways.[14]
>
> [i]t is important to distinguish between a conceptual analysis of a concept and an account of the nature of a phenomenon. A central difference is that the latter is not constrained by our concept of the phenomenon.[15]
>
> It would still not follow from the fact that an explanation tracked the common conception that we were not dealing with a case of medieval influenza.
>
> [common] conceptions do not possess, as such, explanatory privilege, and the same holds for the attitudes that may make them up.[16]

As is discussed further in sub-section (c) below, and in section 3 of this chapter, both Greenberg and Stavropoulos contend that, in light of these concerns, we should reject methodological approaches which—in their view—give too much weight to existing self-understandings of those living under law.

(b) Active elucidation

As noted above, the first concern mentioned—that self-understandings in terms of the concept of law and related concepts are too indeterminate/inchoate/divided to do the job required of them—assumes something, or some things, about the job required of them. In my view, an erroneous picture of the role that self-understandings should play in a theory of law stands behind and influences this concern. This picture can be understood as having three main

---

[13] B Leiter, 'Postscript to Part II: Science and Methodology in Legal Theory' in B Leiter, Naturalizing Jurisprudence: Essays on American Legal Realism and Naturalism in Legal Philosophy (OUP 2007) 189–90. The discussion in the present chapter builds on the account of Leiter's views offered in ch 3, s 3(c).

[14] M Greenberg, 'How to Explain Things with Force' (2016) 129 Harvard Law Review 1932, 1949.

[15] ibid 1950–51.

[16] Stavropoulos (n 12) 85. The reference to 'medieval influenza' relates to an earlier claim by Stavropoulos in the same article: 'The ancients collectively thought, after all, that stars were holes in the sky and the medievals thought that influenza was a kind of adverse astral influence that affected large numbers of people.' See ibid 83.

elements: (a) that the self-understandings of relevance to legal philosophy are to be ascertained on some sort of 'vox-pop' basis; (b) that, thus ascertained, those self-understandings are simply to be described by theorists and inserted into their accounts of law; and (c) that doing (a) and (b) constitutes the core of any methodological approach—such as my own—which accords a central and constraining role to self-understandings in terms of the concept of law and related concepts.

Each element of this picture is misleading. In discussing them in turn, I make recurring use of an example drawn from the work of HLA Hart. Probing the issues that this example raises can improve our understanding of the constraints on a successful theory of law that flow from doing adequate justice to the self-understandings of those living under law.

(i) *Taking Hart's example*
The example in question was briefly referred to in section 1 above.[17] It arises in the context of Hart's argument in *The Concept of Law* that power-conferring legal rules (such as those regulating wills, marriages, and contracts), and duty-imposing legal rules (such as those of the criminal law) each serve a distinctive social function, and are, in certain relevant respects, irreducibly different from one another:

> If we look at all law simply from the point of view of the persons on whom its duties are imposed, and reduce all other aspects of it to the status of more or less elaborate conditions in which duties fall on them, we treat as something merely subordinate, elements which are at least as characteristic of law and as valuable to society as duty. Rules conferring private powers must, if they are to be understood, be looked at from the point of view of those who exercise them. They appear then as an additional element introduce by the law into social life over and above that of coercive control ... Why should rules which are used in this special way, and confer this huge and distinctive amenity, not be recognized as distinct from rules which impose duties ... Such power-conferring rules are thought of, spoken of, and used in social life differently from rules which impose duties, and they are valued for different reasons. What other tests for difference in character could there be?[18]

---

[17] See n 5 and accompanying text.
[18] Hart (n 5) 41.

The contention here is that any theory of law that denies these important differences between power-conferring and duty-imposing laws—for example by insisting that the 'deep structure' of all laws is 'really' of the form of authorizations to legal officials to apply sanctions under certain conditions, or is 'really' of the form of 'orders backed by threats'—does so at the peril of unacceptably distorting the phenomena the theory seeks to explain.[19]

Distortion according to whom, though? As Hart is well aware, legal philosophers who disagree with him on this point do not believe that they are distorting anything. Rather, they embrace the revisionist character of their accounts, such revisionism being necessary to reveal the true structure of all laws that is obscured by superficial apparent differences.[20] For Hans Kelsen, the beliefs, attitudes, and understandings of those living under law are irrelevant material to be filtered out in his pursuit of a 'pure theory' of law which seeks to reveal the uniform structure of, and relations between, legal norms.[21] Jeremy Bentham is concerned with how ordinary people living under law view it, but holds that the theorist's task includes unmasking and demystifying law, and, crucially, disabusing those living under it from false impressions that law itself may have helped instil.[22]

For Hart, however, we are not free to filter out, or radically to revise, how those subject to and using legal rules view them. The distortion Hart counsels against arises when legal philosophers significantly depart from how users of legal rules understand the character of those rules, and how they understand the different functions they play in their lives. Legal philosophers are significantly constrained by, and should not distort, how various aspects of law's operation are perceived and understood by those living under and using it.

---

[19] ibid 26–42, especially at 38–42. At the point in the discussion where the quotation appears, Hart particularly has in mind the views of Hans Kelsen, but in more general terms the points he makes apply also to command theories of law, such as those espoused by John Austin and Jeremy Bentham.

[20] ibid 37–38.

[21] For the first edition of Kelsen's Pure Theory of Law see H Kelsen, Introduction to the Problems of Legal Theory (1934, BL Pauslon and SL Paulson trs, Clarendon Press 2002) chs I and II; H Kelsen, Pure Theory of Law (first published 1960, 2nd edn, M Knight tr, University of California Press 1967), chs I and II. For discussion see J Raz, 'The Purity of the Pure Theory' (1981) 138 *Revue internationale de philosophie* 441, reprinted in R Tur and W Twining (eds), Essays on Kelsen (Clarendon Press 1986) 79–97, and in SL Paulson and BL Paulson (eds), Normativity and Norms: Critical Perspectives on Kelsenian Themes (Clarendon Press 1999) 237–52.

[22] See eg JH Burns and HLA Hart (eds), The Collected Works of Jeremy Bentham: A Comment on the Commentaries *and* A Fragment on Government (OUP 1977) 124; HLA Hart, 'The Demystification of the Law' in HLA Hart, Essays on Bentham (Clarendon Press 1982) essay I; and the discussion of Bentham's views in ch 5 of this book.

(ii) *Not vox-pop*

But how should the self-understandings of those living under law be used by legal philosophers in their theories? In my view, it is important to emphasize that they are not to be lifted wholesale or in a 'vox-pop' manner from those holding them. This point holds even in respect of the self-understandings of those who create and administer law, such as legislators or judges, who have the training and cause to possess a relatively fine-grained and technical set of understandings of aspects of law's operation. And it is particularly apposite, and holds a fortiori, in the case of the self-understandings of citizens living under and using law.

Hart's example is helpful in illustrating this point. In claiming that '[p]ower-conferring rules are thought of, spoken of, and used in social life differently from rules which impose duties',[23] Hart is referring to the self-understandings of those ordinary users of such rules, ie those living in law-governed societies who make wills, conclude contracts, get married. We should not interpret Hart as contending that such persons understand and think about their goals, intentions, and actions under different types of legal rules in the exact manner, let alone the terminology, that Hart develops in his theoretical account. People leading busy lives infused with their own interests, commitments, and specialisms almost certainly do not, and definitely need not, think to themselves, 'in making this will I am utilising aspects of the distinct social function of a power-conferring rule, which I regard as being different in significant respects from what I do when I follow a duty-imposing rule of the criminal law'. Moreover, in my view, nor are such persons' self-understandings in terms of power-conferring rules well-characterized in terms of what they would say if some passing legal philosopher were to stop them as they were going about their business and ask a series of questions designed to elicit their intuitions about whether this or that aspect of what they are doing falls under the category of power-conferring rules, or their intuitions about whether they conceive of their actions and intentions in terms of a hidden coercive or sanction-based element underlying the superficial power-conferring form of such rules.[24]

Rather, the self-understandings of those living under law are more implicit, and diffuse, than the 'vox-pop' or 'eliciting intuitions' notions connote. Such self-understandings are *manifest* in aspects of the *use* made of power-conferring rules by those engaging with them; what those persons find

---

[23] Hart (n 5) 41.
[24] cf Murphy (n 11) 78; Leiter, Part III of 'Beyond the Hart/Dworkin Debate: the Methodology Problem in Jurisprudence' in Leiter, *Naturalizing Jurisprudence* (n 13).

important and unimportant about the experience of using law to make a will or enter into a marriage; the distinctions they draw as regards the role of law in various different areas of their lives. The self-understandings in question do not come pre-packaged and explicit such that the legal philosopher's job is merely to record and reproduce them. A significant part of the task of a theory of law is to identify and interpret those self-understandings from how they manifest in a range of attitudes and behaviours exhibited by those living under law. It is important to note that, in making these points, I am not advocating a wholesale rejection of, for example, 'vox-pop' or survey data or experimental philosophy techniques in legal philosophy.[25] My point is rather than such data could at best be a starting point, and something for the legal philosopher to work with, interpret, and extrapolate from. This being so, any characterization of or terminology in respect of the methodological approach that I adopt which leans heavily on characterizing it as 'descriptive', as if legal philosophers need merely to record and insert in their theories what people living under law may or may not say about it, is—as is discussed further below—significantly misleading.

This being so, the task of legal philosophers in identifying, interpreting, and extrapolating from these often implicit and diffuse self-understandings is active, not passive in character. Moreover, as is explored in sub-section (iii) below and in Chapter 7, aspects of that task are evaluative in character. The legal philosopher must make evaluative judgements in sifting for relevance and importance amongst the self-understandings of those living under law. They must take a stance on which aspects of the relevant self-understandings are of most significance in revealing aspects of law's operation, and home in on and grant appropriate explanatory weight to those in developing an account of law.

Once we understand that the legal philosopher's job is not passively to record and reproduce the self-understandings of those living under and using law, the concern that such self-understandings may be indeterminate, inchoate, or divided in character takes on a different hue. It is the theorist's task to work with that 'raw material' and to extract from it what is most important, significant, and revelatory about the character of law. At times, this may involve generating a more fine-grained understanding and set of distinctions than is contained in the 'raw material'. An explicit and self-aware example of this can be found in Joseph Raz's discussion of legal positivism's sources thesis, and how it can be supported and defended. After claiming that three sets of distinctions can be

---

[25] For an interesting example of the latter see R Donelson and I Hannikainen, 'Fuller and the Folk: The Inner Morality of Law Revisited' in T Lombrozo, J Knobe, and S Nichols (eds), Oxford Studies in Experimental Philosophy, *vol 3* (OUP 2020).

discerned in our common understanding about aspects of the judicial function that we regard as important in social life, Raz makes the point that:

> One need not assume complete convergence between the distinctions mentioned above and the sources thesis. If, in fact, the sources thesis coincides with the way these distinctions are generally applied, it has explanatory power and is supported to that extent. It can then be regarded as being a systemizing or a tidying-up thesis where it goes beyond the ordinary use of these distinctions. This argument for the sources thesis is not an argument from the ordinary sense of 'law' or any other term. It relies on fundamental features of our understanding of a certain social institution.[26]

Various of the examples discussed in the remainder of the current chapter, and in Chapter 7 illustrate further the process of active elucidation that legal philosophers should undertake, and the role of evaluative judgements within it.

(iii) *Not well-characterized as descriptive*
It is also important to clarify that, despite sometimes being characterized as such, the methodological approach I advocate is not well characterized as descriptive in character. It is especially misleading to think in terms of the self-understandings of those subject to and administering law simply being described by legal philosophers in their theories. This can be illustrated by considering why—in both past and current work—I avoid characterizing my stance in the terms which Brian Leiter has suggested that I should characterize it, namely as a 'descriptive theory of a hermeneutic concept'.[27]

Leiter takes the view that, in my past writings on jurisprudential methodology, I have failed to do what he thinks I claim to have done: to map out a kind of 'third way' methodological stance which lies in between a descriptive theory of law, such as Hart was offering in *The Concept of Law*, and a normative justificatory theory of law such as features in the work of Ronald Dworkin or John Finnis. He is correct that I regard it as unhelpful and inaccurate to characterize

---

[26] J Raz, 'Legal Positivism and the Sources of Law' in J Raz, The Authority of Law (OUP 2009) 50. See ibid 48–52 for fuller discussion.
[27] Leiter, 'Beyond the Hart/Dworkin Debate: The Methodology Problem in Jurisprudence' in Leiter, *Naturalizing Jurisprudence* (n 13) 175 and, more generally 172–75. For various of the exchanges between Leiter and myself on this and related methodological issues see ibid 172–75; J Dickson, 'Methodology in Jurisprudence: A Critical Survey' (2004) 10 *Legal Theory* 117 133; Leiter, 'Postscript to Part II: Science and Methodology in Legal Theory' in Leiter, *Naturalizing Jurisprudence* (n 13) 194–99; J Dickson, 'On Naturalizing Jurisprudence: Some Comments on Brian Leiter's View of What Jurisprudence Should Become' (2011) 30 *Law and Philosophy* 477; B Leiter, 'Naturalized Jurisprudence and American Legal Realism Revisited' (2011) 30 *Law and Philosophy* 499, 510–16.

my methodological stance as 'descriptive': as I have consistently argued, it requires legal philosophers to make various 'indirectly evaluative' judgements about aspects of law in the course of constructing their theories.[28] However, he is wrong insofar as I regard my approach as much closer to Hart's than Leiter seems to allow: Hart, too, acknowledged that evaluation of certain kinds was an indispensable element in theories of law.[29] Wherever my views stand in relation to Hart's, Leiter claims that, *contra* how I understand it, my stance is best characterized as a kind of descriptive legal philosophy. It is just that (according to Leiter) I regard law as a hermeneutic concept, ie a concept which is used by people to understand themselves. As a result, he contends, I believe that it is necessary to describe law in terms of the self-understandings of those administering and living under it. In Leiter's terminology, I thus espouse a descriptive theory of a hermeneutic concept.[30] Leiter also claims that the key issue, methodologically speaking, is whether it is correct that law is a hermeneutic concept.[31]

Leiter's thought-provoking views on this and other issues in jurisprudential methodology have frequently prompted me to further, and better, reflection on aspects of my own views. My understanding of him on this point is that he thinks he is restating what I am already doing, but in more perspicuous terms. I take a different view, however, and believe there are two main reasons to resist what I regard as a significant revision of my position.

The first—relatively minor—reason for resisting Leiter's recharacterization of my view has to do with the uncertainties and potential complications arising from the term 'hermeneutic'. This term is used in different ways in different traditions of thought, reflecting a plethora of issues concerning meaning and understanding in the human sciences.[32] Given this, and because I am trying to pin down those methodological constraints which are incumbent specifically on *legal* philosophers, some of which I believe stem from the distinctive character of law as a social institution, I find it better to avoid using this term.

---

[28] See especially J Dickson, Evaluation and Legal Theory (Hart Publishing 2001) chs 3 and 4; Dickson, 'Methodology in Jurisprudence' (n 27); and chs 7 and 8 of the present work.
[29] For my views on this point see Dickson, *Evaluation and Legal Theory* (n 28) 35, n 9; Dickson, 'Methodology in Jurisprudence' (n 27) 122–23. For Hart's views see HLA Hart, 'Comment' in R Gavison and HLA Hart (eds), Issues in Contemporary Legal Philosophy: The Influence of HLA Hart (Clarendon Press 1987) 39; D Sugarman, 'Hart Interviewed: H.L.A. Hart in Conversation with David Sugarman' (2005) *32 Journal of Law and Society* 267 288. I return to this point in ch 7.
[30] Leiter, 'Beyond the Hart/Dworkin Debate' in Leiter, *Naturalizing Jurisprudence* (n 13) 172–75.
[31] B Leiter, 'Naturalized Jurisprudence and American Legal Realism Revisited' (n 27) 512–16.
[32] See T George, 'Hermeneutics' in E Zalta (ed), *The Stanford Encyclopedia of Philosophy* (Winter 2021 Edition) https://plato.stanford.edu/archives/win2021/entries/hermeneutics/

The second—and far more important—reason to resist Leiter's recharacterization is because I regard 'descriptive' as an inaccurate and misleading way to understand my approach to legal philosophy. My contention—in this chapter and the two which follow—is that a successful theory of law is imbued through and through with, and rests on, the evaluative judgements of the legal philosopher, and that such judgements are vital to illuminate what matters about law and to offer a cogent account of what matters about it. As was noted in sub-section (ii) above, the legal philosopher must make evaluative judgements in extrapolating, sifting and sorting in terms of their relevance and importance for understanding law, the self-understandings of those living under it. But she must also make further significant evaluative judgements about what use to make in her arguments of those self-understandings, even after she has extrapolated and sifted them. She must decide what distribution of emphasis is required in terms of using those self-understandings in various arguments, and must make judgements concerning their explanatory role, and concerning what they can and cannot be used to establish, and how conclusively they establish that which they can establish.[33]

To illustrate better what I have in mind here, it is useful to return to the example drawn from Hart outlined in sub-section (i) above and, more specifically, to Leslie Green's illuminating commentary on it in his Introduction to the third edition of *The Concept of Law*. Green agrees with Hart that power-conferring rules differ significantly from, and cannot be reduced to, duty-imposing rules. He also discerns that a key reason why this is so lies with an aspect of Hart's methodology—that we as legal philosophers are constrained in our theories to offer accounts which make sense of law as it appears to and is used by those living under it.[34]

However, Green adds an important caveat to his support for Hart on these issues:

> All that is correct as far as it goes. However, if we want to attend to *all* the 'principal functions of the law as a means of social control' we must go further than Hart does here. It is indeed a mistake to try to reduce power-conferring rules to duty-imposing rules, or to represent nullity as a kind of sanction. But it is not a mistake to notice the ways that power-conferring rules are bound up with social power.[35]

---

[33] See also the discussion of distribution of emphasis selectivity in ch 4.
[34] L Green, *Introduction* to the third edition of Hart, *The Concept of Law* (n 5) xxx–xxxiii.
[35] ibid xxxii.

Green then goes on to point out that power-conferring legal rules, such as laws concerning marriage, in sometimes excluding from their ambit persons or relationships with certain characteristics—for example excluding same-sex couples from being able to marry and rendering any attempted such marriages legally null and void[36]—can function so as to 'express and channel social power'[37] and so operate to signal approval of, and to validate, certain forms of relationships, and certain personal characteristics, over others.

In methodological terms, Green's point can be understood as follows. Hart's theory under-attends to certain aspects of power-conferring rules by under-attending to certain self-understandings in terms of law. The self-understandings in question perhaps most readily feature in the beliefs and attitudes of those who have been on the receiving end of, or who have attained a sensitive understanding of the experience of being on the receiving end of, the part that law plays in channelling social power. Recalling the discussion of 'distribution of emphasis selectivity' in Chapter 4,[38] we might view these as 'experience-sensitive self-understandings in terms of law and related concepts'.

This example demonstrates that legal philosophers must make evaluative judgements in order to identify and bring out the meaning of a wider range of self-understandings than Hart originally had in mind in making his point concerning the differences between power-conferring and duty-imposing rules. Moreover, it shows that, even once the legal philosopher has done this, there is yet more evaluative work to be done, in deciding how much emphasis should be given to these facets of law's operation in their theories, and in deciding how they should be reflected in the explanatory balance of the theory as a whole. In this instance Green contends, rightly in my view, that greater explanatory weight and emphasis ought to be accorded to the 'social power channelling' aspects of law's operation, especially in terms of the function of power-conferring rules, than is present in Hart's account.

(iv) *Constraining nonetheless*
With the clarifications emerging from the discussion above in hand, it is important to return to the point that the self-understandings elucidated by legal

---

[36] As at 2020, only 14% of states in the United Nations (ie 28 out of 193 UN states) have marriage laws enabling same sex couples to marry. See the ILGA (International Lesbian, Gay, Bisexual, Trans and Intersex Association) 'State Sponsored Homophobia' annual report: L Ramon Mendos and others, State-Sponsored Homophobia 2020: Global Legislation Overview Update (ILGA, December 2020) 277 https://ilga.org/downloads/ILGA_World_State_Sponsored_Homophobia_report_global_legislation_overview_update_December_2020.pdf.
[37] Green (n 34) xxxiii.
[38] See ch 4, s 4.

philosophers in the active manner just discussed do result in methodological constraints on successful theories of law. This is well-illustrated in the example drawn from Hart's work referred to throughout this section. Hart's charge against those who would reconstruct power-conferring laws in duty-imposing terms is not one of impossibility of so doing, or of outright falsehood of the resulting account of law. Hart acknowledges that, if one is so minded and has the time to do so, one *can* rearrange and recast all the laws of a legal system in the form claimed for them by sanction-based accounts of law, and indeed he offers his own such illustrative recasting to show us how that might go.[39] But while we can, if we so wish, engage in, for example, a Kelsenian reconstruction of all the laws of a legal system into the form of authorizations to officials to apply coercive sanctions under certain conditions, we should not do so. We should not do so because there are strong methodological constraints steering us away from such a course. We should not do so because, if we do, we will significantly, and unacceptably, put the emphasis in our theories of law in the wrong place. We will significantly under-emphasize the empowering and facilitative aspects of law's character, and significantly over-emphasize its ordering and duty-imposing aspects. The 'litmus test' for appropriate emphasis lies with how those living under and using law view it, with those distinctions they draw regarding aspects of its operation, and with their understanding of the different roles that various types of legal rules play in their lives.

(c) Concept and nature

Ascertaining, and making use of in their theories, the self-understandings of those living under law, is an active, evaluative process for legal philosophers. However, we may still wish to probe further the question of exactly *why* the self-understandings of those living under law play such an important role in theories of law. The way forward with this question dovetails with the second concern canvassed in sub-section 2(a) above, namely that a methodological approach focusing on our self-understandings in terms of the concept of law is problematically limiting in that it will not yield an understanding of what law itself is really like. Rather, so the objection goes, such a focus will yield only an understanding of what our understanding of law is like: it will not take us 'all the way' to that which the concept of law picks out, ie the nature of law itself.[40]

---

[39] See Hart (n 5) 36, 38.
[40] See s 2(a) for references to this concern in certain works by Brian Leiter, Nicos Stavropoulos, and Mark Greenberg.

The rejoinder to both these points is: we should grant weighty explanatory significance to the self-understandings of those living under law, because in the case of law, those self-understandings form a vitally important part of the data we seek to explain, such that explaining our self-understandings in terms of law *is* explaining (aspects of) the nature of law. The concern that examining our self-understandings in terms of the concept of law and related concepts will not take us 'all the way' to identifying and understanding the nature of law itself has built into it an assumption that, to put things metaphorically, there is considerable space, or distance, between the concept of law, and that which it is a concept of, ie the nature of law.[41] This assumption is particularly clear in a quote from Mark Greenberg mentioned earlier:

> [i]t is important to distinguish between a conceptual analysis of a concept and an account of the nature of a phenomenon. A central difference is that the latter is not constrained by our concept of the phenomenon ... Many of the reasons why we might move away from traditional conceptual analysis do not apply to accounts of the nature of a phenomenon ... rather than being tied to ordinary classifications, one can study explanatorily deeper phenomena.[42]

As Joseph Raz notes, however, some philosophers and legal philosophers, including Hart, did not understand the relation between concept and nature in this way:

> When Ryle wrote about the concept of mind, or Hart the concept of law they meant, in advancing explanations of the concepts of mind and of law, to offer explanations of the nature of mind and of the law ... For them as for many other philosophers there was no difference between an explanation of concepts and of the nature of things of which they are concepts.[43]

It is well beyond the scope of the present work to examine in depth the considerable range of philosophical views on the correct way to understand the relations between concepts and that which they are concepts of. However, in keeping with the aims of this book, I believe that something illuminating can be said as regards the specific case of the relation between the concept of law,

---

[41] See also the discussion in ch 3, s 3(c).
[42] Greenberg (n 14) 1950–51.
[43] J Raz, 'Can There Be a Theory of Law?' in J Raz, Between Authority and Interpretation (OUP 2009) 19. Raz makes it clear in this article that his view differs somewhat from Hart's on this issue.

and that which it is a concept of, ie law. In the example discussed throughout this chapter, Hart concludes his discussion on the differences between power-conferring and duty-imposing rules as follows: 'Such power-conferring rules are thought of, spoken of, and used in social life differently from rules which impose duties, and they are valued for different reasons. *What other tests for difference in character could there be?*'[44]

I have emphasized the final line in this quotation because it takes us to the crux of the matter. The self-understandings of those living under and using law play such a weighty role in legal philosophers' accounts of aspects of law's nature—in this case, the social functions of different sorts of legal rules—because those self-understandings simply are part of the data, or the explanandum, that we seek to explain. This being so, the concern that focusing on our self-understandings in terms of the concept of law and related concepts will not take us 'all the way' to an understanding of aspects of the nature of law dissolves—the nature of law is *constituted* in significant part by how those who create, administer, and live under law understand themselves in terms of law. Why so? Because of the character of law itself. Law is a human-made social construction. It comes into being, is maintained in being, is applied, executed, altered, etc. by virtue of the attitudes, beliefs, actions, intentions, and self-understandings of those human beings whose law it is. All these phenomena, therefore, are precisely what a theory of law attempts to characterize and constitute the explanandum for legal philosophers seeking to identify and explain law's nature. If, by contrast, we were considering the nature of a biological medical phenomenon, such as the nature and causes of multiple myeloma, we would not ask: 'what other tests could there be regarding important features of this disease, and important distinctions to be drawn in understanding this disease, beyond how patients living with this condition think about and understand the character and course of their illness?' We would not ask this because we know that there *is* something else, something beyond those patients' self-understanding, which comprises the 'data set' of this disease (for example, the link, established in scientific studies, although not fully understood, between multiple myeloma and a condition called monoclonal gammopathy of unknown significance (MGUS), this latter occurring where there is an excess of protein molecules in the blood, and with one in every 100 persons with MGUS in any given year going on to develop multiple myeloma).[45]

---

[44] Hart (n 5) 41 (my emphasis).
[45] See eg O Landgren, RA Kyle, and SV Rajkumar, 'From Myeloma Precursor Disease to Multiple Myeloma: New Diagnostic Concepts and Opportunities for Early Intervention' (2011) *17*(6) *Clinical Cancer Research* 1243; J Sanders and others, 'Is There a Case for the Early Use of Bisphosphonates in

Law, however, is not like this. There is no further 'data set' lurking behind the actions, attitudes, beliefs, and practices of human beings that together constitute the human social practice of law. It is for this reason that the self-understandings of those who create, administer, and are subject to law impose significant and weighty constraints on what counts as an accurate and explanatorily powerful theory of aspects of law's nature. As I have sought to explain in Chapters 2, 3, and 5, however, and as is explored further below, once the relevant actions, attitudes, beliefs, and practices have constituted a social institution with certain features, that social institution—law—forms a distinctive social reality which our theories of law must capture and explain.[46]

3. Self-understandings as Constraints on Successful Theories of Law II: What *Not* to Do with Them and Why

Some legal philosophers espouse a view very different from mine as regards the proper role in our theories of law for self-understandings in terms of law and related concepts held by those living under law. In their view, such self-understandings should not be accorded so central, or so constraining, a role. They view theories of law—including their own—as being relatively free to be revisionist as regards how law is thought of, spoken of, and used by those who create, administer, and live under it. In exploring such views, I focus here on aspects of the work of Nicos Stavropoulos and of Mark Greenberg, although as the discussion proceeds, given the issues I wish to focus on, it is Greenberg's work which receives most attention. There is much to admire in certain aspects of these theorists' powerful and original work, and it is not my aim to offer a comprehensive critique of either of their positions. My focus lies only with the issue which has concerned me in this chapter, namely how constraining or otherwise on our theories of law are self-understandings in terms of law and related concepts held by those who create, administer, and are subject to it.

Smouldering Myeloma and MGUS? (Bisphosphonates in SMM & MGUS)' (2007) 29(5) *International Journal of Laboratory Hematology* 395.

[46] It is interesting to note that some of the points argued for above appear to accord with Brian Leiter's recent views on these issues, as expressed in for example, Leiter, 'Naturalized Jurisprudence and American Legal Realism Revisited' (n 27) 513, notwithstanding that, as I noted in s 2(a) above his earlier views (see n 13 above and accompanying text) appeared to be significantly at odds with them.

(a) Slipping the leash

Despite some important differences in the substance of their views, both Stavropoulos and Greenberg hold that, methodologically speaking, it is a mistake to regard existing self-understandings in terms of the concept of law and related concepts as supplying constraints on our theories of law of the sort and in the manner I advocate. In understanding their views, it is important to note that their doubts about granting the relevant self-understandings such a constraining role do not stem from any scepticism about it being an important task of theories of law to identify and explain the nature of law, nor from any doubts that this is an achievable goal. Stavropoulos and Greenberg both regard their work as having gone a significant way to doing just that: they have offered what they regard as true and explanatorily powerful theories which reveal important aspects of law's nature.[47]

As was noted in Chapter 4 in discussing some issues surrounding subject-matter selectivity in legal philosophy,[48] both Stavropoulos and Greenberg regard their theories of law as swimming against the prevailing jurisprudential tide. Stavropoulos claims that his understanding of law is opposed to a position that he calls 'the orthodox view',[49] and Greenberg sees his theory as offering an alternative to what he terms 'the standard picture'.[50] Although both to a significant extent define their own position by explaining it in opposition to, respectively, 'the orthodox view' or 'the standard picture', it is not always straightforward to grasp the precise commitments of the view(s) they take themselves to be opposing, or to understand to whom, exactly, they ascribe these views, and the basis of the ascription in question. Stavropoulos sometimes refers to the orthodox view as 'a version of legal positivism',[51] has attributed this view to Joseph Raz's account of legal obligation,[52] and has also claimed that the orthodox view is 'reflected in Hart ... and developed in its strongest form in Raz'.[53] Greenberg tells us that the standard picture is a 'vague picture—I hesitate to call it a theory'[54] and claims that this picture, despite its

---

[47] On this point see the quotations from their work at the outset of s 2 of ch 2.
[48] See ch 4, s 3.
[49] See eg Stavropoulos (n 12) 86–88.
[50] See eg M Greenberg, 'The Standard Picture and Its Discontents' in L Green and B Leiter (eds), Oxford Studies in Philosophy of Law, vol 1 (OUP 2011) passim; M Greenberg, 'The Moral Impact Theory of Law' (2014) 123 Yale Law Journal 1288, 1296–99.
[51] Stavropoulos (n 12) 76.
[52] ibid 86–88.
[53] N Stavropoulos, 'Legal Interpretivism' in E Zalta (ed), The Stanford Encyclopedia of Philosophy (Spring 2021 Edition) s 2 https://plato.stanford.edu/archives/spr2021/entries/law-interpretivist/.
[54] Greenberg, 'The Moral Impact Theory of Law' (n 50) 1296.

vagueness, is assumed by 'many lawyers, judges, and law professors (other than legal philosophers)'[55] as well as being assumed by HLA Hart and John Finnis, but rejected by Scott Shapiro.[56]

What is clearer, however, is that both Stavropoulos and Greenberg place considerable emphasis on explaining and justifying why normative considerations, especially moral considerations, play a different and more significant role in determining what the law is, and, importantly, in determining which factors play precisely what roles (and why they play those roles) in determining what the law is, than is the case according to the orthodox view or the standard picture. The alternative views that they offer are termed 'interpretivism' in Stavropoulos' case, and, in the part of his work I shall focus on, 'the moral impact theory of law' in Greenberg's:

> [f]or interpretivism, the justifying role of principles is *fundamental*: for any legal right or obligation, some more principles ultimately explain how it is that institutional and other nonmoral considerations have roles as determinants of the right or obligation ... The relevant notion of justification has two aspects. First, the principles and therefore the moral facts that they reflect give reasons *why* any aspect of institutional practice ... bears on legal rights and obligations ... Second, the principles thereby determine *how* any such consideration bears on rights and obligations.[57]
>
> According to my view, legal obligations are a subset of moral obligations. Legal institutions—legislatures, courts, administrative agencies—take actions that change our moral obligations. They do so by changing the morally relevant facts and circumstances ... My theory holds ... that the resulting moral obligations *are* legal obligations. I call this view the *Moral Impact Theory* because it holds that the law is the moral impact of the relevant actions of legal institutions.[58]

Both accounts offer thought-provoking reflections on the nature of law, some of which resonate strongly with me. Of particular note in this regard is Stavropoulos' emphasis on the relevance of law's claimed right to coercively enforce demands against individuals, and the sense in which this puts those

---

[55] ibid 1297, n 19.
[56] ibid 1298, n 23. Although I cannot discuss this further here, I have significant doubts as to the accuracy of some of the ascriptions which Stavropoulos and Greenberg make.
[57] Stavropoulos (n 53) s 1 (emphasis in original).
[58] Greenberg, 'The Moral Impact Theory of Law' (n 50) 1290 (emphasis in original; internal footnote reference omitted).

subject to law in a position of standing moral vulnerability,[59] and Greenberg's valuable point that part of the nature of law might include those standards that law is supposed to live up to, including any moral task it ought to perform.[60]

Notwithstanding these points, however, I disagree strongly with a core methodological claim made by both theorists: that theories of the nature of law ought not to be tied to and constrained by existing common conceptions of law or self-understandings in terms of law. According to Stavropoulos and Greenberg, legal philosophers should be free to 'slip the leash' of those ties in developing their accounts of law's nature:

> Many of the reasons why we might move away from traditional conceptual analysis do not apply to accounts of the nature of a phenomenon ... rather than being tied to ordinary classifications, one can study explanatorily deeper phenomena.[61]
>
> [common] conceptions do not possess, as such, explanatory privilege, and the same holds for the attitudes that may make them up.[62]

One motivating factor for this methodological stance appears to be that both theorists harbour suspicions that remaining tied to and constrained by existing self-understandings in terms of law will:

(i) limit theories of law to attaining a relatively shallow and superficial understanding of law's nature;
(ii) hamstring those theories as regards accessing explanatorily 'deeper' truths about law's nature; and
(iii) run a significant risk of leading us to erroneous conclusions about law's nature.

This being their view they regard their own theories—in being free to transcend existing self-understandings—as able to offer explanatorily deeper accounts of law than theories which grant those self-understandings a significantly constraining role.

---

[59] See eg Stavropoulos (n 12) 88–89.
[60] Greenberg (n 14) 1951–54. I discuss some matters related to this point in chs 5 and 8.
[61] Greenberg (n 14) 1950–51. It should be noted that, in this work, I largely try to sidestep the issue of exactly what conceptual analysis as a philosophical technique may or may not amount to. This is not an accidental omission. I believe that the methodological position I advocate in legal philosophy, including the role for self-understandings in terms of law and related concepts within that methodological position, is better characterized in other terms, ie in the way I explain and defend it in this chapter and the two which follow.
[62] Stavropoulos (n 12) 85.

(b) The consequences of revisionism

Although they advocate that theories of law should be free, as I have put it, to 'slip the leash' of existing self-understandings in terms of law, both Stavropoulos and Greenberg raise some qualms about the possible consequences of so doing. Their respective concerns—which they attempt to lay to rest—share certain features, but seem to place the emphasis regarding the worry of 'slipping the leash' in somewhat different places. In the remainder of this section, I argue that Stavropoulos misidentifies what is of most concern as regards the revisionism he advocates, while Greenberg correctly identifies some significant worries in this regard but fails in his attempt to defuse them. The discussion also throws more light on why respecting the constraints stemming from self-understandings in terms of law held by those who create, administer, and live under it, is of distinctive importance in the philosophy of law.

Stavropoulos notes the concern that, in advocating a theoretical account that is not constrained by existing common conceptions or self-understandings (which he refers to in the quotation below as 'the substantive approach'), legal philosophers risk the charge that they are problematically changing the subject, and failing to engage with and explain law as it is, and as it features in the lives of those whose law it is:

> [a] theory that takes the substantive approach might succeed in spite of contradicting the common conception. How could theory share some subject matter with ordinary thinkers and speakers, even as it purports to correct them individually or even collectively? Wouldn't the revisionary character of some theory rather entail that the theory and the ordinary folk talk past each other?[63]

In addressing this concern, Stavropoulos focuses on that aspect of it which involves ensuring that it is the same subject matter being focused upon by (i) those 'ordinary folk' possessing self-understandings in terms of the concept of law, and (ii) a theoretical account of law such as Stavropoulos advocates that has the potential to be significantly revisionist as regards those self-understandings. He tells us that:

> It is now a familiar point that sharing a subject matter is *easy*. Two parties can disagree about some object, including its nature, by finding *some* common

[63] ibid 83.

ground, eg by sharing some distinguishing properties or examples (those not in dispute). Disagreement is premised on understanding that is good enough for competence, not complete understanding. But competence is easy.[64]

Stavropoulos then goes on to reference some points made by Tyler Burge and by Timothy Williamson to provide support for his stance.[65]

In my view, there are some concerns with Stavropoulos' approach here. One is that Stavropoulos' claim that solving the issue of talking past one another by means of finding the requisite basis for assurance that we are all talking about the same thing is '*easy*' and is a familiar point, sits ill at ease with his own statement in the immediately preceding paragraph where he refers to this matter as a 'profound and highly controversial issue'[66] which needs considerable further investigation to resolve.

A second concern—that will emerge more fully in analysing Mark Greenberg's views below—is that Stavropoulos appears to contend that his claims hold generally, methodologically speaking, across a variety of different subject matters. I infer this from the fact that in the work under discussion, he refers with approval to, and seeks to use as support for his own views, both Burge's claims as regards artefact concepts such as sofas, and Williamson's claims as regards the non-artefact concept of 'vixens'.[67] The view that one set of methodological precepts can be generalized across several domains and/or across several different kinds of concepts seems also to be evidenced by the fact that Stavropoulos believes that the points he makes in respect of promising apply easily and equally well to law, and to legal obligation.[68] My worry about this approach stems from the fact that I believe, and argue throughout this book, that many of the methodological constraints incumbent on legal philosophers are so *as a result of the distinctive character of law*. In Chapter 5, for example, I argued that the social reality of law as an institutionalized and systemic social practice of a particular sort justifies legal philosophers in adopting certain attitudes in respect of it (such as an attitude of due wariness), and imposes significant constraints as regards the need to do adequate justice to both law's social and normative character.[69] In the present chapter, I have argued

---

[64] ibid 83 (emphasis in original).
[65] ibid 83–84.
[66] ibid 83.
[67] ibid 83. See also N Stavropoulos, Objectivity in Law (Clarendon Press 1996), especially chs 2, 4, and 5, where he relies on views regarding how concepts refer held by Saul Kripke in respect of names and naming, and by Hilary Putnam in respect of natural kinds, and believes that these views can usefully be employed in understanding law.
[68] Stavropoulos (n 12) *passim*.
[69] See ch 5, ss 2, 3, and 5.

that the role and character of, and constraints imposed by, self-understandings in terms of law and related concepts take on a particular hue because of the specific character of legal philosophy's explanandum: a social practice significantly constituted by the attitudes, beliefs, actions and intentions of those who create, administer and live under law.[70] This being so, in my view, arguments in favour of or against the existence of certain sorts of methodological constraints in legal philosophy must, to be persuasive, be couched in terms of, and show adequate sensitivity to, the particular character of law as an explanandum.

Finally, I have some doubts as to whether Stavropoulos has placed the emphasis in the right place as regards the concern he raises. His worry is that, by departing significantly from existing self-understandings and common conceptions regarding law, we may have difficulty in tethering our explanations to the same object of inquiry, ie in being able to show that we are all starting on, and remaining on, the same page, in terms of that which we are seeking to explain. It is my view, however, that the emphasis of the concern Stavropoulos raises should lie less with ensuring we all start in the same place, and more with the plausibility of where we end up, and of the account of law which we end up with, at the conclusion of our inquiries.

This last point can be unpacked and explored by examining certain aspects of Mark Greenberg's views. As has already been noted, according to Greenberg:

> [l]egal obligations are a subset of moral obligations. Legal institutions—legislatures, courts, administrative agencies—take actions that change our moral obligations ... My theory holds ... that the resulting moral obligations *are* legal obligations. I call this view the *Moral Impact Theory* because it holds that the law is the moral impact of the relevant actions of legal institutions.[71]

Towards the end of 'The Moral Impact Theory of Law', Greenberg considers some objections he thinks may arise in respect of the conclusions mandated by the above view.[72] Of particular relevance for present purposes is the potential objection that it counts against his account of law that it has the following consequence: 'Because my theory holds that the law is a certain part of the moral profile, my theory has the consequence that the law can never include truly evil norms. Such norms can never be part of the moral profile.'[73]

---

[70] See ss 1 and 2 of this chapter.
[71] Greenberg, 'The Moral Impact Theory of Law' (n 50) 1290, emphasis in original; internal footnote reference omitted.
[72] ibid 1337–41.
[73] ibid 1337.

Before turning to Greenberg's attempted rebuttal of this objection, we should note that it is significantly indeterminate. He claims that 'truly evil norms' cannot count as law on his approach, but that, due to legal institutional considerations (for example, that a legal institution has enacted, or adjudicated on, certain legal norms, together with the need to respect a certain understanding of democracy, and/or the need for law to bring coordinated solutions to otherwise intractable problems) seriously morally flawed norms *can* count as part of law.[74] But where does the line between these lie? To give but a few examples: are laws criminalizing same sex sexual acts between consenting adults in private, which still exist in some sixty-seven UN states around the world—more than one-third of all UN states—and which, in some cases, authorize decades' long or life jail terms and/or the death penalty, only 'seriously morally flawed' or are they 'truly evil norms'?[75] Are the norms criminalizing same sex relations in Cameroon's 2016 penal code which authorize punishment of between six months and five years in prison, plus substantial fines, 'truly evil norms' or only 'seriously morally flawed'?[76] What about analogous provisions in the Gambian criminal code of 1965, as amended in 2005, which authorize fourteen years of imprisonment?[77] Or Iran's Penal Code of 2013 according to which same sex sexual relations are punishable by death in some cases, and by thirty-one to seventy-four lashes in others?[78] What of the laws in the forty-two UN states which restrict freedom of expression in relation to sexual orientation issues, including in the form of restrictions on expressions of same-sex intimacy and restrictions on expressions of support or positive portrayals of non-heterosexual identities and relationships?[79] Such restrictions are present in at least four European states (and are under consideration at present in several more),[80] and, at state level, in several states in the United States of America.[81]

Does the extent to which various conceptions of democracy hold or do not hold in states which criminalize homosexual acts and/or the promotion of

---

[74] ibid 1302, 1304, 1312, 1314, and 1337.
[75] See Ramon Mendos and others (n 36) 113–41 https://ilga.org/downloads/ILGA_World_State_Sponsored_Homophobia_report_global_legislation_overview_update_December_2020.pdf. It should be noted that this report draws extensively on local knowledge and concrete experience on the ground in the relevant jurisdictions. It reports what happens, not merely what might happen, as a result of the provisions of the law of each jurisdiction covered.
[76] ibid 114.
[77] ibid 116.
[78] ibid 131. The report cited here notes that: 'as of November 2020, there is full legal certainty that the death penalty is the legally prescribed punishment for consensual same-sex sexual acts in six (6) UN Member States, namely Brunei, Iran, Mauritania, Nigeria (12 Northern states only), Saudi Arabia and Yemen.' See ibid 31.
[79] ibid 145–63.
[80] ibid 159–62.
[81] ibid 151.

homosexual acts change the classification from truly evil and so not part of the law, to seriously morally flawed but part of the law on the Greenberg approach? Can legal institutional decision or practice ever render morally obligatory a duty to commit someone to death or subject them to seventy-four lashes for certain expressions of their sexuality? Can it render morally obligatory the prosecution of persons for presenting LGBT people and their lives in a positive light? In his adjectival qualification of the norms he has in mind as 'truly evil', the impression is created that Greenberg may regard such norms as relatively rare, and, if so, perhaps he would view the examples I cite above as extreme. But they are sadly neither. The laws I have cited above hail from all continents of the world, and are only a tiny tip of a very large iceberg.[82] Moreover, these examples only refer to one area amongst very many where laws are used to ensure that fundamental parts of human beings' personality and/or attributes, such as their gender, caste, race, sexual orientation, religious belief etc. are either criminalized, with attendant punishments prescribed that may devastate their lives, or are rendered a legally authorized reason to discriminate against them.

Wherever the line precisely falls, a not insignificant proportion of the laws in the penal and criminal codes of UN states around the world would seem to qualify as truly evil norms on Greenberg's approach. Greenberg claims that we should not hold such norms to be part of the law in the jurisdiction in which they appear. Pointing out that this flies significantly in the face of the social reality of the existence of the numerous provisions of penal and criminal codes, and their devastating effects of the lives of those who fall foul of them, meets with the following response:

> [m]y theory does not deny that there are evil laws, where 'laws' is used in the sense of *statutes or other authoritative legal texts*. It should be uncontroversial that there are bad statutes, ordinances, regulations, and so on. The issue is the much more theoretical one of what impact on the content of the law such statutes have—in particular, whether such statutes give rise to evil legal norms.[83]

This embrace of a significant divorce between the social practice of law, and the theory of law which attempts to identify and explain that social practice, should give us cause for concern. Moreover, this is not the only instance where

---

[82] As the ILGA 2020 report indicates, in addition to laws delineating specific acts which are criminalized, other laws use vague terms such as 'acts against nature', 'indecency', 'immoral acts', that can be interpreted in a variety of ways, and frequently lead to the discretionary use of these norms to persecute LGBT people: see ibid 113.
[83] Greenberg, 'The Moral Impact Theory of Law' (n 50) 1338.

Greenberg advocates it: he also argues that as his theory of law requires a complex, wide-ranging, and ambitious moral theory, there may be a significant number of occasions when, despite its theoretical correctness, judges should not use his theory to determine the law as it will be applied to parties in cases coming before them, and should turn to another, more pragmatic, method instead.[84]

This cannot be a sound approach. As I have argued throughout this and the preceding chapter, the specific character of our explanandum is that which drives the methodological constraints that ought to be observed by legal philosophers in constructing their theories. We are not free to claim that, no matter what is happening in the actual social and institutional practice of our societies, and no matter the prevalence of legal norms such as those I have referred to above, and no matter their consequences, including their devastating effect on the lives of those who experience living under them, that these are not part of our 'real' explanandum because we are interested in law primarily in a 'theoretical' sense. Furthermore, when we take a closer look at what that theoretical sense is for Greenberg, he makes it clear in passages such as that quoted above, that it concerns the content of the law. So his claim is that—despite being created by the actions of legal institutions, despite appearing in penal and criminal codes, despite hundreds of thousands of individuals worldwide being imprisoned or discriminated against and understanding only too clearly that what is happening to them is happening because of the law of their jurisdiction—laws such as those referenced above criminalizing homosexual conduct or prohibiting the positive portrayal of LGBT persons and their lives, have little and in some cases no impact on the content of the law, and that the content of the law should be explained in a different, theoretical sense which does not include them.

As was noted earlier in this chapter, Greenberg claims that 'slipping the leash' of existing common conceptions of law and existing self-understandings in terms of law leads us to a more profound level of understanding because, '[r]ather than being tied to ordinary classifications, one can study explanatorily deeper phenomena'.[85] But in the case of law—an explanandum significantly constituted by, and sustained in place by, the beliefs, actions, attitudes, and understandings of human beings and their social practices—it is difficult to understand how he thinks he can justify his claims that his theory is correct of some phenomenon which not only goes beyond those things, but may

---

[84] ibid 1334–37.
[85] Greenberg (n 14) 1950–51.

be significantly divorced from them. This raises the question: in what sense is Greenberg explaining that which I take to be our explanandum in legal philosophy—the social practice and social reality of law as it actually exists in, and has significant effects in, our society—rather than some other explanandum, for example, what would count as morally justified law, or what would count as morally obligatory law?

Greenberg does not adequately address these issues nor explain how his account is sufficiently attuned to the specific character of his alleged explanandum: law as it exists in the social reality of our societies. Instead, he offers a generalized methodological precept that he claims is 'fairly banal'[86] and presents as if it were uncontroversial, and largely agreed upon:

> Ultimately, the way to determine whether there can be truly evil legal norms is not to consult English usage or even lawyers' intuitions. True theories often have counterintuitive consequences—a great deal of what we now think about the world and about human beings would once have been thought to be absurd. We have to evaluate how successful theories are on a wide range of criteria, and once we have decided in this holistic way which theory is most successful, we then have to accept whatever counterintuitive consequences that theory has (at least until a better theory comes along).[87]

This stance is neither uncontroversial nor banal. Many theorists in many areas of philosophy would dispute it, and still more would require, at the very least, that it be considerably qualified. Moreover, as a methodological precept purporting to apply to the relations between theoretical accounts, and common conceptions of and self-understandings in terms of that which they are an account of, it is breath-taking in its seeming domain-generality. Why should we believe this same precept applies as regards theories of phenomena as diverse as quarks, justice, planetary orbits, Scottish humour, biological taxa, social alienation, the wandering albatross, law, and the character of photography as an art form? Why should we accept that in all these cases it is not a negative that might count against it, that a theory has highly counter-intuitive consequences and offers an account significantly divorced from how the explanandum is currently conceptualized, and how it features in our existing thoughts and beliefs about it, and actions in terms of it? Why should we be persuaded of such a

---

[86] Greenberg, 'The Moral Impact Theory of Law' (n 50) 1338.
[87] ibid (internal footnote reference omitted).

sweeping claim in favour of revisionism, asserted with very little argument, and falsely characterized as 'fairly banal'?

In this and the preceding chapter, I have argued to the contrary. I have sought to explain and defend the view that law is a distinctive sort of explanandum, one which has in several senses a social reality to it that plays crucial roles in the lives of those who create, administer and live under it. I have contended that these distinctive features of law as an explanandum ought significantly to constrain legal philosophers in their theoretical attempts accurately to identify and adequately explain aspects of its nature. Greenberg's approach, which advocates 'slipping the leash' of existing conceptions of and self-understandings in terms of law, results in his espousal of a theory of law which, far from being (as Greenberg claims), 'simple and natural'[88] in fact rides roughshod over how law is thought of and operates in the lives of those whose law it is, and cannot appropriately identify and explain our explanandum in the terms in which it requires to be explained. This approach offers us a stark illustration of the limits of revisionism in legal philosophy, and of the consequences of proceeding in disregard of those limits.

4. Conclusion: Self-understandings and the Limits of Revisionism

The discussion in this chapter illuminates further aspects of the IELP that I espouse. That methodological approach features a strong commitment to observing the constraints that the self-understandings of those who create, administer, and live under law, impose on theories of law. Elucidating law is an active process: it is not accurately characterized as descriptive, and it does not involve legal philosophers merely ascertaining and 'lifting' wholesale into their theories the views of those living under law. But those self-understandings are constraining nevertheless, and they are so in significant part because they part-constitute the very data, the very explanandum, that we seek to explain. Disregarding and/or riding roughshod over these self-understandings, in a misguided search for allegedly explanatorily deeper phenomena than the concrete social and institutional practice of law as it exists in our societies, results in accounts of law which are unacceptably divorced from law's social reality. In pressing these points, I have sought to show that law is a distinctive sort of explanandum, which places concomitantly distinctive constraints on theories

[88] Greenberg, 'The Moral Impact Theory of Law' (n 50) 1341.

attempting to identify and explain its nature. Whatever place there may be in theoretical accounts of other phenomena for the extensive sort of revisionism advocated by a theory such as Greenberg's, I maintain that it should not feature in the philosophy of law, for it results in theoretical accounts which fail to explain law in its concrete social reality and as it functions in the lives of those whose law it is.

7
Indirectly Evaluative Legal Philosophy
The Value of Staged Inquiry

Chapters 5 and 6 introduced and developed aspects of the approach to legal philosophy that I champion—indirectly evaluative legal philosophy (IELP)—by considering several constraints that are incumbent on legal philosophers as they approach and attempt to characterize law. The constraints in question concern the need to acknowledge and explain each aspect of an important duality running through law, the desideratum of adopting an attitude of due wariness in approaching law, and the requirement that a theory of law do adequate justice to the self-understandings in terms of law held by those living under it.

This chapter explores another key feature of IELP which is responsible for its name: legal philosophers must make evaluative judgements in constructing and defending their accounts of law, but in the earlier stages of their inquiries the evaluative judgements concerned can and should be 'indirectly evaluative' in character.[1] This approach both allows for and facilitates a certain kind of 'staged inquiry' wherein important aspects of law's nature can be identified and understood in a way which leaves open until an appropriate point in the investigation questions of their moral value or justification. IELP thus enables legal philosophers to proceed in appropriate stages in understanding what law is, what law ought to be, and what is relevant to assessing law according to the standards by which it should be judged.

1. Evaluation in Legal Philosophy

Throughout this book I have emphasized that legal philosophy about the nature of law involves theorists in an active process requiring them to make evaluative judgements of certain kinds.[2] The discussion of subject-matter selectivity

---

[1] See the six tenets of IELP identified in ch 5, s 1.
[2] I have also emphasized this aspect of the philosophy of legal philosophy in earlier work, eg J Dickson, Evaluation and Legal Theory (Hart Publishing 2001) passim, but especially chs 2, 3, and 7; J Dickson, 'Methodology in Jurisprudence: A Critical Survey' (2004) 10(3) Legal Theory 117.

and of distribution of emphasis-selectivity in Chapter 4 highlighted the ways in which legal philosophers must make evaluative judgements in selecting which aspects of law to focus on, and in deciding where and how to place the emphasis in their accounts of law.[3] The exploration of various constraints incumbent on legal philosophers in Chapters 5 and 6 also indicated that legal philosophers must make evaluative judgements in constructing and defending their theories: for example, in identifying and interpreting the self-understandings in terms of law held by those living under it.[4]

This emphasis on and embrace of the role of evaluative judgements in legal philosophy should readily indicate why—as I discussed in Chapter 6[5]—I regard the term 'descriptive' as a misnomer when applied to the kind of methodological approach I champion.[6] But what sort of evaluative judgements are these, exactly, and what is meant by referring to them as 'indirectly evaluative' in character?

(a) Indirectly versus directly evaluative judgements in legal philosophy

One promising place to start in exploring the character of indirectly evaluative judgements is by contrasting them with what they are not. We can usefully do so in the context of various approaches to legal philosophy with which we are familiar, and which have already featured in this book.

Some theories of law take the view that questions concerning law's moral value and moral obligatoriness ought to take their place front and centre from the outset. Such theories embrace the idea that legal philosophers need to make what I will refer to as 'directly evaluative judgements' from an early stage in their inquiries. Examples of this kind of approach can be found in the work of John Finnis, Mark Greenberg, and Ronald Dworkin.

Finnis contends that we must embark upon our theories of law from the starting point of examining, and taking a stance on, what law's moral point or value is, why we have law, and why, morally speaking, we should comply with

---

[3] See ch 4, ss 2–4.
[4] See ch 6, s 2.
[5] See ch 6, s 2(b)(iii).
[6] Tendencies to refer to certain approaches to legal philosophy as descriptive in character can be found amongst both supporters and critics of such approaches. See eg J Waldron, 'Normative (or Ethical) Positivism' and SR Perry, 'Hart's Methodological Positivism', both in JL Coleman (ed) Hart's Postscript: Essays on the Postscript to 'The Concept of Law' (OUP 2001); A Marmor, 'Legal Positivism: Still Descriptive and Morally Neutral' (2006) 26 *Oxford Journal of Legal Studies* 683.

it, rather than by attempting to characterize law without yet considering these matters:

> Suppose we tried to think about law without trying first to describe it or to work out what of the concept of it is. Suppose we asked instead whether, and if so why, and when, we—or more precisely each one of us—should favour having, endorsing, maintaining, complying with, and enforcing it.[7]

Finnis claims that if we proceed from the 'why have/endorse/comply with law?' starting point, we will come to understand that law is uniquely well-placed to make a positive moral contribution to our lives, and that it is, by its nature, morally valuable.[8] He contends that law has, and should be characterized in terms of, a moral point or objective; that is, reasonably to resolve the coordination problems of a political community and provide a set of framework conditions enabling and assisting its members to lead morally valuable lives. Moreover, it is Finnis' view that, at the unit level of political society, *only* law can bring about the conditions in which these morally valuable aims can be achieved.[9]

As was discussed in Chapter 6, Mark Greenberg contends that we should understand law such that legal obligations are a subset of moral obligations because law is the moral impact of the relevant actions of legal institutions.[10] For his part, Ronald Dworkin contends that any successful theory of law must 'explain how what it takes to be law provides a general justification for the exercise of coercive power by the state'.[11] Dworkin accordingly takes his task in *Law's Empire* to be to constructively interpret our legal practices by putting them in their best moral light in terms of their ability properly to police and constrain state coercion, and so set the terms on which law is morally justified in imposing duties on those individuals subject to it.[12]

Each of these accounts of law contains and is supported by what I refer to as directly evaluative judgements. Directly evaluative judgements are judgements that examine, and take a stance on, whether and to what extent some

---

[7] J Finnis, 'Law and What I Truly Should Decide' (2003) 48 *American Journal of Jurisprudence* 107, 107.
[8] ibid 111.
[9] See J Finnis, Natural Law and Natural Rights (1st edn, OUP 1980; 2nd edn, OUP 2011) *passim*. The very first sentence in the book serves well as its leitmotif: 'There are human goods that can be secured only through the institutions of human law, and requirements of practical reasonableness that only those institutions can satisfy.'
[10] M Greenberg, 'The Moral Impact Theory of Law' (2014) 123 *Yale Law Journal* 1288, *passim*, but especially at 1290.
[11] R Dworkin, Law's Empire (Fontana Press 1986) 190.
[12] ibid 93 and *passim*.

X, or some feature of some X, is good or valuable. In the case of law, as the examples above indicate, directly evaluative judgements include: that law by its nature is uniquely able to achieve the moral purpose of reasonably resolving coordination problems for the common good in political society; that law by its nature generates moral obligations to obey it; that law by its nature comprises those rights and duties which are justifiably imposed on individuals because they flow from the morally best interpretation of their community's legal and political practices.[13] Accounts of law's nature which contain and are supported by directly evaluative judgements concerning law's moral value, goodness, or obligatoriness are, in the terminology employed in this book, examples of directly evaluative legal philosophy.

Directly evaluative judgements, and directly evaluative legal philosophy (DELP), can be contrasted with the methodological approach I advocate, and which I term indirectly evaluative legal philosophy (IELP). This approach involves—at least in the earlier stages of inquiries into law's nature—evaluative judgements of a different character. In engaging in IELP, theorists do make evaluative judgements from the outset, but those evaluative judgements are *not* directly evaluative judgements concerning the value or goodness of aspects of law. Rather, and as I have argued in previous work,[14] according to IELP, legal philosophers should begin their inquiries by making indirectly evaluative judgements: judgements that pick out those aspects or features of law that are important and significant to explain, but which do not involve, or entail, taking a stance on the goodness or value of those aspects or features. In the case of law, indirectly evaluative judgements would include: 'one thing that it is important to explain about law is that, like morality, it uses normative terminology, but that, unlike morality, the norms of law are created and modified by social institutions such as legislatures and courts'; 'a significant feature of law is that it presents itself as justified in enforcing its norms using the coercive apparatus of the state'; and 'law's claim that it has moral authority over us is important in understanding law's nature, and is relevant to considering how we ought to take its claims'. This third example is intentionally suggestive of a point discussed further in sections 2(b) and 3 below: that one factor which can support the making of an indirectly evaluative judgement that a given feature of law is important and significant to explain is that the feature in question is relevant to normative questions concerning law's goodness or value and concerning what

---

[13] See also Dickson, *Evaluation and Legal Theory* (n 2) ch 3. Note that directly evaluative judgements could also be to the effect that some X, or some feature of some X, is bad, and/or is not valuable. This point resurfaces in sub-s (b) below.
[14] Dickson, *Evaluation and Legal Theory* (n 2) 52–57 and, more generally, ch 3.

we ought to do given the presence of law, its character, and its claims. IELP insists, however, that it is possible to know that some feature of law is *important*, and is *relevant* to an eventual direct or moral evaluation of that feature and/or of the phenomenon exhibiting it, without yet knowing, and without yet having to consider or to take a stance on, that eventual direct or moral evaluation.[15]

Examples of indirectly evaluative judgements can be found in the work of several legal philosophers, including HLA Hart, Joseph Raz, Wil Waluchow, Leslie Green, and myself:

> It [Hartian legal theory] wouldn't be morally evaluative. It's evaluative in a sense, but any theory that tries to define or explain a complex activity would have to select some items out of it as important enough to be focused upon. I mean, if I'm watching a game, if I'm describing the game as a game, I won't pick out in order to describe the game the size of the players, because it doesn't throw light on any major question. Whereas I will pick out that they are not only struggling to get hold of the ball, but if they put it in a certain place then that counts as a point towards winning. So it's evaluative in a sense that you pick out features of the complex activity, not because it justifies it morally, but because these would be relevant to among other questions what moral questions you ask. But it doesn't give the answer.[16]

A theory of what the law is strives to identify its central, prominent, important features. What makes a feature prominent or important or central is inescapably and inevitably an evaluative question. It is important if it bears upon what matters. In large measure it is precisely the fact that certain features are relevant to what one ought to do which marks their importance.

It is crucial to remember, however, that we can and often do know that a feature of a scheme or institution is relevant to its evaluation without knowing whether that makes it good or bad.[17]

Discovering certain elements of legal practice worth highlighting because they are morally relevant in no way commits one to saying that these are elements in virtue of which the practice is actually justified (or unjustified) morally. One can see that the use of coercion is morally relevant without

---

[15] ibid ch 7. This is explored further in ss 2(b) and 3 of the present chapter.
[16] Words of HLA Hart in D Sugarman, 'Hart Interviewed: H.L.A. Hart in Conversation with David Sugarman' (2005) 32(2) *Journal of Law and Society* 267, 288. Note that the above is from a transcript of an interview; Hart in his own words is available here in the audio files of the interview: H.L.A. Hart in conversation with David Sugarman by Oxford Academic (OUP) | Free Listening on SoundCloud. Hart on the sense in which his theory is 'evaluative-but-not-morally-evaluative-or-justificatory' is in Part 6 of the interview, starting at 3 mins 40 secs into Part 6.
[17] J Raz, 'The Morality of Obedience' (1985) 83 *Michigan Law Review* 732, 735. See also J Raz, 'Authority, Law, and Morality' in J Raz, Ethics in the Public Domain (Clarendon Press 1994) 236–37.

knowing whether and when coercion is ever justified morally ... one can see moral relevance without making a moral commitment.[18]

Each of these accounts contains and is supported by indirectly evaluative judgements concerning the importance, centrality, and significance of certain features of law. In the terminology employed in this book, they are instances of IELP. Moreover, as the quotations above indicate, and as I will explore in the remainder of this chapter and in Chapter 8, IELP is committed to a staged approach to legal philosophical inquiry. At the first stage, theories of law should pick out certain features of law, and certain aspects of those features, which are important and significant to explain. At this stage in the inquiry the theory of law does not yet take a stance on the goodness or value of what has been picked out. Once an account of law has identified those important features of law and has given an explanatorily robust account of their character at the first stage of inquiry, it can then move on—at a later stage in the inquiry—to consider the goodness or value of those features, and to assess what contribution, if any, they make to rendering law overall good, valuable, and worthy of obedience.

(b) Are indirectly evaluative legal philosophy and directly evaluative legal philosophy rivals?

It is important to consider and clarify the sense in which IELP and DELP are rival methodological approaches. On first encounter, it may sound as if this is not the case, because, as is mentioned above, and explored in greater depth in the remainder of this chapter and the next, IELP, like DELP, regards it as extremely important that legal philosophers explore whether various properties of law are such that they render law good, valuable, justified, or generate obligations to obey it. The approaches differ significantly, however, as regards the route they take in approaching these questions.

DELP insists that legal philosophers must begin their inquiries by proceeding directly to questions of law's moral value, worth, and obligatoriness. Moreover, theorists adopting this approach tend to reject the idea that there is any room for, or point in, other methodological approaches to ascertaining

---

[18] W Waluchow, Inclusive Legal Positivism (Clarendon Press 1994) 22–23. See more generally ch 2 of that work. See also Dickson, *Evaluation and Legal Theory* (n 2) 137 and, more generally, chs 3 and 7 of that work, and L Green and T Adams, 'Legal Positivism' in E Zalta (ed), *The Stanford Encyclopedia of Philosophy* (Winter 2019 Edition) s 4.3 https://plato.stanford.edu/archives/win2019/entries/legal-positivism/

law's nature, such as IELP. Legal philosophy, in their eyes, *must* begin by making, for example, judgements regarding law's moral point or value, and by explaining how law generates moral reasons for action. This point is made explicitly by Finnis, and features strongly in the work of others espousing a DELP approach:

> In short, a complete and fully realistic theory of law can be and in all essentials has been worked out from the one hundred percent normative question, what should I decide to do ... I can think of no interesting project of inquiry left over for a philosophical theory of law with any different starting point.[19]

IELP on the other hand, contends that the route to answering such question should be indirect in character, and that theories of law should proceed in stages. At the first stage, the legal philosopher makes indirectly evaluative judgements picking out certain features of law as significant and important to explain. IELP acknowledges and indeed embraces the point that one reason why certain aspects of law should be picked out as important and significant to explain is because of the relevance those features have to an eventual consideration of those features' and law's goodness or value.[20] But to pick out certain things as *relevant* to an eventual evaluation of them as good or bad is not yet actually to evaluate them as good or bad. This point is emphasized by Hart in a passage from his work already quoted in sub-section (a) above:

> [i]t's [Hart's legal philosophy] evaluative in a sense that you pick out features of the complex activity, not because it justifies it morally, but because these would be relevant to among other questions what moral questions you ask. But it doesn't give the answer. Whereas Dworkin is saying any worthwhile jurisprudence is a blend of description and moral evaluation—it's got to show the law in its best light. Why not show it in the worst light?'[21]

In posing the question at the end of the above passage, Hart also highlights another important distinction between the IELP and the DELP approaches, at least in the form that they assume in the work of the three proponents of DELP discussed earlier in this chapter. All three of those theorists believe that law's inherent moral qualities are positive in character: Finnis holds that only law

---

[19] Finnis (n 7) 115. See also G Webber, 'Asking why in the study of human affairs' (2015) *60 American Journal of Jurisprudence* 51; G Duke, 'Law's Normative Point' (2019) *38 Law and Philosophy* 1.
[20] This point is explored further in ss 2(b) and 3 of the present chapter, and in ch 8.
[21] Hart (n 16) 288.

can bring about the conditions of valuable human flourishing in political societies; Dworkin contends that law upholds individual rights and responsibilities and ensures that citizens are only subject to state coercion when this is morally justified; Greenberg regards legal obligations as a subset of moral obligations. However, Hart's worry in the final sentence of the passage quoted above is one which I share: the concern that some approaches to understanding law do not sufficiently leave room for the possibility that law is, in some aspects of its nature, morally bad, and/or morally risky, and/or morally something to be wary of, and cautious about obeying.

It is important to acknowledge, however, that although Finnis, Dworkin, and Greenberg believe that law's inherent moral qualities are positive in character, this need not be an inevitable feature of the DELP approach.[22] Moreover, and importantly, on the IELP approach, it is both a possible and a welcome situation if a legal philosopher, after they have made indirectly evaluative judgements regarding those aspects of law which are important to explain and after they have explained them, wishes to mount an argument at the second stage of their inquiries capable of supporting the conclusion that law possesses some features which are inherently morally good, or bad. As this way of proceeding goes via the indirect route that IELP advocates, it would be terminologically misleading to refer to this second stage of inquiries on the IELP approach as DELP. In my view, it is better to think of such inquiries as belonging to the latter stages of IELP, and to say that they form the second stage of that methodological approach, which turns to questions of law's goodness, value, and justification only after we have a cool-headed and morally neutral understanding of some of law's important and significant properties.

2. Indirectly Evaluative Judgements in Staged Inquiry

The preceding section introduced and began to explore the character of IELP. But can that methodological approach substantiate its claims? Is it possible to make indirectly evaluative judgements concerning the significance and importance of features of law which do not involve or entail directly evaluative judgements of those features' goodness or value? Even if it is possible, can we explain the basis on which we are to make such judgements, and why we ought to proceed in this 'staged inquiry' manner? This section explores these questions by

---

[22] Some radically critical approaches to theorizing about law may be examples of DELP, which hold that the character of various of law's features render it an inherently bad phenomenon.

considering some examples of phenomena that I contend can and should be understood using the staged inquiry approach

(a) Some examples of indirectly evaluative judgements and their role in staged inquiry

(i) Example 1: academic dress requirements

At the university where I work—the University of Oxford—there are certain requirements regarding forms of academic dress that must be worn by certain categories of persons on certain occasions.[23] One set of requirements concerns what must be worn by those attending in-person university examinations. Student members of the university are required to wear academic dress with sub fusc clothing when attending a university examination. Academic dress consists of the appropriate academic gown plus mortar board or soft cap. Sub fusc clothing is a dark suit with dark socks, or a dark skirt with black stockings or trousers with dark socks and an optional dark coat; black shoes; plain white collared shirt; a black tie or white bow tie.[24] Until relatively recently, academics at the university required to attend university examinations for the first thirty minutes—this is usually the academic who set the examination paper or a substitute designated by them—were subject to the same rule as student members. There has now been a small change to this latter rule, and 'examiners attending the first thirty minutes of a taught course examination for the purpose of resolving any queries about the examination paper may, if they wish, wear academic dress with formal clothing rather than with sub fusc'.[25] Another set of requirements concerns which forms of academic dress, including gowns and hoods, must be worn to degree ceremonies and other formal university occasions.[26]

These are but a small sample of a voluminous set of requirements relating to academic dress at the University of Oxford. Suppose that, for some reason, I wish to write an article on academic dress requirements at the university. Assume that I am open, eventually, to offering assessments of whether this phenomenon is good or bad, justified or unjustified, worth preserving, or

---

[23] See 'Regulations relating to Academic Dress, made by the Vice-Chancellor, as Authorised by Council' of 2002, amended 2008, 2012, 2015, https://governance.admin.ox.ac.uk/legislation/vice-chancellors-regulations-1-of-2002; See also https://www.ox.ac.uk/students/academic/dress
[24] ibid reg 5.
[25] ibid reg 7.
[26] ibid regs 3 and 4.

something that should be abandoned/reformed. Such eventual assessments would, in the terminology employed in this book, involve directly evaluative judgements of the value or goodness of aspects of the academic dress requirements. In terms of exploring the idea of 'staged inquiry'—that inquiries into certain phenomena are to be approached in stages, and, at the first stage, by making indirectly evaluative judgements—the relevant question is: can I engage in such staged inquiry with regard to understanding academic dress requirements at the University of Oxford?

In my view, yes. What are some of the important and significant features of the academic dress rules at the University of Oxford? It is important that these rules state requirements that are mandatory rather than being mere guidelines which one can opt in to or out of as one chooses. It is significant that the requirements are enforceable, and enforced, and are so by a group of officials within the university known as the Proctors, who can, inter alia, restrict entry to certain occasions, and/or issue fines to, and/or take other disciplinary action against, those who do not comply with the rules. Knowing and complying with the rules hence bears upon students' being able to attend and complete university examinations whilst avoiding disciplinary measures. It is significant that according to guidance accompanying the rules, it falls to students' colleges to advise them as regards the gowns they are entitled to wear, as this entails that compliance with the mandatory rules is partly the responsibility of colleges and college tutors, of whom I am one. It is important that these rules are available for both academic and students to consult and to identify their contents and that we can do so by consulting the statutes and regulations of the university which are available on its website.

It seems, therefore, that I am able to make a range of indirectly evaluative judgements regarding what is important and significant about Oxford University's academic dress code, including what is important in terms of what it tells me about responsibilities I have due to my job, including responsibilities to students. Can I do this without those indirectly evaluative judgements containing or entailing directly evaluative judgements concerning the goodness or value or obligatoriness of those academic dress requirements? I contend that I must be able to do so. For I personally have never considered whether these academic dress requirements are good, or valuable, or obligatory, and as things stand I have no idea what any such value or obligatoriness might consist of, or what might explain it. I am not claiming that considering such questions is impossible or inappropriate. But I have never considered them, and I do not have an inkling as to what the answers to them might be. Nonetheless, it seems to me that I have identified above some matters which are important in respect of Oxford University's academic dress requirements, including some matters which are of importance as regards the advice I should give to students as part of my job. I can ascertain that these requirements exist, I know that certain aspects of them are significant and important,[27] and I can identify what they require of my students and myself, all without having any idea whether they are valuable or justifiable, or even what factors might contribute to them being valuable or justifiable or otherwise. Indeed, I believe that I have done my job and advised my students diligently in these matters for two decades whilst never considering, let alone taking a stance on, whether the rules in question are valuable or justified.

(ii) Example 2: the tutorial system of university teaching
The University of Oxford also employs a distinctive method of teaching undergraduate students known as 'the tutorial system'.[28] According to this system, undergraduates are taught in tutorials which are very small groups of just two or three students to one tutor. Students are asked to produce a piece of written work before each tutorial, which their tutor will mark and give individually tailored feedback on. This piece of written work is also used to structure and influence what is discussed in the tutorial. As applied to the undergraduate law curriculum at Oxford University, students in their first two years have one tutorial in one subject every week of term, and one tutorial in another subject every two weeks of term. Lectures also exist, but are viewed as secondary to, and less compulsory than, tutorials.[29] The tutorial system can be contrasted with a different system of university teaching used at many other UK universities. This second system features a series of integrated lectures and tutorials, with tutorials happening after the lectures in the relevant topic has taken place. Lectures are held every week, but tutorials are held only once every two weeks or so. Tutorials contain between eight and fourteen students to one tutor. Students typically do not produce a piece of written work before each tutorial, and tutorial discussion centres around pre-circulated questions for consideration by the group in the tutorial.[30]

---

[27] I explore some factors that support the indirectly evaluative judgements legal philosophers make in s 2(b) of this chapter.
[28] The documentation available as part of the Oxford tutorial system teaching recording system gives some information on the tutorial system's operation: https://www.oxcort.ox.ac.uk/documents.html
[29] Note that, although highly distinctive, this approach is not unique to Oxford: in the UK, the University of Cambridge employs a similar method.
[30] There are no doubt many variants of this system. In constructing the general outline above, I draw on my experience as a student, and as an academic, at the University of Glasgow, the University of Leicester, and at University College London.

Suppose that I want to understand the Oxford University tutorial teaching system, and that I am open to considering in due course whether it is good and valuable in ways which indicate that Oxford University should retain its commitment to it, or whether it needs to be reformed or even replaced by something akin to the system used at other UK universities. Can I proceed in my quest by making only indirectly evaluative judgements at the first stage in a staged inquiry? Once again, it seems to me that I can. It is important that the Oxford tutorial system features exceptionally small group teaching, with a ratio of students to tutor that is considerably smaller than at almost all other UK universities. It is significant that students produce a piece of written work for every tutorial, and that they receive feedback on that written work. It is important to note that the Oxford tutorial system is very resource-intensive: on the comparison numbers mooted above, it requires approximately five to six times more person hours of teaching than the system employed at many other UK universities.

It seems, therefore, that I am able to make indirectly evaluative judgements regarding what is important and significant about Oxford University's tutorial teaching system, including what is important because it tells me something about the responsibilities I have in virtue of my job, including my responsibilities to students. Can I do this without those indirectly evaluative judgements containing or entailing directly evaluative judgements concerning the educational value or worth of Oxford's tutorial system? So far as my own reflections are concerned, this case is a little different from Example 1. This time it so happens that I have spent some time considering whether the tutorial teaching system has educational value, and whether Oxford University should persist in using it. Moreover, and as the points made below should indicate, I also have some, albeit rather vague, ideas regarding what any such value might consist of, and regarding which criteria we should use in considering whether to stick with, reform, or abandon the system. For all this, however, I believe that I can pick out, as I have above, features of the tutorial system which are *relevant to considering* its educational value or worth, and are *relevant to considering* whether Oxford University ought to persist with it, without yet knowing the answers to those directly evaluative questions. Because although—as it happens—I have considered such directly evaluative questions from time to time over two decades in teaching in the system, I still do not know the answers to them, or indeed whether conclusive such answers are possible, and for several years of teaching in the system, I did not have the time to consider them at all.

Here are some illustrations of what I mean by this. That the Oxford tutorial teaching system is extremely small group teaching with just two or three students to one tutor, that students produce written work in advance of each tutorial and receive feedback on it, and that the system is extremely resource-intensive strike me as relevant factors in considering whether that system possesses distinctive educational value. These features of the system could contribute to the tutorial system realizing educational value through offering students an individually tailored learning experience which fosters independent thinking and research and affords them the opportunity to develop and discuss their own views on complex topics. However, these features may also contribute to rendering the system very work intensive for students during term time, contributing to already significant levels of stress and anxiety. Students may have to use a variety of 'short-cuts' to keep up with the amount of work required each week in term time, and students may miss out on the opportunity to learn from more of their peers in a tutor-facilitated larger group discussion situation. Moreover, these features of the tutorial system also render it expensive for the university and extremely repetitive for the tutors who teach the same thing some six times over to students two by two, where in another UK university they could teach it once to a group of twelve. This may deleteriously affect teaching quality, and contribute to the problems which the university has as regards retention of Oxford academics who carry a very high load of tutorial teaching as compared with their colleagues at other universities. Is there a distinctive educational value realized by the Oxford tutorial teaching system? If there is, is there sufficient gain in terms of educational value when set against the disadvantages and potential downsides of the system—for students, for tutors, and for the university, in educational and other value terms? Despite considering these questions, at least from time to time during two decades teaching within the Oxford tutorial system, I do not know the answers. I do not have a conclusive view as to which factors—in terms of the positive, and the negative, values realized by the Oxford tutorial system—should predominate, let alone carry the day in any consideration of whether to persist with the system. Moreover, as it seems plausible to me that pervasive incommensurability of values exists, I am open to the possibility that there is no conclusive correct answer to these questions.

Do I understand the rules and the character of the tutorial system, including what is important and significant about it in terms of my own job and my duties to students? I think that I do. Indeed, I believe that I could and did make such indirectly evaluative assessments of aspects of the tutorial system during my first few years of teaching in it, and diligently fulfilled my duties to the students, when I certainly had no time to consider the value or goodness of the system, or whether my new employers were doing the right thing in persisting with it.

(iii) Example 3: law's authority claim

As has been emphasized throughout this book, law is a complex and multifaceted phenomenon, and theories of law, in order to be successful, must select just some aspects of law upon which to focus.[31] One such aspect which has received much theoretical attention is law's authority claim. Law has been regarded by a variety of legal philosophers as making a claim to be authoritative, and to provide us with reasons for action which stem in significant part from its status as law. Theories highlighting this feature of law often take it to be a mark of law's claim to authority that it requires us to do as it says because it says so:

> Obedience is not a matter of doing what someone tells you to do. It is a matter of doing what he tells you to do *because he tells you to do it*. Legitimate, or de jure, authority thus concerns the grounds and sources of moral obligation.[32]
>
> [m]arking a rule as legally binding is marking it as an authoritative ruling. This marking-off of authoritative rulings indicates the existence in that society of an institution or organization claiming authority over members of the society that is holding them bound to conform to certain standards just because they were singled out by that purported authority regardless of whether or not they are justifiable standards on other grounds.[33]
>
> In any event, authority is useless for the common good unless the stipulations of those in authority ... are treated as exclusionary reasons, i.e. as sufficient reason for acting notwithstanding that the subjects would not themselves have made the same stipulation and indeed considers the actual stipulation to be in some respect(s) unreasonable.[34]

According to such views, law's claim to authority is an important and significant feature of law to explain. I agree with these theorists on this point, although, given the focus of this book, I cannot argue in support of it here.[35] Rather, I offer it as an example to illustrate two things:

(1) that in the domain of theorizing about law, it is possible to make indirectly evaluative judgements concerning the importance and significance of a given feature of law, without these judgements containing or

---

[31] See especially the discussion in ch 4.
[32] RP Wolff, In Defense of Anarchism (Harper & Row 1970) ch 1 9.
[33] J Raz, 'Legal Positivism and the Sources of Law' in J Raz, The Authority of Law (2nd edn, OUP 2009) 51.
[34] Finnis (n 9) 351–52.
[35] See further the discussion in s 3(a) of this chapter.

entailing directly evaluative judgements of the moral value or justifiability of the feature of law in question, and

(2) that, sometimes, these judgements of importance and significance rest on the fact that the feature of law picked out is *relevant* to eventual direct evaluations of it in terms of its moral value or justifiability, but that such relevance can be ascertained without yet making such direct evaluations.

To explain further: law's claim that we ought to put aside our own judgement of the merits of some course of action and do as law requires because law requires it clearly has an impact on our autonomy, and upon our practical reasoning processes. If we accept law's claim then it would seem that, in some sense, we are ceding some of our autonomy as regards matters falling within the scope of law's authority, and are no longer acting on our own assessment of what the balance of reasons requires. The existence, and character, of law's claim to authority is important because of its bearing on and relevance to these morally significant matters. The character of law's claim reveals the manner in which it purports to bear upon our practical reasoning, and the way in which this impinges upon our autonomy and upon the exercise of our capacities to deliberate, judge things for ourselves, and act on the conclusions of our deliberations. This renders law's claim to authority important, and morally relevant, and gives us reason as legal philosophers to try to pin down and understand this claim further. To do so is also to engage in the first stage of an inquiry which can then later go on to consider, inter alia: when (if ever), and on what grounds, law's authority claim is justified and when (if ever) we ought to do as law says because law says so.

Moreover, the idea that 'first stage' indirectly evaluative judgements concerning the *importance* of law's claim to authority can be made prior to, and, in some sense, *relatively* independent of,[36] 'second stage' directly evaluative judgements concerning whether and when the claim is true, gains plausibility from the fact that quite different 'second stage' positions are held by legal philosophers who agree on the 'first stage' judgements of importance and significance.

Robert Paul Wolff famously contends that law's authority claim is never justified, and that we ought never to do as law (or indeed any purported authority) says because it says so. According to his view, if we accept something as an

---

[36] This point is discussed further in s 3 of the current chapter, and in ch 8.

authority and act accordingly, we unacceptably relinquish our duties to act as autonomous rational agents.[37]

Joseph Raz reaches a different directly evaluative conclusion. On his view, law's claim to authority can *sometimes* be true, and we who are subject to law can *sometimes* be justified in doing as law says because law says so. The justification conditions are given by Raz's 'normal justification thesis': we are justified in accepting law's claim to authority when we will do better at acting in accordance with those reasons that apply to us anyway when we follow the purportedly authoritative directive than if we try to follow those reasons directly.[38]

Both Wolff and Raz, however, proceed from similar analyses of the importance and character of authority claims. As the quotations from their work mentioned above indicate, both theorists maintain that accepting a person or institution as having practical authority is a matter of doing as that person or institution requires *because they so require it*.[39] For Raz, this feature of law is highly significant as regards law's ability to play a mediating role between people and the reasons which apply to them. It marks the fact that the function of an authority is to sum up, balance, and replace the reasons which apply to people anyway, and that, when the conditions for the justification of authority are met, people are then meant to take their cue from what the authority requires because it so requires it, rather than themselves going back to, deliberating on, and acting on their own judgement of, the reasons that apply to them anyway.[40] For Wolff, the 'because it so requires it' feature of practical authority of the kind claimed by law is important because of the impact on our autonomy which he believes ensues if we accept authority claims on the terms on which they are made.[41] Raz and Wolff hence both proceed from very similar understandings of the character of claims to authority, and both regard the 'because it so requires it' condition as vitally important, before reaching very different conclusions as to whether, and, if so, under what circumstances, such claims can be justified.

The three examples discussed in subsections (i) to (iii) above tell strongly in favour of the possibility of staged inquiry wherein indirectly evaluative judgements about the importance and significance of certain features of some phenomenon are made prior to and, in some sense, *relatively* independent of,

---

[37] See Wolff (n 32) ch 1.
[38] See eg J Raz, The Morality of Freedom (Clarendon Press 1986), chs 2, 3, 4, 14, and 15; J Raz, 'The Obligation to Obey: Revision and Tradition' and J Raz, 'Authority, Law, and Morality' both in Raz, *Ethics in the Public Domain* (n 17).
[39] See nn 32 and 33 and accompanying text.
[40] See Raz, 'Authority, Law, and Morality' in Raz, *Ethics in the Public Domain* (n 17) s I.
[41] Wolff (n 32) ch 1.

directly evaluative judgements of whether those features are good or valuable. It should be noted, however, that the relative independence of each stage does not mean that the stages are unconnected. Indeed, adopting a staged inquiry approach to understanding law is helpful in facilitating and advancing our eventual inquiries into what may be good, and valuable, about it, in a manner which lessens certain of the risks we might otherwise run.[42]

(b) Supporting indirectly evaluative judgements in staged inquiry

A further question presents itself as regards the indirectly evaluative judgements which I contend legal philosophers should undertake in the first stage of their inquiries: on what basis are these judgements to be made? What lends support to a judgement that X feature of law is important and significant to explain? In discussing the three examples above, I began to illustrate, or at least to hint at, some possible answers, albeit tailored to the particularities of the phenomena considered. In the academic dress example, I suggested that aspects of it were important to explain because they bear upon the vital matter of students being able to complete university examinations whilst avoiding disciplinary measures. I also suggested that aspects of the phenomenon are important due to the guidance role envisaged for colleges, and for college tutors, and because of the implications of this for the job duties of any academic holding the kind of post that I do in the University of Oxford. In the tutorial teaching system example, I drew attention to features of the system that are important because they have a bearing on the quality of the working lives of those students and tutors participating in it, and features of the system which would be relevant to assessing whether it possesses sufficient educational value to be worth persisting with when its negative qualities are also taken into account. In the case of law's claim to authority, I highlighted aspects of this claim that are important to explain due to their bearing on law's ability to impinge on things that matters deeply to us: our practical rationality; our autonomy; our capacity to decide for ourselves what we ought to do.

We can still ask, however, whether there is anything *general* to be said about the basis or bases on which we make indirectly evaluative judgements of the kind that feature in IELP. While, as the discussion thus far indicates, and as I have considered in previous work,[43] there may be several factors supporting

---

[42] These points are explored further in the remainder of this chapter, and in ch 8.
[43] See Dickson, *Evaluation and Legal Theory* (n 2) 58–65.

the making of indirectly evaluative judgements, in the context of the aims of the present work—to explore the character of IELP and situate it within the landscape of theorizing about law—one factor can be emphasized as having key importance. Indirectly evaluative judgements are made on the basis that they pick out and direct our attention towards understanding those features of law which are relevant to eventual direct evaluations of law's moral goodness, justifiability, and obligatoriness.[44]

This is so because of the kind of thing that law is, and the effects it both purports to and can have on the lives of those living under it. As I emphasized in Chapter 5, law does not approach us in a neutral manner. Rather, it comes at us claiming to state what ought to be done and claiming that it is justified in so doing. Law also claims for itself the right to authorize the use of coercion against those who do not comply with its view of what ought to be done. Furthermore, as was highlighted in Chapters 5 and 6, law operates via social institutions and processes. The social reality of law manifests itself not as an ideal or as an abstraction but as a socially instantiated institutionalized normative system. Because of this, law can reach deep and wide into whole swathes of our lives and can use a host of compliance techniques if we fail to act in accordance with its directives. The examples discussed in Chapter 6 regarding the effect various laws can have on the lives of LGBT individuals in various jurisdictions, including subjecting them to lengthy terms of imprisonment, and, in some jurisdictions, to corporal or even capital punishment, should bring this home to us in stark terms.[45]

That law has these features and operates in this manner means that it is vitally important—at an appropriate stage in our inquiries—to ask directly evaluative questions of it regarding its moral value, justifiability, and obligatoriness. Given how pervasive and far-reaching law's effects can be, it is crucial that we—we citizens, lawyers, legal officials, and legal philosophers—hold law to account in virtue of the kind of thing that it is and according to the standards to which it ought to be held. Indeed, as was discussed in Chapter 5, and as is further explored in Chapter 8, we do not fully understand law unless we understand those values and ideals to which it aspires—as well as those aspects of its social reality which endure irrespective of whether it reaches them.

---

[44] In addition to the present discussion, I have also emphasized this point in those works cited in n 2 above, and in J Dickson, 'Methodology in Legal Philosophy' in M Carpentier (ed), *Meta-theory of Law* (forthcoming 2022), to be published in French by ISTE Editions, and in English by Wiley Press. This point is also highlighted by several of those theorists identified previously as adopting a methodological stance akin to my own. See eg Sugarman (n 16) 288; Raz, 'The Morality of Obedience' (n 17) 735; Waluchow, *Inclusive Legal Positivism* (n 18) ch 2.

[45] See ch 6 s 3(b).

Indirectly evaluative legal philosophy proceeds by picking out, focusing on, and understanding the character of those features of law which are of relevance to an eventual assessment of it in terms of those standards it ought to live up to. It is vital to appreciate—and, as I discuss in Chapter 8, it is often greatly underappreciated—that the indirectly evaluative approach to legal philosophy is acutely intensely interested in asking and attempting to answer questions such as whether law possesses certain distinctive moral values, whether law serves a particular moral purpose, whether law's claim to authority over us is ever justified, and, if so, in virtue of what, and whether, morally speaking, we ought to obey the law. As the final tenet of the IELP approach mentioned at the outset of Chapter 5 states: IELP aims to facilitate and engender moral and other evaluation, criticism and reform of law, tasks which are a vital part of legal philosophy, and which have significant relations of continuity and complementarity with the task of identifying and explaining law's nature.[46]

The issue, then, is not *whether* such matters should be explored, but *the route we should take* in exploring them. The claim of IELP is that the route should be indirect, and that the investigations along that route should proceed in stages. Indirectly evaluative judgements at the first stage of inquiry are made on the basis that they pick out and explain those aspects of law that are important, significant, and relevant in terms of subjecting law to appropriate directly evaluative scrutiny at a later stage. But why proceed thus? Why is 'the indirect route' the appropriate way to arrive—eventually—at the directly evaluative questions of law's value, justifiability, and obligatoriness?

3. The Advantages of the Indirectly Evaluative Approach to Legal Philosophy

(a) These arguments and their limits

Before offering my view of the advantages of elucidating law via the staged inquiry route of IELP, it is important to acknowledge some of the limitations of the arguments that follow. There are limits as regards how conclusive certain of the arguments in this book can be for the reason that it is not possible in a work focused on methodology in legal philosophy to also develop and defend my own theory of the nature of law as regards all those features of law that I refer to

---

[46] See ch 5, s 1, tenet 6.

and/or use as examples.[47] This point is particularly pertinent, because, as I have sought to explain in previous work,[48] and as I re-iterate here, I view questions of methodology and questions of substance in legal philosophy as being intricately linked. To illustrate further by way of contrast, consider two possible models of the relation of methodological stances to the theories of law which those stances support. According to Model 1, the correctness of a given methodological approach is independent of, and can be ascertained prior to, the correctness of the substantive account of aspects of law's nature which rests upon that methodology. If this model held good, it would be possible to adjudicate between alternative jurisprudential methodologies on purely methodological grounds. The success of a theory of certain aspects of law's nature would then be dependent on its at least employing what has, on methodological grounds, been determined to be the correct jurisprudential methodology. However, on an alternative model—Model 2—the relation between a given methodological approach, and the substantive account of aspects of the nature of law that it supports, is more holistic and mutually reinforcing. On this view, jurisprudential methodologies and the theories of law that employ them must be evaluated together, and each can derive support from the other. On this model, a given methodology can receive support from the theory that employs it: for example (and it is only an example for the purposes of illustration) it can receive support to the extent that the theory employing it accords with our pre-theoretical understanding of the phenomenon in question.[49]

In my view, something along the lines of Model 2 most plausibly captures how things stand as regards the relation between a given jurisprudential methodology, and the theory of aspects of the nature of law which employs that methodology. This being so, there are limits to the conclusiveness of some of the arguments offered in this book—including those in the remainder of this chapter—because I do not (and cannot, within the confines of the current work) offer my own fully-fledged substantive theory of relevant aspects of the nature of law alongside my view of the jurisprudential methodology—IELP— that I believe legal philosophers should adopt. Another way to put this—to mangle a saying more than somewhat—is to say that the proof of the methodological pudding is in the producing of illuminating and persuasive accounts of aspects of the nature of law.[50]

---

[47] See eg n 35 and accompanying text.
[48] See Dickson, *Evaluation and Legal Theory* (n 2) ch 1, s B.
[49] This is not intended as an in-depth discussion of the various possibilities in this regard. My aim is only to illustrate some factors affecting how conclusive certain of the arguments in this book can be.
[50] An entertaining explanation of this saying is available at https://www.phrases.org.uk/meanings/proof-of-the-pudding.html.

I regard it as important in a work focused on the philosophy of legal philosophy to be aware of these points, but also not to overstate them. This book does offer arguments on aspects of the substance of law's nature, including, for example, on its character as a social and institutional fact, and on aspects of its relations with morality. It contends, for example, that failing to realize any moral purpose that law may have does not thereby render it any less law.[51] Moreover, some of the arguments offered tell in favour of and provide support for, other of my views on aspects of the substance of law's nature, such as law's existence conditions and identification conditions—matters which I have also written about elsewhere.[52] In addition, even if sometimes non-conclusive, arguments can offer us interesting and persuasive food for thought on the matters they concern, and, as I noted in Chapter 4, part of the strength of jurisprudential inquiry, and an indicator of progress within it, is its ability to open up, explore, and highlight the importance of yet further questions that we cannot yet answer, or cannot yet answer within our current work.[53]

(b) Mitigating risks and advancing consideration of what law ought to be

IELP, with its commitment to 'staged inquiry' can mitigate some significant risks as regards our attempts to elucidate law and can appropriately facilitate and advance consideration of what law ought to be, and of those standards to which law should be held in critically evaluating it. The first risk which the staged inquiry approach helps to mitigate is that of being too quick to credit law with the moral value, authority, and obligatoriness that it claims. As is noted both earlier in this chapter,[54] and in Chapter 5 in discussing the desideratum that legal philosophers adopt an attitude of due wariness in approaching law,[55] law does not approach us in a neutral manner. Rather, it comes at us claiming to state what ought to be done and claiming that it is justified in so doing. Law presents itself as a valuable and justified phenomenon which ought

---

[51] See ch 5, and ch 6 especially s 3.
[52] See eg J Dickson, 'Is the Rule of Recognition Really a Conventional Rule?' (2007) 27(3) *Oxford Journal of Legal Studies* 373; J Dickson, 'The Idea of a Legal System: Between the Real and the Ideal' in N Walker (ed), MacCormick's Scotland (Edinburgh University Press 2012); J Dickson, 'Legal Positivism: Contemporary Debates' in Andrei Marmor (ed), The Routledge Companion to Philosophy of Law (Routledge 2012); J Dickson, 'Towards a Theory of European Union Legal Systems' in J Dickson and P Eleftheriadis (eds), Philosophical Foundations of European Union Law (OUP 2012).
[53] See ch 4, especially s 3.
[54] See s 2(b).
[55] See ch 5, s 5.

to be understood as such, and ought to be obeyed on the terms in which it presents itself. If we accept law's claims at face value, and especially if we do so at too early a point in our inquiries into its character, there is a risk that we may fail to see it as it really is and may fail to make sufficient space to consider whether law possesses all, or perhaps any, of the qualities it claims for itself. The staged inquiry approach of IELP mitigates that risk, allows us that space for consideration, and enables us to begin to identify and explain law's distinctive properties whilst leaving it—for now—an open question what, if any, moral value, moral authority, or moral obligatoriness, it possesses. The IELP approach hence makes room for thoughts such as the following, and for investigation into the important matters that the legal philosophers whose thoughts they are rightly draw to our attention:

> [Dworkin] is saying any worthwhile jurisprudence is a blend of description and moral evaluation - it's got to show the law in its best light. Why not show it in the worst light?[56]
>
> *wherever there is law*—new moral risks emerge as a matter of necessity. There are not only more efficient forms of oppression, there are also new vices: the alienation of community and value, the loss of transparency, the rise of a new hierarchy, and the possibility that some who should resist injustice may be bought off by the goods that legal order (in some cases, necessarily) brings.[57]

Stemming in part from my views—noted in section 3(a) above—regarding the interdependence of methodological approaches and the substance of the theories of law they support, I cannot conclusively argue that *only* the IELP approach can mitigate the risk outlined above and can make space for consideration of the matters that Hart and Green draw to our attention. It is the case, however, that several of the DELP approaches considered in this book provide evidence that this risk is real and actualized. As I have argued in the present chapter and the two which preceded it, John Finnis, Ronald Dworkin, and Mark Greenberg are proponents of DELP, who insist that the directly evaluative judgements about law they make in their theories yield the conclusion that law's inherent moral qualities are positive in character. Finnis holds that only law can bring about the conditions of valuable human flourishing in political

---

[56] Sugarman (n 16) 288.
[57] L Green, 'Positivism and the Inseparability of Law and Morals' (2008) 83 *New York University Law Review* 1035, 1054.

societies. Dworkin contends that law upholds individual rights and responsibilities and ensures that citizens are only subject to state coercion under conditions where this is morally justified. Greenberg regards legal obligations as a subset of moral obligations: they tell us what we have moral reason to do. In approaching law asking as their primary question(s) from the outset: what is law such that it can justify the application of state force against individuals? (Dworkin); what is law such that it necessarily establishes a presumptive general moral obligation to obey it? (Finnis); what is law such that its obligations are a subset of moral obligations and that law is the moral impact of actions of legal institutions? (Greenberg), these proponents of DELP load the dice significantly in favour of law living up to the claims it makes, and do not allow their jurisprudential inquiries the space or the possibility to come to a negative or neutral conclusion in moral terms about these facets of law. Indeed in Dworkin's case, there appears to be a sort of intellectual hostility to anyone who tries to explore such possibilities: he claims that the first and main duty of legal philosophers is to seek to justify law, and to put it in its best light, and that anyone doing otherwise is either being disingenuous or has shady political aims.[58] As Hart and Green's points above remind us, however, there is nothing wrong with legal philosophers asking whether law has facets which are, or which at least run the risk of, being necessarily *bad*. Indeed, and as I explored in the context of the work of Bentham, Hart, and Raz in Chapter 5, there is nothing wrong with, and much that is positive in, legal philosophy taking a key part of its task to be exploring and exposing such matters.[59]

This first risk that the IELP staged inquiry approach helps to mitigate is, in a sense, two risks in one: (i) the risk of being too quick to accord to law the moral value and obligatoriness it claims for itself, and (ii) the risk of not leaving sufficient time and space for legal philosophers to consider whether aspects of law's nature are, or run the risk of being, morally bad. To this we can add a further important point: mitigating these risks is particularly at a premium in the case of law. Law is a wide-ranging and far-reaching practical normative phenomenon which claims authority over us in many morally significant areas of our lives. If we are too quick to accept its claims as true, then we may also be too quick to jump when it calls, and to do that which it asks of us. This comes with

---

[58] See Dworkin (n 11) 271–74, where Dworkin contends that: 'Nothing is easier or more pointless than demonstrating that a flawed and contradictory account fits as well as a smoother and more attractive one. The internal skeptic must show that the flawed and contradictory account is the only one available' (at 274), and then accuses some proponents of the Critical Legal Studies movement of seeking '[t]o show law in its worst rather than its best light, to show avenues closed that are in fact open, to move toward a new mystification in service of undisclosed political goals' (at 275).

[59] See ch 5, s 5.

its own morally weighty set of risks and consequences, as I have argued in previous work, and as both Hart and Raz remind us:

> Wicked men will enact wicked rules which others will enforce. What surely is most needed in order to make men clear-sighted in confronting the official abuse of power, is that they should preserve the sense that the certification of something as legally valid is not conclusive of the question of obedience, and that, however great the aura of majesty or authority which the official system may have, its demands must in the end be submitted to a moral scrutiny.[60]
>
> There are risks, moral and other, in uncritical acceptance of authority. Too often in the past, the fallibility of human judgment has led to submission to authority from a misguided sense of duty where this was a morally reprehensible attitude.[61]

A further risk which the IELP staged inquiry approach can help to mitigate is that of failing to do adequate justice to the social fact properties of law in our theoretical accounts of it. The DELP accounts of Dworkin, Finnis, and Greenberg each manifest this risk, and, in my view, it is neither a coincidence, nor unrelated to their methodological approach, that they do so. As was discussed above, these accounts maintain that their inquiries into the nature of law must begin with and be shaped by certain directly evaluative questions: what is law such that it can justify the application of state force against individuals? (Dworkin); what is law such that it necessarily establishes a presumptive moral obligation to obey it? (Finnis); what is law such that its obligations are a subset of moral obligations and that law is the moral impact of actions of legal institutions? (Greenberg). They each then produce a theoretical account which regards law as morally justified and as establishing the moral obligations that it claims to. But they do so at a cost: the cost of relegating to a 'not law' or 'not really law' status any phenomena constituted as law by the relevant social and institutional facts, but which does not live up to the moral values they contend that law must have:

> [w]e have no difficulty in understanding someone who does say that *Nazi law was not really law*, or was law in a degenerate sense, was less than fully law.[62]

---

[60] HLA Hart, *The Concept of Law* (3rd edn, OUP 2012) 210.
[61] J Raz, 'The Obligation to Obey: Revision and Tradition' in Raz, *Ethics in the Public Domain* (n 17) 351. See also Dickson, 'Legal Positivism: Contemporary Debates' (n 52) s 2(c).
[62] Dworkin (n 11) 103–104 (my emphasis).

Posited (enacted or judicially pronounced) rules of the latter kind [unreasonable laws whose moral claim over us is defeated] are analogous to contracts which have been made in full compliance with every formality and other procedural condition specified by the law of contract but are void for illegality. Or, to take two perhaps closer analogies, they are like medicines which prove futile or lethal and are thus not medicinal at all, or like arguments whose formal elegance only masks their invalidity: no argument. *Unjust laws are not laws*, though they may still count in reasonable conscientious deliberations, and certainly warrant attention and description.[63]

Because my theory holds that the law is a certain part of the moral profile, my theory has the consequence that the *law can never include truly evil norms*. Such norms can never be part of the moral profile.[64]

As I argued in Chapters 5 and 6, it is vital that our theories of law do adequate justice to law's social fact properties—such as the social and institutional facts by which law is created, modified, applied, and enforced—and to the significance and importance of how those properties are understood by, and impact upon the lives of, those living under law. The IELP staged inquiry approach respects this constraint. Social fact properties of law are picked out as important and significant by means of indirectly evaluative judgements in the first stage of inquiry. Then, at a later stage in the inquiry, we can explore and come to a view on how various of those properties impact upon the moral value, worth, accountability, and obligatoriness, of aspects of law. Moreover, as the staged inquiry approach picks out various of law's social fact properties as significant and important at the first stage of inquiry, and as that approach leaves open until a later stage in the inquiry whether law has any of the moral value or obligatoriness that it claims, it does not the run the risk of brushing under the theoretical carpet inconvenient facts about law and instances of law—such as the laws criminalizing homosexuality sadly still so prevalent around the world that I discussed in Chapter 6[65]—which do not fit the morally valuable picture of law certain DELP theories are wedded to. This is a risk which it is important to mitigate if we are to do justice to law *as it is* not as we wish it might be, and if we are to do justice to its impact upon the lives those living under it.

The IELP staged inquiry approach can help to mitigate the above risks. But the advantages of it do not stop at risk mitigation. For this approach is also

---

[63] Finnis (n 7) 114 (my emphasis).
[64] Greenberg (n 10) 1337 (my emphasis). As I argued in ch 6 s 3(b), Greenberg's stance must in fact deny the status of law to a significantly wider category than 'truly evil norms'.
[65] See ch 6, s 3(b).

capable of appropriately and effectively advancing consideration of what law ought to be, and which values and standards law should be held to. As this chapter has demonstrated, it is possible for legal philosophers to make indirectly evaluative judgements of the importance and significance of certain features of law prior to and relatively independent of making directly evaluative judgements concerning the moral worth and justifiability of those features. Such indirectly evaluative judgements can be made on the basis that they pick out those features of law which are relevant to its eventual moral evaluation. IELP hence focuses and facilitates consideration of what law ought to be, and of those standards to which law should be held, in a way which does not run the risk of prejudging these matters, or of allowing our views of how law ought to be to cloud our understanding of what it is. These points are explored further in this book's final chapter.

8
Continuity and Complementarity in Legal Philosophy

1. Introduction

This chapter continues the task of exploring various aspects of indirectly evaluative legal philosophy (IELP). Following on from the discussions in Chapter 7, it considers further the relationship between the IELP approach, and the asking and answering of what I have termed directly evaluative questions concerning the moral value, justification, and obligatoriness of law. As I have discussed already, I embrace the idea that legal philosophy is a 'broad church' in the sense of including within its ambit many different theoretical inquiries regarding law.[1] This discussion which follows brings out one important sense in which the IELP approach embraces this point. As indicated by its sixth tenet, IELP aims to focus, facilitate, and engender moral and other evaluation, criticism, and reform of law, tasks which are a vital part of legal philosophy, and which have significant relations of continuity and of complementarity with the task of identifying and explaining law's nature.[2]

Some critics of the methodological approach that I advocate strongly disagree, however, and charge that approach with being intellectually isolationist and insular in character. In keeping with my reasons for writing this book,[3] it is important to acknowledge and engage with such challenges, which I do in section 2 below. Having defended IELP from the charges levelled at it by certain of its critics, I then turn in section 3 to explore further the point with which Chapter 7 closed: the sense in which the IELP approach can aid and advance consideration of issues such as how law ought to be, those standards to which law ought to be held, and the conditions, if any, under which it is morally valuable and ought to be obeyed. Section 4 brings the book to its conclusion.

---

[1] See ch 3, ss 1 and 2; ch 4, ss 3 and 4. See also J Dickson, 'Ours Is a Broad Church: Indirectly Evaluative Legal Philosophy as a Facet of Jurisprudential Inquiry' (2015) 6 *Jurisprudence* 207.
[2] See ch 5, s 1, where I outline the six tenets of IELP.
[3] See ch 1, s 3.

Elucidating Law. Julie Dickson, Oxford University Press. © Julie Dickson 2022.
DOI: 10.1093/oso/9780198727767.003.0008

2. Some Challenges Considered

Some theorists would regard my contention that IELP is committed to the task of focusing and facilitating the moral evaluation of law with considerable scepticism. An accusation not infrequently made is that theories of law which seek first to identify and explain aspects of law's nature without yet taking a stance on law's moral value, justification, or obligatoriness are thereby guilty of a pernicious insularity, and of problematically truncating the ambit of legal philosophical inquiry.

This line of thought features strongly in Ronald Dworkin's defence of his own methodological approach and in his critical appraisal of certain other methodological approaches:

> They [legal philosophers who defend versions of legal positivism, such as Jules Coleman and Joseph Raz] make little attempt to connect their philosophy of law either to political philosophy generally or to substantive legal practice, scholarship, or theory...
>
> ... I now suspect that at least part of the explanation is to be found in the appeal not of positivism as a theory of law, but of legal philosophy as an independent, self-contained subject and profession. Positivists since Hart (including Hart in the Postscript to his book, *The Concept of Law*, which was published after his death) have defended with great fervor a guild-claim: that their work is conceptual and descriptive in a way that distinguishes it from a variety of other crafts and professions. On their understanding, legal philosophy is distinct not only from the actual practice of law, but also from the academic study of substantive and procedural fields of law because both practice and academic study are about the laws of some particular jurisdiction, whereas legal philosophy is about law in general. It is also distinct from and independent of normative political philosophy because it is conceptual and descriptive rather than substantive and normative ... It is, in short, a discipline that can be pursued on its own with neither background experience nor training in or even familiarity with any literature or research beyond its own narrow world and few disciples.[4]

---

[4] R Dworkin, 'Thirty Years On: A Book Review of Jules Coleman's *The Practice of Principle: In Defence of a Pragmatist Approach to Legal Theory*' (2002) *115 Harvard Law Review* 1655, 1678–79 (internal footnote reference omitted).

Dworkin is not alone in at least some of his views:

> An unsound jurisprudential method will seek to banish the question [how does injustice affect the obligation to obey the law?], in some of its senses, to 'another discipline.'[5]
>
> The mark of contemporary analytic jurisprudence is its intellectual isolation.[6]
>
> [t]he artificial boundary between political theory and legal philosophy which I have been deploring in this chapter has meant that the jurisprudence of theorists like Plato, Cicero, Machiavelli, Hobbes, Locke, Hume, Kant, Hegel, and Savigny, is largely neglected.
>
> I have heard it said that this is a good thing: it means we can study the problems of legal philosophy directly, undistracted by a purely antiquarian interest in the history of ideas. But these analytic discussions tend to be flat and repetitive in consequence, revolving in smaller and smaller circles among a diminishing band of acolytes. Worse still, they are in danger of becoming uninterestingly parochial from a philosophical point of view, as we distance ourselves from the intellectual resources that would enable us to grasp conceptions of law and controversies about law other than our own.[7]

Do any of these charges stick against the methodological approach I champion? The 'guild-exclusivity' charge was discussed and repelled in Chapter 3.[8] What of the related charge(s) of intellectual isolationism and neglect of cognate disciplines? An important initial question, of course, is: which theorists are supposed to be guilty of these charges, and as regards which aspects of their work? In the passage quoted above and in much of the article from which it is drawn, Dworkin singles out Jules Coleman and Joseph Raz as targets for his criticism.[9] Other critics are somewhat opaque as regards their intended targets, but earlier in this book I claimed that—in addition to Raz—Les Green, HLA Hart, and Wil Waluchow also espouse an IELP-type methodological

---

[5] J Finnis, Natural Law and Natural Rights (2nd edn, OUP 2011) 354.
[6] D Priel, 'Positivism and the Separation of Law and Jurisprudence' 1 http://papers.ssrn.com/sol3/papers.cfm?abstract_id=1951912.
[7] J Waldron, 'Legal and Political Philosophy' in J Coleman and S Shapiro (eds), The Oxford Handbook of Jurisprudence and Philosophy of Law (OUP 2002) 380. See also SR Perry, 'Method and Principle in Legal Theory' (book review of Jules Coleman, *The Practice of Principle: In Defence of a Pragmatist Approach to Legal Theory* (2002) 111 *Yale Law Journal* 1757, especially at 1809–13; M Köpcke Tinturé, 'Positive Law's Moral Purpose(s): Towards a New Consensus?' (2011) 56 *American Journal of Jurisprudence* 183; N Stoljar, 'In Praise of Wishful Thinking: A Critique of Descriptive-Explanatory Theories of Law' (2012) 6 *Problema: anuario de filosofía y teoría del derecho* 51, especially s III.
[8] See ch 3, s 2.
[9] See n 4 and accompanying text.

approach.[10] Can any of these theorists plausibly be accused of intellectual isolationism and/or of failing to engage with work in disciplines such as political philosophy or substantive legal scholarship?

Raz has written extensively in both political philosophy and in moral philosophy, as well as in legal philosophy, in a variety of works throughout his long career.[11] Green's work is of impressive breadth: he has written on the justification of the authority of the state, on political obligation and the duties and limits of government, and on particular doctrinal areas of law such as taxation and marriage and the effect that their structure, content, and justifications have on our societies and on lives lived within them.[12] Hart, in addition to practising law as a Chancery barrister, spent a significant portion of his academic career thinking about and writing about matters such as causation in the law,[13] mens rea in criminal law,[14] the nature and justification of punishment,[15] and the proper moral and other limits of legal intervention in our lives.[16] Waluchow's work on constitutionalism engages significantly with theories and themes in political philosophy, and mounts arguments drawing on, and embedded within, the constitutional law, theory, and doctrines of various jurisdictions.[17] Coleman spent a considerable part of his academic career writing about contract law and tort law and engaging with their theoretical underpinnings.[18] Given the volume of clear counter-evidence, seemingly groundless accusations

---

[10] See ch 7, especially s 1.

[11] Raz's voluminous publication list can be found at https://sites.google.com/site/josephnraz/publicationlist. To mention but a few examples see eg J Raz, The Morality of Freedom (Clarendon Press 1986); J Raz, 'Liberty and Trust' in RP George (ed), Natural Law, Liberalism, and Morality (OUP 1996); J Raz, Engaging Reason: On the Theory of Value and Action (OUP 1999); J Raz, 'Agency and Luck' in U Heuer and G Lang (eds), Luck, Value and Commitment: Themes from the Ethics of Bernard Williams (OUP 2012); J Raz, 'Intention and Value' (2017) 20 Philosophical Explorations 109.

[12] See eg L Green, 'Are Language Rights Fundamental?' (1987) 25 Osgoode Hall Law Journal 639; L Green, The Authority of the State (Clarendon Press 1990); L Green, 'Concepts of Equity in Taxation' in A Maslove (ed), Fairness in Taxation: Exploring the Principles (University of Toronto Press 1993); L Green, 'The Duty to Govern' (2007) 13 Legal Theory 165; L Green, 'Sex-Neutral Marriage' (2011) 64 Current Legal Problems 1.

[13] HLA Hart and T Honoré, Causation in the Law (1st edn, Clarendon Press 1959; 2nd edn, Clarendon Press 1985).

[14] HLA Hart, 'Negligence, Mens Rea, and Criminal Responsibility' in HLA Hart, Punishment and Responsibility: Essays in the Philosophy of Law (1st edn, Clarendon Press 1968; 2nd edn, OUP 2008).

[15] See eg HLA Hart, 'Essays I, III, V, VII, and IX' in HLA Hart, Punishment and Responsibility: Essays in the Philosophy of Law (1st edn, Clarendon Press 1968; 2nd edn, OUP 2008).

[16] See eg HLA Hart, Law, Liberty, and Morality (Stanford University Press 1963); HLA Hart, The Morality of the Criminal Law (OUP 1965).

[17] See eg W Waluchow, A Common Law Theory of Judicial Review: The Living Tree (CUP 2007); W Waluchow, 'Constitutionalism in the European Union: Pipe Dream or Possibility?' in J Dickson and P Eleftheriadis (eds), Philosophical Foundations of European Union Law (OUP 2012); W Waluchow, 'Constitutional Rights and the Possibility of Detached Constructive Interpretation' (2015) 9 Problema anuario de filosofía y teoría del derecho 23.

[18] See eg JL Coleman, Markets, Morals, and the Law (CUP 1988; OUP 2002); JL Coleman, Risks and Wrongs (CUP 1992; OUP 2002).

such as those levelled by Dworkin in the passage quoted previously[19] cannot hope to persuade.

But could the charge of ignorant neglect of the literature and research in, for example, political philosophy and substantive legal scholarship be recast in more nuanced form? The concern then might not be that legal philosophers adopting an indirectly evaluative methodological approach lack knowledge of, and/or fail to engage with issues in neighbouring and cognate disciplines, but that when they engage with such matters they do not correctly perceive or sufficiently illuminate the connections between their legal philosophical stances, and their views in political philosophy or in areas of substantive legal scholarship.

Even this more subtle variation on a critical theme is not well-founded. For, *contra* its claims, the theorists whose work is mentioned above do not merely happen—in addition to their work in legal philosophy—also to have devoted significant portions of their careers to engaging in moral philosophy, political philosophy, and substantive or doctrinal legal scholarship. On the contrary, their work in legal philosophy and in these cognate fields is often deeply interlinked, and theses established in one area provide support for and shape the direction of their arguments in another area. Raz's views on the morally purposive role of the state, and on the scope of and reasons for the moral authority of its legal directives, stand in a relation of mutual support with Raz's 'exclusive legal positivist' espousal of the sources thesis, ie the view that the existence and content of the law can be fully determined by reference to social facts.[20] Leslie Green's work exhibits a standing ability skilfully to weave together and illuminate various connections between legal philosophy, political philosophy, and scholarship regarding particular areas of law and their operation in society. This pervasive feature of Green's work imbues it with particular richness and depth and is present within many of his writings. If a specific example is needed, then the knitting together of and deriving mutual support from and between arguments concerning aspects of the nature of law, arguments from work in legal sociology, points of moral philosophy and of political philosophy concerning the limits of state action, and arguments about what might be appropriate and beneficial legal regulation of sexual morality, including in doctrinal areas such as sexual assault legislation, which we find in his article

---

[19] See n 4 and accompanying text.
[20] There is voluminous literature on this relation of mutual support. For one statement of Raz's own view of it, see J Raz, 'Authority, Law, and Morality' in J Raz, *Ethics in the Public Domain* (Clarendon Press 1994); for some commentary see W Waluchow, 'Authority and the Practical Difference Thesis: A Defense of Inclusive Legal Positivism' (2000) 6 *Legal Theory* 45; E Himma, 'The Instantiation Thesis and Raz's Critique of Inclusive Positivism' (2001) 20 *Law and Philosophy* 61.

'Should Law Improve Morality?' amply provides it.[21] Both Hart himself, as well as commentators on his work, draw out the influences of aspects of his work in general jurisprudence on his work in normative jurisprudence and in substantive legal scholarship.[22] Waluchow's work on constitutional interpretation, and on the justification of certain varieties of judicial review is both framed by, and draws some of its justification from, his views on the nature of law, including aspects of his inclusive legal positivism.[23]

What of the charge that an IELP methodological approach truncates legal philosophical inquiry and banishes to other disciplines some of the most important questions about law's character? For reasons already discussed in Chapter 7, and which are illuminated further in the remainder of this chapter, I regard this charge, too, as false. IELP does hold that legal philosophical investigations into law's character should adopt what I refer to as 'staged inquiry'. During the first stage, legal philosophers make indirectly evaluative judgments concerning those features of law are important and significant to explain. However, they do so in significant part based on which features of law will be relevant to law's eventual evaluation in terms of its moral and/or other goodness. This being so, IELP can focus and facilitate inquiries into law's moral value, justification, and obligatoriness.[24]

Does this staged inquiry approach truncate legal philosophical inquiry and banish to other disciplines those vital questions to be asked in the second stage? To contend that it does would be a gross caricature of the IELP approach's commitments and aims. As was argued in Chapter 7[25] IELP holds that there are good reasons why inquiry into law's character should be conducted in stages. It contends that this approach can successfully aid and advance eventual inquiries into law's moral value, justification, and obligatoriness. Moreover, as is evidenced in the discussion above, many legal philosophers adopting an IELP approach do go on to engage in such inquiries. This is very far from the

---

[21] L Green, 'Should Law Improve Morality?' (2013) 7 *Criminal Law and Philosophy* 473. There are many more examples, and indeed in my view it is difficult to find an example of Green's work which does not feature interwoven arguments across neighbouring and cognate disciplinary areas.
[22] See eg HLA Hart, 'Prolegomenon to the Principles of Punishment' in HLA Hart, Punishment and Responsibility: Essays in the Philosophy of Law (1st edn, Clarendon Press 1968; 2nd edn, OUP 2008) 6–7; HLA Hart, 'Postscript: Responsibility and Retribution' in HLA Hart, Punishment and Responsibility: Essays in the Philosophy of Law (1st edn, Clarendon Press 1968; 2nd edn, OUP 2008) 226–27, 229; HLA Hart in conversation with David Sugarman by Oxford Academic (OUP) | Free Listening on SoundCloud; J Gardner, 'Hart on Legality, Justice, and Morality' in J Gardner, Law as a Leap of Faith (OUP 2012); MH Kramer and others, The Legacy of H.L.A. Hart: Legal, Political, and Moral Philosophy (OUP 2008) Introduction.
[23] See eg Waluchow, *A Common Law Theory of Judicial Review* (n 17), especially ch 5, ss B–E inclusive.
[24] See the discussion in ch 7, especially ss 2 and 3, and in the remainder of the present chapter.
[25] See ch 7, s 3.

picture painted by some critics of unjustified truncation of lines of inquiry and banishing of questions to another discipline. Indirectly evaluative inquiries into significant and important aspects of law's nature on the one hand, and inquiries into law's moral value, justification, and obligatoriness on the other are connected to, are in a sense continuous with, and serve to complement, one another.

3. IELP and Law as It Ought to Be

We can begin to highlight aspects of the complementarity that I have in mind by returning to an example which featured in Chapter 7: law's claim to authority, and certain theorists' views of whether, and, if so, under what conditions, this claim could be true. As was noted in the earlier discussion, a variety of legal philosophers view law as claiming to be authoritative and claiming to provide us with reasons for action which stem in significant part from its status as law.[26] According to such views, law's claim to authority is an important and significant feature of law to explain.

In Chapter 7, the focus of the discussion was on showing how it is possible for theorists such as Joseph Raz and Robert Paul Wolff to make indirectly evaluative judgements regarding the importance of law's claim to authority, and to analyse the character of that claim (and indeed to agree on certain parts of their analysis), without yet taking a stance on whether law's claim is ever true, and, if it is, under what conditions it is true. In the context of the current discussion, the focus is slightly different: this example can be used to illustrate how focusing in on certain of law's important and significant features at the first stage of inquiry can aid and advance consideration of how law ought to be, and of those values and standards law should be held to, at a later stage in the inquiry.

(a) Setting the standard

This line of thought runs as follows. As was discussed in Chapter 7, Raz and Wolff give very different answers to the morally evaluative question: 'when, and under what conditions, is law's claim to possess legitimate authority over us justified?' For Raz, the answer (roughly) is: sometimes, for some people, with regard to some laws, under certain conditions, ie when we will do better

---

[26] See ch 7, s 2(a)(ii).

at acting in accordance with those reasons that apply to us anyway when we follow the purportedly authoritative directives of the law than if we try to follow those reasons directly.[27] For philosophical anarchist Wolff, however, the answer is: never, because if we take law's directives to be authoritative over us, and do as law says because law says so, we unacceptably relinquish our duties to act autonomously.[28]

Raz and Wolff give very different answers to the directly evaluative question of when law's claim to authority is justified. But in both of their cases, the indirectly evaluative judgements they make concerning those features of law's authority claim which are important to explain, and their explanation of those features prior to considering the impact of the character of authority claims on questions of their value and justifiability, focus and aid their consideration of the latter.

Wolff's analysis of the important features of authority claims reveals that authorities demand that those subject to them do as they require *because they require it*.[29] This understanding brings into focus aspects of the standard which an authority must meet and aids our understanding of what it would be to accept something or someone as a practical authority in our lives: to take something as an authority on the terms in which it presents itself is to do as it says because it says so. With these points brought more clearly into focus, Wolff can then go on to ask the directly evaluative question: 'can it ever be morally justified, given our duties of autonomy, to do as law says because law says so?'—a question which he answers in the negative.

Raz's analysis of the character of reasons for action and of how such reasons interact in the situation of certain sorts of conflict proceeds from picking out important features of our self-understanding in the domain of our practical reasoning.[30] The analysis reveals that in addition to first order reasons, there also exist second order reasons to act for a reason or to refrain from acting for a reason. Raz argues that one category of second order reasons are exclusionary reasons: reasons to refrain from acting for a reason, and that purportedly authoritative directives are instances of exclusionary reasons, such that to take someone or something as having practical authority over us is to treat their directives as exclusionary reasons.[31] This understanding brings into focus

---

[27] See Raz, *The Morality of Freedom* (n 11) chs 2–4, 14, and 15; and Raz, 'Authority, Law and Morality' (n 20), especially s I for fuller explanation of what Raz terms the normal justification thesis.
[28] RP Wolff, In Defense of Anarchism (Harper & Row 1970) ch 1.
[29] ibid especially at 9.
[30] See J Raz, Practical Reason and Norms (Princeton University Press 1990 (reprint with new postscript; original edition by Hutchinson 1975)) 37–39.
[31] ibid 63–65.

the standard an authority must meet, and what it is to take something as an authority: it must somehow and under some conditions be justified to take authoritative directives as reasons to exclude acting on one's own view of the balance of first order reasons. With this analysis of the character of authoritative directives in hand, Raz can then go on to consider whether there are circumstances where it is justified to refrain from acting on our own view of the first order balance of reasons, and he concludes that this will be justified when we can better conform to right reason indirectly, by following an intermediary directive of an authority rather than trying to act directly in accordance with our own view of what we ought to do.[32]

For present purposes, the issue is not whether Wolff or Raz are correct in the answers they give.[33] Rather, their views can help to illuminate the way in which picking out as important to explain and analysing certain features of law in the first stage of inquiry can focus and facilitate engaging with those normative and justificatory questions to be asked and answered at a later stage. In the case of law's claim to authority, the first stage analysis furnishes us with the standard that law claims to be able to meet, and aids our understanding of what it would be for someone to take law as having authority over them. This being so, this first stage analysis helps to focus which morally evaluative questions it is important to ask of law, what it would be for law's claims to possess legitimate authority to be justified, and hence what it would be for law to meet one vitally important standard according to which it should be judged.

(b) Some clarifications

The discussion above further emphasizes that indirectly evaluative inquiries into aspects of law's nature are connected to, and complement, inquiries concerning law's moral value, justification, and obligatoriness. However, a few points of clarification are needed in order not to misstate matters.

First, although I have contended that, in the case of law's claim to authority, identifying and analysing important aspects of the character of that claim can assist in bringing into focus some of the standards that law ought to live up to, and in terms of which it should be judged, I am not contending that every feature of law which IELP may highlight and analyse has this character. Plausibly, some aspects of law—such as, for example, that its directives can be identified

---

[32] See further those works cited in n 27 above.
[33] See ch 7, s 3(b) for discussion of the limits of some of the arguments in this book.

ultimately by reference to social fact and not moral argument—are not such that they will furnish us with such normative standards.[34]

Furthermore, even in respect of those facets of law which can furnish us with some of the standards that law ought to live up to, I am not claiming that those aspects of law, or law as a whole, can or should *only* be evaluated in terms of those particular standards. Assume for the sake of argument that part of the nature of law is that it consists of directives which can be identified ultimately by reference to social facts, and that such directives claim, and aim, to have legitimate authority over us and to operate by attempting to exclude, and replace, some of the reasons for action we would otherwise have. Given these aspects of law's nature, *one of the* important normative standards law should be evaluated in terms of is whether it succeeds in being what it purports to be, ie whether and under what conditions it does have legitimate authority over us and does generate reasons for action of certain kinds. That normative standard, however, is not exhaustive of those standards that we can, and, depending on the purposes of our inquiry, should, evaluate law in terms of. We may also want to ask, for example, whether law treats those subject to it in a dignified and humane way, and we can evaluate it in terms of the extent to which it exhibits these qualities. We can also ask and evaluate whether a legal system is worthy of the respect of those subject to it, and whether it is something with which they can appropriately identify, feel pride in, and regard themselves as belonging to.[35] The claim in sub-section (a) above is only that *some* of the important normative standards which law should be morally or directly evaluated in terms of are, we might say, intrinsic to the claims that it makes over those subject to it.

That said, it nonetheless remains particularly important that law be evaluated in terms of the claims that it makes, such as its claim to possess legitimate authority over us, and to generate reasons for action of a certain kind. Why is this? The answer is given by the character of law itself, and is insightfully explained by George Duke, as follows:

> [l]aw is a normative system—in the minimalist sense of a system of norms or standards for conduct—and that it is understood, pre-eminently by participants in that system, but also by observers, as intended to provide human agents with practical guidance. The assumption that law is a normative system intended to provide practical guidance has significant methodological

---

[34] In the present context, by 'normative standards', I mean what law ought to be/those standards that law ought to live up to.
[35] On this point see further J Raz, 'About Morality and the Nature of Law' (2003) *48 American Journal of Jurisprudence* 1, especially at 13–15.

implications if it is true. If law is a normative system intended to provide practical guidance, then it is hard to see how one could give an adequate theoretical elucidation of law that did not involve an assessment—which might have a positive or negative outcome—of whether the claims made by the law on our practical reason are justified. A theory of a normative system, the normativity of which is among its central features, which did not address the distinctively normative aspects of that system would clearly be an incomplete and inadequate theory. In this respect, a general descriptive theory of law differs from a natural-scientific theory insofar as its object of investigation is a normative system that forms part of our self-understanding.[36]

I agree strongly with Duke on these points (although to do justice to his argument as a whole, it should be noted that one of his aims in the article from which the above quote is taken is to argue against aspects of my methodological stance in previous work in discussing the idea of explanatory priority in understanding law).[37] Law is a normative system which purports to provide practical guidance to those living under it. In the service of this aim, it claims authority over them, and claims to shape their practical reasoning processes in certain distinctive ways. This being so, it is vitally important that philosophy of law grapples with and attempts to answer questions regarding whether and under what conditions law's claims are justified. In the ways discussed above, IELP not only makes room for these questions: it focuses and facilitates addressing them.

(c) An objection considered

Nicos Stavropoulos has developed a rich and important body of work in legal philosophy explaining, developing, and defending Interpretivism in understanding law.[38] Interpretivism draws on aspects of the work of Ronald

---

[36] G Duke, 'Law's Normative Point' (2019) 38 *Law and Philosophy* 1 12–13 (internal footnote reference omitted).
[37] In 'Law's Normative Point', ibid, Duke offers a careful, and generous, discussion of my chapter J Dickson, 'Law and Its Theory: A Question of Priorities' in RP George and J Keown (eds), Reason, Morality and Law: The Jurisprudence of John Finnis (OUP 2013).
[38] See eg N Stavropoulos, Objectivity in Law (Clarendon Press 1996); N Stavropoulos, 'Obligations, Interpretivism, and the Legal Point of View' in A Marmor (ed), The Routledge Companion to Philosophy of Law (Routledge 2012) 76–92; N Stavropoulos, 'Words and Obligations' in A Dolcetti, L Duarte d'Almeida, and J Edwards (eds), Reading the Concept of Law (Hart Publishing 2013); N Stavropoulos, 'Legal Interpretivism' in E Zalta (ed), *The Stanford Encyclopedia of Philosophy* (Spring 2021 Edition) https://plato.stanford.edu/archives/spr2021/entries/law-interpretivist/; N Stavropoulos, 'The Grounds of Law: Morality and History', Oxford Legal Studies Research Paper No 43/2015 https://papers.ssrn.com/sol3/papers.cfm?abstract_id=2638033.

Dworkin, and advocates novel ways to identify law, and to understand how the actions of legal and political institutions impact upon and are relevant to the justification of those legal rights and obligations which the state seeks to impose on individuals. In his article, 'Obligations, Interpretivism and the Legal Point of View',[39] Stavropoulos argues that methodological approaches which first of all identify and analyse law's claim to authority without yet engaging in moral evaluation regarding it, and which then view such inquiries as yielding the relevant moral standard(s) against which law should later be judged, curb and problematically restrict those morally evaluative inquiries that legal philosophers ought to be undertaking. He attributes such a problematically restrictive approach to a stance he terms 'the orthodox view',[40] and contrasts it with the methodological stance of legal interpretivism:

> The orthodox view has it that the explanation must begin in nonnormative elucidation of what is legally significant in legal practice and why, by the lights of the practice itself. From that 'legal point of view' we notice that the practice assigns to some of aspects of itself—institutional directives—a certain kind of binding force. The unqualified normative question of why those parts of the practice should have the contemplated role comes last, and concerns whether the law in fact has the force it claims for itself—whether the law so understood ought to be obeyed. Interpretivism, by contrast, begins by rejecting the claim that nonnormative elucidation of the point of view of the practice determines the correct explanation of the legal relevance of institutional practice. Rather, the explanation of how legal practice matters to legal rights and obligations is an ordinary explanation of the normative effects of action by appeal to the substantive normative considerations that give it that role. For interpretivism, the unqualified question of why legal practice matters must come first.[41]

Stavropoulos regards Raz as subscribing to 'the orthodox view' that he is critical of, and, in my view, given how he puts matters in the quotation above, aspects of the IELP methodological approach would also fall within his target. As can be seen from this passage, an important component in Stavropoulos' understanding of the difference between the orthodox view and Interpretivism lies in how constrained or otherwise legal philosophers should be by their understanding of the character of law's claims, ascertained by, amongst other

---

[39] Stavropoulos, 'Obligations, Interpretivism, and the Legal Point of View' (n 38).
[40] I discuss Stavropoulos' use of 'the orthodox view' as a label for those views he disagrees with in ch 6, s 3(a).
[41] Stavropoulos, 'Obligations, Interpretivism, and the Legal Point of View' (n 38) 77.

things, examining the attitudes of those legal officials who make those claims on law's behalf. I have argued in this chapter that an indirectly evaluative analysis of the claims law makes can assist in focusing, and furnishing, some important standards in light of which law should eventually be morally evaluated. I regard this as a beneficial feature of IELP. For Stavropoulos, however, the idea that the normative part of the inquiry is focused and shaped by the first stage 'nonnormative elucidation'[42] of law's claims—which are in part extrapolated from the attitudes of those legal officials making them on law's behalf—is disadvantageous and stifles the normative inquiries that legal philosophers ought to undertake.[43]

Stavropoulos contends that, in order to avoid what he regards as these methodological disadvantages, legal philosophy ought not to 'privilege' law's claims. Although those claims—as manifest in the attitudes of those legal officials administering and applying law—may serve as a useful starting point, they should not be understood as decisively shaping our inquiries regarding the moral concerns that law's existence generates, the moral standards law should be held to, and what, if anything, might morally justify law's imposition of rights and duties.[44] Rather, law's claims as manifest in legal officials' attitudes should be treated, 'as hypotheses, which theory checks and may correct, rather than as constraints that theory must respect on pain of changing the subject',[45] and legal philosophers should take the view that 'even if a specific explanation [of law's ability to create moral reasons for action] is uniquely picked out by the implied attitudes of official action, it needn't be the correct one. The attitudes are not privileged'.[46]

This aspect of Stavropoulos' argument recalls the discussion of his views, and of those of Mark Greenberg, in Chapter 6. It will be recalled that I argued that these theorists' stance that legal philosophers should be allowed to 'slip the leash' of existing self-understandings in terms of law held by those subject to and administering it had some problematic consequences, including their espousal of accounts of law's nature which end up significantly divorced from the beliefs and attitudes of those working in and living under law.[47] This point can also be pressed against Stavropoulos in the context of the present discussion. Why isn't it an explanatory and/or methodological *disadvantage* that his methodological approach allows for and indeed encourages a theory

[42] ibid.
[43] ibid *passim*, but see especially 77–84, 86–91.
[44] ibid 79–84, 90–91.
[45] ibid 81.
[46] ibid 91.
[47] See ch 6, ss 3(a) and 3(b).

of law to depart significantly from how law is understood by those working in and administering it? Although it is not entirely clear how radical a departure Interpretivism allows in this respect, Stavropoulos' comment that any common understanding—including that held by judges and other legal officials—of what law claims and how it intends its claims to be taken could be merely, '[a] flawed hypothesis about how politics works, a hangover from a time when it was thought that the will of kings created reasons by divine delegation'[48] appears to indicate that legal officials could be very wrong indeed as regards the character and claims of the law that they administer, and that theories of law hence should not regard themselves as constrained by those officials' attitudes, beliefs, and self-understandings.

As has been emphasized throughout this book, however, given the kind of thing that law is, and the manner in which it operates, those attitudes, beliefs, and self-understandings are *part-constitutive* of what legal philosophers are trying to explain. Law is a human-made social phenomenon, and the concept of law is a concept already used by those subject to and administering law to understand themselves, their actions, and aspects of their reasoning in terms of law. As legal philosophers we need to do justice to the lived social reality of law as it features in and is experienced in the lives and understandings of those who work with and are subject to law. Given that this is so, in my view, a significant challenge presents itself for theorists adopting an approach such as Stavropoulos' Interpretivism: to explain why their willingness to depart radically from those self-understandings, and from that lived social reality, is not an explanatory disadvantage of their accounts.

Stavropoulos also regards what he calls 'the orthodox view' as disadvantageous because it restricts legal philosophers' attention to one main issue as regards law's moral evaluation:

> [t]he moral problem that law presents is the problem of (legitimate) authority. What makes this the law's characteristic moral problem is the law's claim ... So the complete orthodox account pairs an explanation of the grounds of legal obligation that appeals to the existence of legal directives with an explanation of the moral problem of the directives' playing the grounding role. But what matters is the order of explanation: the moral problem of authoritative guidance is germane only because analysis of our common conception of law has shown it to be germane.[49]

---

[48] Stavropoulos, 'Obligations, Interpretivism, and the Legal Point of View' (n 38) 91.
[49] ibid 87.

Stavropoulos, however, believes that law's chief moral problem which legal philosophers ought to address in their theories lies elsewhere, namely with the imposition of state coercive force upon individuals in order to direct them to act in accordance with the law. Interpretivism views law as capable of properly constraining and policing this imposition of coercive force, and so ensuring that it is only brought to bear on citizens under conditions where it is justified.[50]

This, however, seems somewhat of a red herring as regards the differences between an IELP staged inquiry approach and Stavropoulos' legal interpretivism. First of all, it is not clear that what Stavropoulos takes to be the chief moral concern arising out of law's presence is so different from or unrelated to puzzles concerning whether, when, and in virtue of what law's claim to authority could be justified. Arguably, whatever might justify law's claim to possess legitimate authority over those subject to it will also be a significant part of the explanation of how law can justifiably impose coercively enforced legal rights and duties on individuals. Secondly, even to the extent that Stavropoulos is drawing attention to a distinct moral concern regarding law, as I argued in subsection (b) above, while *some* important moral questions concerning law, and *some* important moral standards to which law should be held are furnished by identifying and analysing the claims law makes, these questions and standards are not exhaustive of the moral questions that legal philosophers should ask of law, or of the moral evaluations of law that they should undertake.

4. The Province of Jurisprudence Enlarged?

This chapter has explored some aspects of the relations of continuity and complementarity between IELP, and the asking, engaging with, and answering of questions concerning the moral value, justifiability, and obligatoriness of law. Jurisprudential inquiries which begin by picking out and analysing important aspects of the nature of law do not thereby stand in isolation from inquiries concerning the moral evaluation and criticism of law. Rather, the staged inquiry approach of IELP serves to focus and facilitate those latter enterprises as regards some of the important questions they should address. Does this represent an attempt at enlarging the proper province of jurisprudence concerning the nature of law? To my mind, it does not. It merely reemphasizes and reminds us of what has long been the case, and what should, *contra* the views of certain legal philosophers considered in this chapter, have long been understood to be

[50] ibid 88–89.

the case: the task of identifying and analysing those significant and important features of law which make it into what it is, is deeply and significantly tied to the task of engaging with law's moral evaluation, and/or justification, and/or criticism and reform. As was emphasized towards the end of Chapter 5,[51] this view echoes strongly down the tradition in legal philosophy in which IELP takes its place. As Hart reminds us, legal philosophers such as Jeremy Bentham, who were insistent on approaching law without *yet* morally evaluating it, and without *yet* assuming it to have the moral value and obligatoriness it claims for itself, were: '[n]ot dry analysts fiddling with verbal distinctions ... but ... the vanguard of a movement which laboured with passionate intensity and much success to bring about a better society and better laws'.[52]

IELP, with its commitment to staged inquiry, enables legal philosophers to approach law and to begin to understand it in a clear, cool-headed, and unromanticized way which lessens the risk of prematurely assuming law to have the moral value, justifiability, and obligatoriness that it claims for itself. But questions of law's moral value, justifiability, and obligatoriness are vital questions in understanding law, and in the ways explored in this book, IELP focuses and facilitates our engaging with them.

With these discussions undertaken, this book draws to a close. I would like to thank all those who have stuck with it from start to finish, and also all those who have dipped in and out of it as suited their own purposes. Although not conclusive in all of its arguments,[53] I hope that this work contributes in a thoughtful and exploratory way to the ongoing conversation in our discipline about the methodology, or the philosophy, of legal philosophy.

---

[51] See ch 5, close of s 5, and s 6.
[52] HLA Hart, 'Positivism and the Separation of Law and Morals' in HLA Hart, Essays in Jurisprudence and Philosophy (Clarendon Press 1983) 52.
[53] See ch 7, s 3(b) for a discussion of some of the reasons why this is so.

Index

For the benefit of digital users, indexed terms that span two pages (e.g., 52–53) may, on occasion, appear on only one of those pages.

abuse of power 158
acquiescence 76
active elucidation *see* self-understandings
Alexy, Robert 35
analytical jurisprudence *see* jurisprudence
apartheid 98–99
　see also race
artefact/non-artefact concepts 127–28
Artic peoples 73–74
Ashcraft, Richard 56n.8
audience-dependence 65–67, 77–78, 79
Austin, John 4–5, 6, 57, 59, 75, 76, 78–79
authoritative legal texts 130
authority of law 56, 60
　law's authority claim 148–51

Bentham, Jeremy 75, 99, 100, 101, 102, 112, 156–57, 175–76
biological sciences 45–46
biology
　concepts 45–46
　philosophy of 45–46
Blackstone, William 99
boundary fences 31, 34–35
Brunei
　same-sex relations 129n.78
Bulygin, Eugenio 40–41
Burge, Tyler 127–28

capital punishment 152
causation in the law 164–65
chemical sciences 45–46
Cicero 163
citizenship 43
coercion 57, 95
　coercive control 111, 113
　state 98–99
Coleman, Jules 33, 162, 163–64
colonial rule 61

command theory of law 4–5, 59, 63, 75–77, 80, 112n.19
complementarity 35, 36–37, 161–76
　challenges 162–67
　clarifications 169–71
　IELP 167–75
　jurisprudence, province of 175–76
　objections 171–75
　standard-setting 167–69
concept of law *see* nature of law
conceptual analysis
　immodest/modest 49
connective model 3–4
constitutionalism 164–66
constructive interpretation method 65–66
contract law 111, 113, 164–65
corporal punishment 152
Cotterrell, Roger 11–12, 26, 27–28, 51
Court of Justice of the European Union (CJEU) 61–62
courts 138–39
　justice, of 96
　role of 87–88, 93–94
criminal law 111, 113
　mens rea 164–65
Critical Legal Studies movement 72–73, 137n.58

death penalty 129, 152
demarcation problem 57–58
democracy, concept of 129–30
descriptive legal theorists 8–9
　methodological approach 113–14, 115–18, 136
directly evaluative legal philosophy (DELP) 138–39, 156–57, 158, 159
　directly evaluative judgements *see* indirectly evaluative legal philosophy (IELP)
　IELP, compared 140–42

discrimination *see* gender; race
domain-apt approaches *see* nature of law
domestic violence 67–68
duality of law
   examples 84–94
   in indirectly evaluative legal philosophy (IELP) 87–90
   social and normative nature of law 85–87
due wariness *see* indirectly evaluative legal philosophy (IELP)
Duke, George 170–71
duty-imposing rules 111, 112
   see also power-imposing rules
Dworkin, Ronald 12, 47, 48, 59, 77–78, 106–7, 109, 115–16, 136, 137, 141–42, 156–57, 158, 162–65, 171–72
   'one right answer' thesis 65–66

'elucidating' law/philosophy
   active process, as a 2–3, 8, 9
   choice of terminology 3–4
   identifying and explaining law 2, 6, 13
   moral issues 3
   motifs 2–3
   multi-faceted phenomenon, law as a 2, 7–8
   rationale for elucidating law 3–12
emphasis selectivity, distribution of
   constraints 79–80
   distribution of emphasis 56n.8
   evaluation in legal philosophy 135–36
   legal philosophy 55, 56, 79–80
   nature of law 65–80
   subject-matter selectivity, compared 69, 79
   see also experience-sensitive engagement
Endicott, Timothy 56
Engels, Friedrich 70n.42
error theory 19n.12
essentialism 32–33, 38, 40–41, 42
   natural kinds 45–46
European Union (EU)
   legal systems, theory of 61–62
evaluation in legal philosophy *see* indirectly evaluative legal philosophy (IELP)
evil norms *see* 'truly evil norms'

exclusionary reasons 168–69
experience-sensitive engagement 67–74, 78, 79–80, 118
   application 67–68
   see also emphasis selectivity, distribution of
experimental philosophy 113–14
expression, restrictions on *see* freedom of expression

feminist legal theory 67–68, 69–70
   see also gender
fines, requirement to pay 105
Finnis, John 12, 55–56, 74–75, 76–77, 78–79, 80, 90–94, 96, 106–7, 115–16, 123–24, 136–37, 140–42, 156–57, 158
   'collateral obligation' 91n.24
freedom of expression 129
Fuller, Lon 57n.10

Gambia
   criminal code (1965) 129
Gardner, John 35, 75, 78–79, 80
gender 129–30
   discrimination 72–73
   gender-based violence 67–68
   race, and 72–73
   see also feminist legal theory; homosexuality; LGBT community; sexuality
Giudice, Michael 11–12, 36–37, 40, 41–42
governance practices 38–39
Green, Leslie 41–42, 70–71, 117–18, 163–66
Greenberg, Mark 9, 12, 96, 110, 120, 122–26, 128–33, 136, 137, 141–42, 156–57, 158, 159n.64, 173–74
   'standard picture' 59

Hart, H. L. A.
   academic career 164–65
   analytic philosophy 31–32
   Austin, criticisms of 75, 78–79
   coercion in law, role of 99n.48
   command theories of law 75–77, 80, 112n.19
   concept of law 109, 120
   'elucidating' law 3–5

IELP and DELP approaches 141–42, 156–57, 163–64
indirectly evaluative judgements 139
jurisprudence, work on 165–66
legal normativity, character of 102n.58
legal norms 63
legal positivism 101, 102, 123–24, 162
methodological position 99–100
moral evaluation 175–76
nature and system of law 57
necessity, concept of 41
revisionism 112
rules in law 59, 112, 113, 117–19, 120–21
self-understandings 106–7
The Concept of Law 4–5, 76, 111–12, 115–16, 117
'wicked' rules 157–58
Hegel, Georg W. F. 163
hermeneutic concept 115–16
  terminology 116
Hobbes, Thomas 163
homophobia
  ILGA report 98n.44, 129n.75, 130n.82
homosexuality
  criminalization of 98–99, 129–30, 159
  same-sex marriage 118
  see also gender; LGBT community
Hume, David 163

indirectly evaluative legal philosophy (IELP)
  advantages 153–60
    arguments, and limits of 153–55
    'oughtness' of law 155–60, 167
    risk mitigation 155–60
  background 82–85
  central tenets 82–83
  complementarity, and *see* complementarity
  constraints 104, 135
  definition 13
  directly evaluative judgements 136, 137–38
  directly evaluative legal philosophy (DELP), compared 140–42
  duality of law 87–90, 104
  due wariness, attitude of 83–84, 88, 94–102
  evaluation in legal philosophy 135–39
  evaluative judgements 9–10
    direct vs indirect 136–40
    indirectly, as staged inquiry 139–53, 159–60
  nature of law, and 88–89, 92
  prospects, theoretical 101–3
  staged inquiry, and 166
    academic dress requirements 143–45, 151
    indirectly evaluative judgments 139–53
    law's authority claim 148–51
    supporting indirectly evaluative judgments 151–53
    tutorial system of university teaching 145–47, 151
  value of 83, 102–3, 135–60
  theoretical approaches 13–14
  see also directly evaluative legal philosophy (DELP); self-understandings
instrumental argument 47–48
interpretivism 124–25, 171–75
  definition 16
interstitial character of law-making 4–5
Iran
  Penal Code (2013) 129
  same-sex relations 129

judges 65–66, 97
judicial review 165–66
jurisdiction-specific features of law 18
jurisprudence
  analytical 17, 31–32, 33–34, 163
  approaches 11, 35, 38
  boundary fences 34–35
  definition 34
  essentialism, and 32–33
  general 34
  holistic nature of 6
  inquiry, types of 35, 175–76
  methodology of 1–2, 100, 108n.9, 115–15, 154–55
  necessity, human/strict 41
  particular 34
  pluralist 36–37
  'special' 32
  see also nature of law

Kant, Immanuel 163
Kelsen, Hans 40, 76, 112, 118–19
Köpcke Tinturé, Maris 12
Kripke, Saul 45
   a posteriori necessary truths 40n.49
   'Kripke-Putnam semantics' 45–46
Krygier, Martin 34–35, 36–37, 57

Lacey, Nicola 11–12, 35, 36–37, 51
   'intellectual imperialism' 26n.2
   'philosophical imperialism' 26n.2
language
   legal discourse/nomenclature 97, 105
   philosophy of 60
   see also semantic theories
LaPorte, Joseph 45–46
legal obligation, concept of 109n.12
legal philosophers
   a priori arguments 39–40n.48
   due wariness, attitude of 96, 99, 155–56
   legal systems, theory of 61–62
   nature of law, and 22, 23, 60, 62–63
   self-understandings 119
   staged inquiry by *see* staged inquiry
   subject-matter selectivity 61
legal philosophy
   aims and objectives 1–2
   approaches 1, 35
   audience-dependence 65–67
   boundary fences 34–35
   constraints 1–2
   criteria of success 1
   definitions 1–2, 34
   disagreement 77–79
   domain-apt approach *see* nature of law
   emphasis selectivity, distribution of 55, 56, 65–80
      constraints 56, 79–80
   experience-sensitive engagement 67–74
   explanatory depth 74–77, 80
   explanatory power 79–80
   levels of inquiry 1
   methodology of 1–2
   moral philosophy, and 1, 13–14
   nature of law, about the 34
   philosophy of 1–3
   political philosophy, and 1, 13–14
   questions of 54–55
   social philosophy, and 1, 13–14
   subject-matter subjectivity 55–56, 57–65

   theory construction, roles for choice 55–56
   'where to start' 74–77, 80
legal positivism 47, 77, 91, 101, 114–15, 123–24, 162, 165–66
   'exclusive' 47, 165–66
   inclusive 140n.18
   see also sources thesis
legal practice 32
legal systems, theory of 61–62
legal theory
   approaches 35
   definition 34
Leiter, Brian 9, 11–12, 46, 49, 50, 57, 115–17
LGBT community 129–30, 131, 152
   see also gender; homosexuality
liberty, deprivation of 85, 105
Locke, John 56n.8, 163

Machiavelli, Niccolò 163
marriage law 111, 113–14, 118, 164–65
   same-sex marriage 118
Marx, Karl 70n.42
Mauritania
   same-sex relations 129n.78
medieval
   craft guilds 31n.15
   influenza 110n.16
metaphysics 3–4, 15–16
methodology
   concepts, approaches to 110
   descriptive approaches 113–14, 115–18
   distinctive character of law, and 127–28
   jurisprudence, of 1–2, 100
   legal philosophy, of 1–2, 52n.77
mind, philosophy of 60, 120
monoclonal gammopathy of unknown significance (MGUS) 121
Moore, Michael 40–41
Moral Impact Theory 124–25, 128
morality
   law, and 57
   moral argument 90
   moral authority of law 138–39, 165–66
   moral autonomy 60
   moral disagreement 56
   moral error theory 19n.12, 98–99
   moral evaluation 12, 13–14, 175
      insufficiency of 12
      role of 83

moral normativity 10
moral obligations 100, 124, 129, 136, 137–38, 158
moral philosophy 1, 13–14, 165–66
moral reasoning 65–66
moral risk 70–71, 78, 156–58
moral task of law 89, 124–25
moral under-determination 56
moral values 86, 136–37, 152, 159, 166, 176
  sexual 165–66
Murphy, Liam 9, 11–12, 46–50, 108–9

narrative methods 69–70
national identity 61
natural law theory 91
  definition 91
nature of law 6, 13
  abstractness 25
  'actual' 48–49
  boundary fences, disciplinary 31, 34–35
  concept of law 37, 46–50, 105, 106–7, 174
    in toto 106–7
  conflict, points of 23–24
  criminal offences 43–45
  domain-apt approaches 22–24, 25, 41–42, 52–53, 54–55
  general concept 17
  guild exclusivity, guilty of 25, 31–37, 163–64
  IELP, and 88–89, 92
  impossibility 25, 37–50
  law, concept of 15–16
  legal norms, and 43–45, 63
  legal philosophers, and 22, 23, 60
  legal philosophy about the 34
  metaphysical extravagance 37, 38–39
  natural kind terms 45–46, 127n.67
  natural sciences, concepts 45–46
  'natural world' reality 43
  semantic theories 45–46
  social character of law, neglectful of 25, 50–51
  social reality, and 15, 28, 43, 44–45, 46
  social theory, and 32n.19
  socially constructed entities, nature of 37, 42–46, 121
  static and staple questions 25, 52, 57–58, 81

subject-matter selectivity, and 58
theoretical imperialism 25, 26–30
theories of law, and 7, 20
  see also jurisprudence; self-understandings
Nazi law 158
necessary/contingent distinction 19–20, 41–42
Nigeria
  same-sex relations 129n.78
nonnormative elucidation 172–73
normal justification thesis 150, 168n.27
normativity
  law, of 10, 85–87
  moral 10
  normative claims 97
  normative language/ statements 86, 138–39
  normative phenomena 86
  normative point or value 91, 92–94
  normative standards, defining 170n.34
  normative systems, theory of 170–71

'one right answer' thesis 65–66
open texture of law 4–5
'ought-ness' 10, 86, 167

Pashukanis, Evgeny 70n.42
Patterson, Dennis 11–12
philosophy of law
  approaches 35
  definition 34
Plato 163
  Phaedrus 45n.58
pluralism 51
  jurisprudence 36–37
  opportunities 73–74, 77, 81
  'question' 54, 64
  subject-matter selectivity 66
police 93–94, 105
  powers *see* stop and search powers
political philosophy 1, 13–14, 164–65
politics
  law and 57
  political identity 61
positivism *see* legal positivism
power-conferring rules 106–7, 111–12, 113–14, 117, 118, 120–21
  social function of 113
  see also duty-imposing rules

practical-political argument 47–48
Priel, Dan 12
prisons 85
promising, concept of 109n.12
properties of law 16, 17, 60
propositions of law 16, 47
psychology 32
punishment, nature and justification of 164–65
'push back'/corrective 95–96
  definition 95–96
Putnam, Hilary 45
  'Kripke-Putnam semantics' 45–46
  natural kinds 127n.67

race 129–30
  critical race theory 69–70, 77
  gender 72–73
  Jim Crow laws 98–99
  racial discrimination, cases of 72–73
  see also apartheid
rationality 60, 97, 151
Raz, Joseph 156–58, 162
  complementarity 35
  concept of law 27, 33, 48, 106–7, 109–10, 120
  directly/indirectly evaluative judgements 139, 150, 167–68
  duality of law 92–94
  essentialism, on 27, 40–41
  'great tradition' 101
  guild-exclusivity charge 163–64
  'Institutional Nature of Law' 20, 28–30
  'internal' or 'legal' viewpoint 76
  jurisprudential methodology 100–1
  legal obligation, account of 123–24
  legal positivism 162
    sources thesis 47, 114–15
  moral authority of the state 165–66
  moral tasks 89
  normal justification thesis 150, 168n.27
  'orthodox view' 172–73
  properties of law 41–42
  reasons for action 168–69
  scope of academic career 164–65
  'The Institutional Nature of Law' 20, 29
realism 22n.16, 100–1
  character of 22
reason, law and 57
reasons for action 168–69

reductive model of analysis 3–5
reform of law 70
religious belief 129–30
revisionist theory of law/revisionism 13–14, 112
  consequences of 126–33
  limits of 133–34
Rodriguez-Blanco, Veronica 12
Roughan, Nicole 56, 60–61
route-dependence 67
rules see duty-imposing rules; power-conferring rules
'ruling' theory of law 59
Rundle, Kristen 57n.10
Ryle, Gilbert 120

Saudi Arabia
  same-sex relations 129n.78
Savigny, Friedrich Carl von 163
Schauer, Frederick 6–7, 11–12, 26–27, 28, 29–30, 33–34, 38, 39, 41
selectivity see emphasis selectivity, distribution of; subject-matter selectivity
self-understandings 13–14, 23–24, 51, 52–53, 83, 88, 104–34, 173–74
  active elucidation 110–19
  background 104–7
  concept of law 105, 106–8, 109, 119–21, 123
  concept and nature 119–22
  concerns 108–10
  constraints on legal theories 107–33
  constraints, methodological 118–19
  'data points' 107–8
  descriptive approaches 113–14, 115–18
  determinateness, issue of 108
  disagreements 109, 126–27
  evaluation in legal philosophy 135–36
  Hart, examples from 111–12
  revisionism, and:
    consequences of 126–33
    limits of 133–34
  'slipping the leash' 123–26, 133
  vox-pop basis 110–11, 113–15
  see also indirectly evaluative legal philosophy (IELP)
semantic theories 45–46
  see also language, philosophy of
sexual assault 67–68, 165–66

sexual morality 165–66
sexuality
  sexual orientation issues 129–30
  see also homosexuality; gender
Shapiro, Scott 33, 35, 123–24
social fact, law as 77, 85, 86, 87, 88–89, 90, 91, 92, 93–94, 96, 99, 100, 101–2, 105, 158, 159, 165–66, 169–70
social institutions 6–7, 15, 17–18, 19–20, 40–41, 44, 85, 98–99, 115, 116, 122
social character of law 25, 50–51, 83–84, 85–87
social power 117–18
  channelling 118
  see also power-conferring rules
social reality of law 15, 21–22, 35, 39–40, 43, 52–53, 64, 85–86, 87, 96, 100, 131–32, 133–34, 152, 174
social theory 36
socialist law 70n.42
sociology of law 27, 29–30, 32, 36, 52–53, 165–66
  'armchair' sociology 109–10
sources thesis 47, 114–15
  see also legal positivism
South Africa
  apartheid legislation 98–99
staged inquiry 13–14, 75, 166, 175–76
  academic dress requirements 143–45
  indirectly evaluative judgments 139–53
  law's authority claim 148–51
  supporting indirectly evaluative judgments 151–53
  tutorial system of university teaching 145–47
  value of 83, 102–3, 135–60
  see also indirectly evaluative legal philosophy (IELP)
statutes 130
Stavropoulos, Nicos 9, 12, 96, 108–9, 110, 122–28, 171–75
  orthodox view 59, 174
stop and search powers 71
story-telling methods 69–70
Strawson, Peter
  Analysis and Metaphysics 3–4

subject-matter selectivity 55–56, 57–65
  constraints 64–65
  distribution of emphasis selectivity, compared 69, 79
  evaluation in legal philosophy 135–36

Tamanaha, Brian 6–7, 11–12, 26, 27, 28–29, 38, 39, 41
taxation law 85, 164–65
theory of law
  criteria and definition 16–17, 30
  self-understandings 106
  see also nature of law
tort law 164–65
'truly evil norms' 129–30, 132, 159

United Kingdom (UK)
  national identity, issues of 61
United Nations (UN)
  states 129, 130
United States (US)
  freedom of expression 129
  Jim Crow laws 98–99
  racial and gender discrimination 72–73
unjust laws 159

vagueness 56
validity, legal 56, 101
  tests for 92

Waldron, Jeremy 12
Walton, Kevin 6–7, 35–36, 39, 41
Waluchow, Wil 139, 140n.18, 163–66
wariness, due see indirectly evaluative legal philosophy (IELP)
welfare benefits 85
Williams, Patricia
  'The Pain of Word Bondage' 72–73
Williamson, Timothy 127
wills, law of 111, 113
Wittgenstein, Ludwig 3n.5, 60
Wolff, Robert Paul 60, 149–50, 167–68, 169

Yemen
  same-sex relations 129n.78